NORTH END
AND THE
WATERFRONT

OLD BOSTON
AND THE
FINANCIAL
DISTRICT

BEACON
HILL AND
WEST END

CHINATOWN
AND THE
THEATER DISTRICT

**North End and
the Waterfront**
Pages 68–79

**Old Boston and
the Financial District**
Pages 56–67

**Chinatown and the
Theater District**
Pages 80–89

EYEWITNESS TRAVEL

BOSTON

EYEWITNESS TRAVEL

BOSTON

Main Contributors **Tom Bross, Patricia Harris, and David Lyon**

LONDON, NEW YORK,
MELBOURNE, MUNICH AND DELHI
www.dk.com

Project Editor Marcus Hardy
Art Editor Nicola Rodway
Editor Simon Hall
US. Editor Mary Sutherland
Designers Elly King, Nikala Sim
Map Co-Ordinators Dave Pugh, Casper Morris
DTP Maite Lantaron
Picture Researcher Brigitte Arora
Production Michelle Thomas

Contributors
Tom Bross, Brett Cook, Patricia Harris, Carolyn Heller,
David Lyon, Juliette Rogers, Kem Sawyer

Photographers
Demetrio Carrasco, Linda Whitwam

Illustrators
Stephen Conlin, Gary Cross, Richard Draper, Chris Orr & Associates,
Robbie Polley, John Woodcock

Maps
Ben Bowles, Rob Clynes, Sam Johnston,
James Macdonald (Colourmap Scanning Ltd)

Printed and bound in China

First American Edition, 2001
14 15 16 17 10 9 8 7 6 5 4 3 2 1

Published in the United States by Dorling Kindersley Publishing, Inc.,
345 Hudson Street, New York, NY 10014

17 18 19 20 10 9 8 7 6 5 4 3 2 1

**Reprinted with revisions 2003, 2004, 2005, 2006, 2007, 2008,
2009, 2011, 2013, 2015, 2017**

Copyright © 2001, 2017 Dorling Kindersley Limited, London
A Penguin Random House Company

A cataloging in publication record is
available from the Library of Congress.

ISSN 1542-1554
ISBN 978-1-4654-6026-4

Floors are referred to throughout in accordance with American usage;
ie the "first floor" is the floor at ground level.

MIX
Paper from
responsible sources
FSC™ C018179

Front cover main image: Replica of *Beaver*, the Boston Tea Party ship, in Fort Point Channel

◀ Panoramic view of Boston across the Charles river with colorful sailing boats

Contents

Tiffany window in the Arlington Street
Church, Back Bay

Introducing Boston

The opulent Grand Lobby of the Wang
Theatre *(see p88)*

Aerial view of Boston over Back Bay and the Charles river

Survival Guide

Pumpkins for sale, a regular sight in the fall

The 18th-century Old South Meeting House
amid Boston's skyscrapers *(see p61)*

Trinity Church, Back Bay
(see pp96–7)

HOW TO USE THIS GUIDE

This guide will help you get the most from your visit to Boston, providing expert recommendations and detailed practical information. The opening section, *Introducing Boston*, maps the city and sets it in its geographical, historical, and cultural context. *Boston at a Glance* is an overview of the city's main attractions. Section two, *Boston Area by Area*, starts on page 40 and describes all the important sights plus three recommended walks, using maps, photographs, and detailed illustrations. The sights are arranged in two groups: those in Boston's central districts, and those a little farther afield. Tips for hotels, restaurants, shopping, entertainment, and sports can be found in *Travelers' Needs*, while the final section, *Survival Guide*, contains practical advice on everything from public transportation and telephones to personal safety.

Boston Area by Area

Each of the six sightseeing areas is color-coded for easy reference. Every chapter opens with an introduction to the area it covers, describing its history and character. For central districts, this is followed by a Street-by-Street map illustrating a particularly interesting part of the area; for sights farther away, by a regional map. A simple numbering system relates sights to the maps. Important sights are covered by several pages.

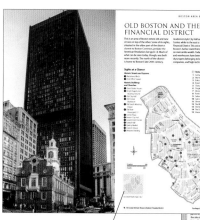

A locator map
shows where you are
in relation to other
areas of the city center.

1 Introduction to the Area
For easy reference, the sights are numbered and plotted on an area map, with "T" stations shown where helpful. The key sights (historic buildings, churches, museums, and open-air sights) are listed by category.

This shaded area
is shown in greater
detail on the Street-
by-Street map.

Color-coded
thumb tabs
mark each area.

Locator map

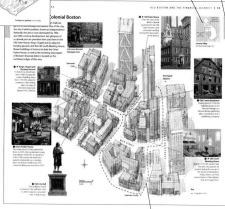

2 Street-by-Street Map
This gives a bird's-eye view of interesting and important parts of each sightseeing area, with accurate drawings of all the buildings within them. The numbering of the sights ties in with the preceding area map and with the fuller descriptions on the pages that follow.

Suggested
walking route

Boston Area Map

The colored areas shown on this map *(see inside front cover)* are the five main sightseeing areas of central Boston (excluding the *Farther Afield* section). Each is covered in a full chapter in the *Boston Area by Area* section *(pp40–129)*. The areas are also highlighted on other maps throughout the book. In *Boston at a Glance (pp28–39)*, for example, they help you to locate the most important sights that no visitor should miss. The maps' colored borders match the colored thumb tabs at the top corner of each page.

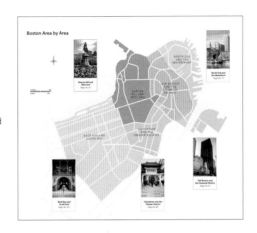

Numbers refer to each sight's position on the area map and its place in the chapter.

Practical information lists all the information you need to visit every sight, including a map reference to the *Street Finder* maps *(pp186–191)*.

3 Detailed Information on each Sight
All the important sights are described individually. They are listed to follow the numbering on the area map at the start of the section. The key to the symbols summarizing practical information is on the back flap.

A visitors' checklist provides the practical information you will need to plan your visit.

Story boxes provide details on famous people or historical events.

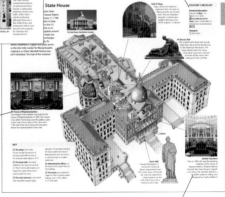

Stars indicate the most interesting sights.

4 Boston's Major Sights
These are given more extensive coverage, sometimes two or more full pages. Historic buildings are dissected to reveal their interiors; museums and galleries have color-coded floor plans to help you find important exhibits.

Captions provide more detailed information about specific sights.

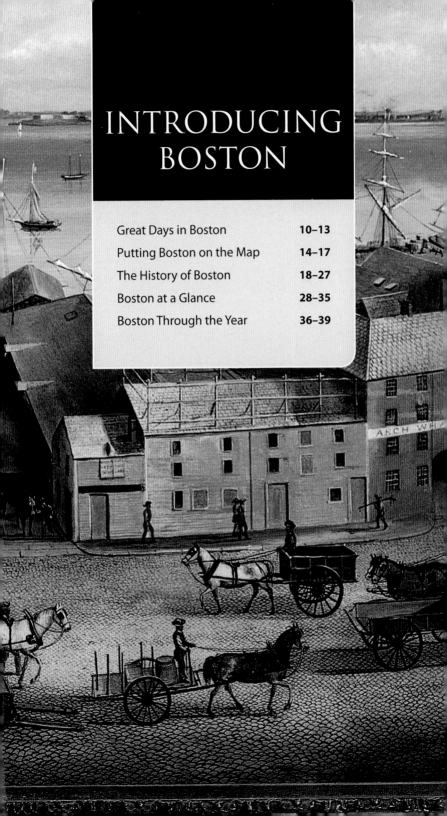

INTRODUCING BOSTON

GREAT DAYS IN BOSTON

As well as being compact and walkable, Boston also has an extensive subway system (the "T"), which makes neighboring Cambridge easily accessible. Here are itineraries for some of the city's prime historical and cultural attractions, arranged first under themes and then by length of stay on pages 12–13. All the places mentioned here are cross-referenced to other parts of the guide so you can ponder over more detailed information and tailor each day's outing to your personal interests. Price guidelines on pages 10–11 include transportation, food, and admission charges.

Bell tower and steeple of the 18th-century Old North Church

Historic Boston

Two adults allow at least $80

- **Historic North End**
- **A walk along the waterfront**
- **Elegant Old State House**
- **King's Chapel**

Morning
Start in the **North End** *(pp70–71)*, Boston's oldest neighborhood. Hanover Street is full of Italian cafés and bakeries, and east from here is the **Paul Revere Mall** *(p74)*, where an equestrian statue commemorates the patriot. Continue to the lovely 18th-century **Old North Church** *(p73)*, followed by a stroll through **Christoper Columbus Park** *(p75)* for great harbor vistas. For lunch, head to **Quincy Market** *(p66)* or **Durgin Park** *(p143)*, with its local specialties.

Afternoon
Refreshed, head to the **Old State House** *(pp62–3)*, the one-time seat of the British colonial government. Nearby is the simple **King's Chapel and Burying Ground** *(p60)*. Continue to the **Old South Meeting House** *(p61)*, where rousing speeches led to The Boston Tea Party *(p77)*. End the day relaxing in popular **Boston Common** *(pp48–9)*.

Culture & Fresh Air

Two adults allow at least $110–125

- **Impressive Trinity Church**
- **Masterpieces in the Museum of Fine Arts**
- **Isabella Stewart Gardner Museum**
- **Boston skyline from Back Bay Fens parkland**

Morning
Start the day on the lovely open space that constitutes **Copley Square** *(p98)*, which is dominated by the beautiful 1877 Neo-Romanesque **Trinity Church** *(pp96–7)*, with its soaring interior spaces richly decorated with murals and stained-glass windows. Then, for a bit of morning retail therapy, walk a short distance to either of two upscale urban malls: **Copley Place** *(p101)* or the **Prudential Center** *(p100)*, where all your needs are catered for under one roof.

Stained glass, Trinity Church

In addition, **Boylston Street** *(p98)* and parallel **Newbury Street** *(p95)* also overflow with some of the city's most stylish stores and fashion boutiques. At the Copley "T" station, board a train for the **Museum of Fine Arts, Boston** *(pp106–9)*, the largest art museum in New England, with collections ranging from the ancient world to the 21st century. After allowing ample time to roam the galleries, head to the upper level of the Linde Family Wing to enjoy a leisurely lunch in Bravo, the MFA's classy restaurant with walls, as one might expect, adorned with a rotating exhibition of some of the museum's contemporary artworks.

Afternoon
After lunch, head to another Boston cultural treasure nearby: the **Isabella Stewart Gardner Museum** *(p105)*. Here, European masterpieces are among the highlights of the collection. After all this culture, take a breath of fresh air and enjoy a stroll amid the waterways, marshes, and footbridges of Back Bay Fens, one of the jewels of the area known as **The Emerald Necklace** *(p105)*. This rambling parkland also has enchanting views of Boston's soaring skyline. If you would like to extend this cultural day into the evening, make your way to Symphony Hall, the acoustically fine-tuned home of the

acclaimed **Boston Symphony Orchestra** *(p160)*, for a classical music fest. Or, just a block away, audiences regularly fill Jordan Hall for concerts and recitals presented by students of the **New England Conservatory of Music** *(p160)*. Alternatively, if you are in the mood for drama, the independent **Huntington Theatre** *(p160)* stages first-rate productions, while the **Colonial Theatre** *(p160)*, in the Theater District, presents tours of recent Broadway hits.

The Boston Symphony Orchestra performing at Symphony Hall

Cambridge Academia

Two adults allow at least $95

- Bustling Harvard Square
- Harvard Yard architecture
- European masterpieces in the Harvard University Art Museums
- MIT campus and museums

Morning
Catch a Red Line train across the river to the college town of **Cambridge** *(pp110–11)*, emerging at Harvard Square. This is the site of the nation's oldest and most prestigious university. Immerse yourself in the scholarly atmosphere by visiting **Harvard Yard** *(pp112– 13)*, surrounded by lecture halls and dormitories that cover a broad spectrum of American architecture. From here, head to the eminent **Harvard University Art Museums**

Majestic façade of the Memorial Hall in Harvard Yard

(p114–15), which assemble all of Harvard's major art collections under one gorgeous roof designed by the Italian architect Renzo Piano. Don't miss the ancient Chinese bronzes, the brash German Expressionist canvases, or the fine examples of Post-Impressionism. Back in Harvard Square, **Grafton Street Pub** *(p149)* offers a good-value lunch.

Afternoon
After lunch, visit the Harvard Museum of Natural History *(p116)* to see the scientifically accurate glass flowers. For another cultural experience, ride a No. 1 bus to the **MIT Campus** *(p123)* to savor avant-garde 20th-century architecture and Alexander Calder's 12-m (40-ft) high stabile *The Big Sail*. Catch the subway back to central Boston from Kendall Station.

A Family Day

Family of four allow $235

- Get wet on the Boston Duck Tour
- Swan Boat lagoon "cruise"
- Tropical fish in the New England Aquarium
- Hand's-on fun in the Children's Museum

Morning
Get children acquainted with this kid-friendly city by joining **Boston Duck Tours** *(p183)*, which provides narrated sightseeing tours in World War II-era amphibious vehicles. The downtown tour includes the Charles River, an exciting way to view the city's skyline. Then stroll through the **Public Garden** *(pp48–9)*, locale of bronze duck sculptures. Real ducks also swim on the park's lagoon, and you can join them aboard a pedal-powered Swan Boat. Take the subway from Arlington "T" station to Aquarium "T" station, where the **New England Aquarium** *(pp78–9)* has a huge tank full of tropical fish, sharks, and stingrays. For lunch, stroll along the waterfront to enjoy fresh local fish at the **Barking Crab** *(p144)*.

Afternoon
Walk across the bridge to the highly interactive **Children's Museum** *(p77)*. Permanent features include a rock-climbing wall, a construction zone, a maze, and a science playground.

Visitors on a relaxing Swan boat cruise in Boston's Public Garden

2 Days in Boston

- Take a stroll through Boston Common and the Public Garden
- Enjoy a behind-the-scenes tour of Fenway Park
- Take a look at some pricey real estate on Beacon Hill

Day 1
Morning Begin your day people-watching at **Boston Common and the Public Garden** (pp48–9). Indulge your inner child with a calming ride on the famous Swan Boats and later go shopping at the nearby **Back Bay's** (pp92–3) world-class shops. Refuel at one of the many lunch spots on Boylston Street.

Afternoon Acquaint yourself with Boston's baseball fervor by taking a tour of **Fenway Park** (p168), the country's oldest baseball park and a city landmark. Continue your culture crawl with an afternoon at the **Museum of Fine Arts** (pp106–9).

Day 2
Morning Explore some of New England's priciest real estate on the historic **Beacon Hill** (p44). Grab a beverage and peruse the many high-end boutiques and antique shops that line the beautiful **Charles Street** (p46). Then head towards the harbor to enjoy lunch alfresco at one of the restaurants on the waterfront.

Afternoon Enjoy one of the city's water-based attractions such as Boston Duck Tours or the **New**

England Aquarium (pp78–9). Sit on a bench at **Faneuil Hall** (p65) or **Quincy Market** (p66) to enjoy two of the city's most popular sights. End the day with a stroll through the atmospheric North End. View the **Paul Revere House** (p75) and **Old North Church** (p73) by moonlight, then choose from the neighborhood's dozens of restaurants and cafés.

3 Days in Boston

- Admire priceless art at the Museum of Fine Arts
- Head to the waterfront New England Aquarium
- Peruse Back Bay's world-class shops

Day 1
Morning The **Old State House** (pp62–63) provides an easy starting point for the **Freedom Trail** (p126–29). Check out the historic **Faneuil Hall** (p65), then walk on to the North End, where you'll see the **Paul Revere House** (p75) and the lovely 18th-century **Old North Church** (p73). Lunch options abound, with dozens of Italian eateries and two bakeries.

Afternoon Take a brisk stroll along the waterfront through **Christopher Columbus Park** (p75) and watch pleasure boats bobbing in the Boston Harbor. At the **New England Aquarium** (pp78–9) you can enjoy face-to-face encounters with harbor seals and stingrays. Later, take in the city's theater scene at top venues such as the **Wang and Shubert Theatres** (p88).

Gold eagle sculpture symbolizing America on the west façade of Old State House

Day 2
Morning Start your day on historic **Beacon Hill** (p44–45). Be sure to check out **Louisburg Square** (p46) and the well-curated boutiques and antique shops that line **Charles Street** (p46). Travel along the waterfront until you reach the seaport district to enjoy water views and a delicious lunch of locally caught seafood.

Afternoon Take a short walk to Fan Pier, where the **Institute of Contemporary Art** (p76) stands facing the harbor. It has become the region's focal point for modern art and also features speakers and live music. Spend the evening at **Faneuil Hall Marketplace** (p66) and enjoy the many street performances.

Day 3
Morning Beat the crowds by taking one of the first tours of the day at Fenway Park. Visit the nearby **Museum of Fine Arts** (pp106–9) next, the largest art museum in New England. Later, take the speedy elevator to the top of the iconic **Prudential Tower** (p100), where you can enjoy unparalleled views from the Skywalk observatory and while dining at Top of the Hub.

Afternoon Take a leisurely stroll through **Boston Common and the Public Garden** (pp48–9), and enjoy a ride on the seasonally operating Swan Boats. Walk up and down **Newbury Street** (p95) and **Boylston Street** (p98), both of which are lined with world-class shops. The trendy South End is great for a walk later on, buzzing with energy from its bars and restaurants.

Fenway Park, a historical landmark and home of the Boston Red Sox Baseball team

5 Days in Boston

- Walk through the Harvard and MIT campuses
- People-watch at Faneuil Hall and Quincy Market
- Enjoy a hearty Italian dinner at the North End

MIT's Great Dome surrounded by other university buildings in the college town of Cambridge

Day 1

Morning Start your day with a visit to one, or both, of the city's most lauded museums: the **Museum of Fine Arts** *(pp106–9)* and the **Isabella Stewart Gardner Museum** *(p105)*. Next, go for a behind-the-scenes tour at Fenway Park that allows visitors the opportunity to touch the famous "Green Monster" outfield wall. Have lunch at the **Prudential Tower** *(p100)* food court that offers several eating options as well as stunning views from the Skywalk observatory.

Afternoon Indulge in world-class shopping by visiting chic **Copley Place** *(p101)* or the two main shopping streets: **Newbury Street** *(p95)* and **Boylston Street** *(p98)*. A short walk away is **Boston Common and the Public Garden** *(pp48–9)* where you can enjoy a ride on the Swan Boats. Round off the day with a stroll through the trendy, lively South End neighborhood.

Day 2

Morning From Boston, hop on the subway's red line until you reach **Harvard Square** *(p110)*, an inviting neighborhood filled with eclectic shops and eateries. To best appreciate **Cambridge's** *(pp110–11)* preeminent standing in worldwide academia, explore the campus of Harvard University. Enjoy lunch in **Harvard Square** while watching the bustling crowds of students and tourists.

Afternoon Visit one of the **Harvard University Art Museums** *(pp114–16)*, then make the short journey to the **Massachusetts Institute of Technology** *(p111)*, whose campus is filled with fascinating architecture, museums, and art.

Day 3

Morning Grab a coffee or tea in one of **Beacon Hill's** *(p44)* several coffee shops, then stroll through the handsome cobblestone streets lined with impressive million-dollar real estate, especially in the exclusive **Louisburg Square** *(p46)*. Next, visit the acclaimed boutiques and antique shops along the scenic **Charles Street** *(p46)*. The many popular cafés here offer sidewalk views.

Afternoon Walk along the waterfront until you reach the **Institute of Contemporary Art** *(p76)*, a go-to destination for lovers of modern art. Special exhibits, speakers, and live music performances are commonplace. Then follow the crowds to the charming North End, where popular Italian eateries have lines out the door most nights.

Day 4

Morning Hop on one of the frequent, inexpensive boats that shuttle visitors to the Boston

The entrance to Quincy Market, a hub of social activity in the Financial District

Harbor Islands. Take a step back in time and enjoy a visit to Georges or Castle Islands, and snap stunning pictures of the Boston skyline from Spectacle Island. Upon returning to the Boston waterfront, head straight to the North End for a bite.

Afternoon A short stroll from the North End, **Charlestown** *(p117)* exudes history. Simply follow the **Freedom Trail** *(p126–29)* and you'll arrive at the **Bunker Hill Monument** *(p117)*, site of the infamous Battle of Bunker Hill. Head back towards the water to visit the historic **Charlestown Navy Yard** *(p117)* and the **U.S.S. Constitution** *(p117)*.

Day 5

Morning Greet the day with a walk through **Christopher Columbus Park** *(p75)*. Then walk to the **New England Aquarium** *(pp78–9)* to see the giant ocean tank or watch a 3D film on the huge IMAX screen. Then hop aboard a Boston Duck Tour. Enjoy tasty dishes of locally caught seafood at one of the Seaport District's waterfront eateries.

Afternoon Take a walk on the famous **Freedom Trail** *(p126–29)* and visit the **Old State House** *(pp62–3)*, then visit the iconic **Faneuil Hall** *(p65)*. Next, you'll reach the North End, where you can sit and relax outside the **Old North Church** *(p73)*. Later, laugh the night away by catching a big-name comedian at the Wilbur Theatre. Or, if the weather allows, catch a lively rock concert at the city's largest waterfront venue, the Blue Hills Bank Pavilion.

Putting Boston on the Map

Boston is situated along the United States'
northeastern Atlantic coast on Massachusetts Bay.
Founded in the early 17th century around a large
natural harbor at the mouth of the Charles River,
the modern city now covers an area of 49 sq miles
(127 sq km) and has a population of 600,000.
Boston is the capital of Massachusetts and a major
center of American history, culture, and learning.

Cornwall

St Lawrence

Fort Drum

Watertown

Lester B
Pearson

Toronto

Lake Ontario

Mississauga

Adirondack Mountains

Burlington

St Catharines

Niagara Falls

Rochester

Syracuse

Utica

Buffalo

Geneva

Auburn

NEW YORK

Lake Erie

Cortland

Oneonta

Ithaca

Catskill Mountains

CANADA

Elmira

Binghamton

UNITED STATES
OF AMERICA

○ Boston

Mansfield

Atlantic
Ocean

Gulf of
Mexico

Scranton

MEXICO

Caribbean Sea

Williamsport

Wilkes-Barre

Delaware

Hazleton

PENNSYLVANIA

Phillipsburg

Pittsburgh

Allegheny Mountains

Altoona

Allentown

Reading

Harrisburg

Trenton

Bedford

Lancaster

Philadelphia

York

Philadelphia

Camden

NEW
JERSEY

Cumberland

Hagerstown

Wilmington

MARYLAND

Frederick

Winchester

Baltimore

Dover

Delaware
Bay

WEST
VIRGINIA

Strasburg

Washington
Dulles

Baltimore-
Washington

Annapolis

Washington, DC

DELAWARE

VIRGINIA

For keys to symbols *see back flap*

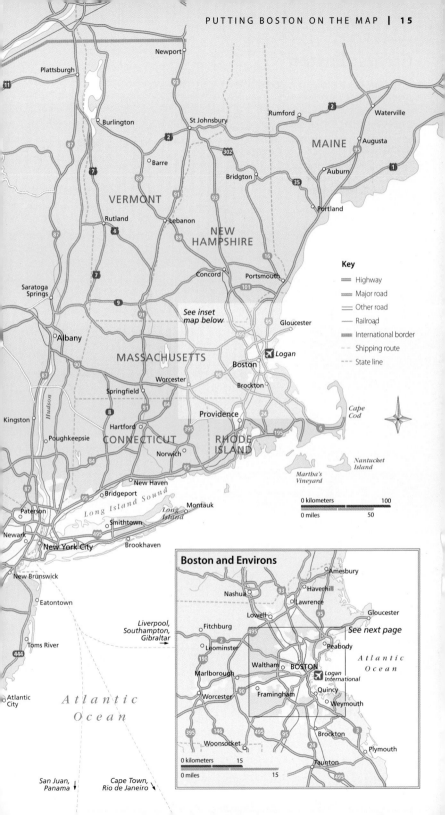

Key

- ▬▬ Highway
- ▬▬ Major road
- — Other road
- — Railroad
- ▬▬ International border
- - - - Shipping route
- - - - State line

Boston and Environs

See next page

Greater Boston

The city of Boston is made up of 20 separate districts, with the central city focused around the harbor on the Shawmut Peninsula. Much of the city lies within Suffolk County, although the greater Boston area also covers parts of Norfolk and Middlesex Counties. Boston is well served by major road, rail, air, and sea links, and has a good public transportation system, including a modern subway network.

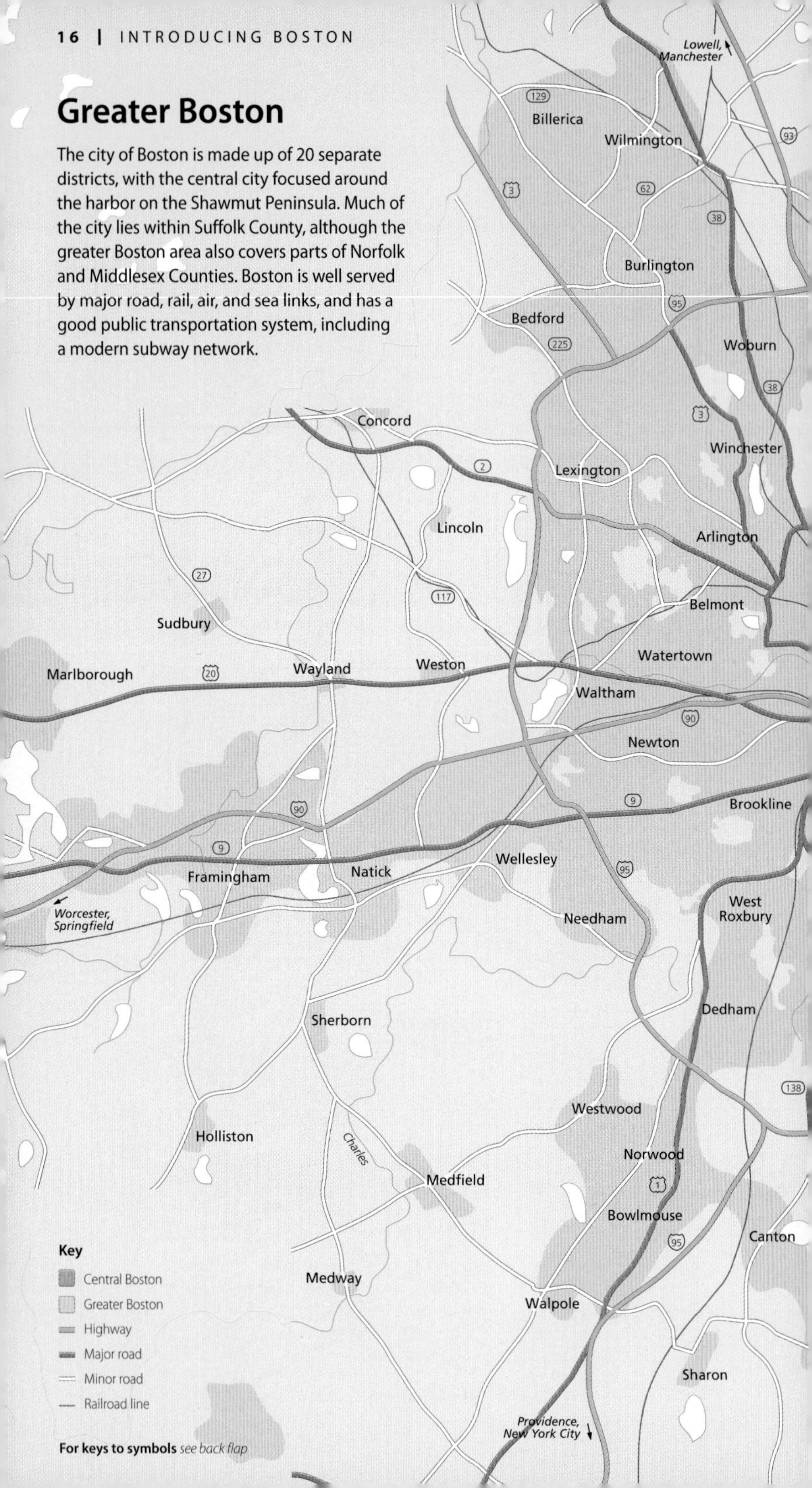

Lowell, Manchester

129
Billerica
Wilmington
93
3
62
38
Burlington
95
Bedford
225
Woburn
3
Concord
2
Lexington
Winchester
Lincoln
Arlington
27
117
Belmont
Sudbury
Weston
Watertown
Marlborough
20
Wayland
Waltham
90
Newton
9
Brookline
90
9
Wellesley
95
Framingham
Natick
West Roxbury
Worcester, Springfield
Needham
Sherborn
Dedham
138
Westwood
Holliston
Charles
Norwood
Medfield
1
Bowlmouse
Canton
95
Medway
Walpole
Sharon
Providence, New York City

Key

■ Central Boston
■ Greater Boston
▬ Highway
▬ Major road
= Minor road
- Railroad line

For keys to symbols *see back flap*

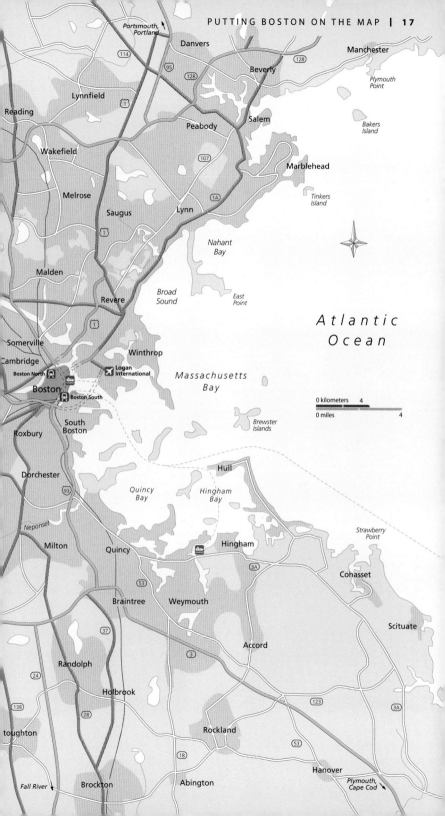

HISTORY OF BOSTON

Evidence of human occupation in Massachusetts dates from around 7500 BC. By around AD 500 Algonquin Indians were widespread in the region. Hunter-gatherers, they fished, farmed beans and pumpkins, and hunted moose and deer. They were made up of seven tribes, the closest geographically to present-day Boston being the Massachusetts, Wampanoags, and Nipmucks.

Other tribes in the region included the Nausets around Cape Cod, the Pennacooks farther north, and Pocumtucs and Mohicans to the west. Their dialects came from the same language, and their physical features were similar. Each tribe lived in close-knit communities of approximately 250 people.

The First Europeans

During the Age of the Vikings, Norsemen from Scandinavia adventured far from home, reaching North America. The coastal land of Vinland discovered by Leif Erikson in around AD 1000 may well have been on the Massachusetts coast. French and Spanish fishermen fished here in the mid-15th century and the Italian-born explorer John Cabot led an English expedition to the New England coast once in 1497 and again in 1498. A few years later Miguel Cortereal sailed from Portugal to Massachusetts, where his ship was wrecked. His name was found carved on a granite rock with the year 1511. Throughout the 16th century, the English, French, Portuguese, Spanish, and Italians explored the East Coast, whaling, fishing, and trading with the natives. In 1602 the English man Bartholomew Gosnold sailed to Massachusetts, landing on the peninsula he called Cape Cod and traversing the island he would name Martha's Vineyard after his daughter. He returned to England with furs from the natives and *sassafras* (bark of a North American tree) to be used medicinally.

In 1607 James I of England offered land in the New World to two companies. What is now Virginia he gave to the London company, led by Captain John Smith. To a group from Plymouth, England, he assigned New England and land as far south as what is now Delaware. The Plymouth Company set out in 1607 to found a colony along the Kennebec River in present-day Maine, but the harsh winter led the company to return to England. John Smith's Virginia expedition was more successful. In May 1607 he arrived in Jamestown, where he founded a permanent colony.

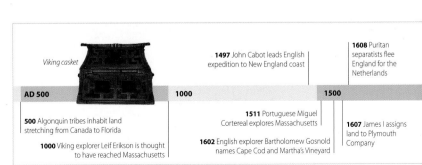

Viking casket

1497 John Cabot leads English expedition to New England coast

1608 Puritan separatists flee England for the Netherlands

AD 500

1000

1500

500 Algonquin tribes inhabit land stretching from Canada to Florida

1000 Viking explorer Leif Erikson is thought to have reached Massachusetts

1511 Portuguese Miguel Cortereal explores Massachusetts

1602 English explorer Bartholomew Gosnold names Cape Cod and Martha's Vineyard

1607 James I assigns land to Plymouth Company

◄ Inhabitants of Boston watching the Battle of Bunker Hill *(see p22)*

The first Thanksgiving at Plymouth, Massachusetts, celebrated by the Pilgrim Fathers in 1621

The Pilgrim Fathers

In 1614 John Smith traveled to the northeast and published his findings in a book entitled *A Description of New England*. This land would become a haven for people who were victims of religious persecution, especially Puritans, who did not adhere to all the beliefs and rituals of the Church of England. One group of Puritan separatists had already left England to seek greater freedom in The Netherlands, but had faced economic hardship there. Lured by Captain Smith's reports, they returned to England to seek a grant for land in the New World. Joining other Puritans led by William Bradford, they set out from Plymouth in two ships, the *Mayflower* and the *Speedwell*. Quickly discovering that the *Speedwell* was leaking, they returned to Plymouth, crammed into the *Mayflower*, and set sail again on September 16, 1620.

Meeting of John Winthrop with local native chief in around 1630

Two months later the 102 Pilgrims arrived at Cape Cod. Before disembarking, they formulated the "Mayflower Compact," agreeing to govern themselves democratically with "just and equal laws…for the general good of the colony." The Pilgrims named their new home Plymouth and soon made friends with the natives. On April 1, 1621, Governor John Carver and Chief Massasoit signed a peace treaty. They celebrated the first Thanksgiving that year sharing provisions with their native hosts.

Founding of Boston

Charles I assigned land 40 miles (65 km) north of Plymouth colony, near the Charles River, to the Massachusetts Bay Company, a large group of Puritans. In the spring of 1630 over 1,000 Puritans departed in 11 ships bound for Massachusetts. Some settled in Salem and other

1614 Captain John Smith explores the Northeast

1630 John Winthrop and Puritans settle in Boston

1636 Harvard University is founded

1652 First American coin produced in Boston

Pine-tree shilling, the first U.S. coin

1686 James II appoints Sir Edmund Andros as governor

1610 **1630** **1650** **1670**

1620 The Pilgrims settle in Plymouth

1621 Governor John Carver and Chief Massasoit sign peace treaty

1640 First English-language book printed in America

1638 Anne Hutchinson banished from Boston for religious beliefs

1660 Quaker Mary Dyer hanged on Boston Common

1684 Charles II nullifies the Massachusetts Bay Charter

1635 Boston Latin School opens

communities along the Massachusetts Bay. The vast majority, however, followed John Winthrop, their newly appointed governor, to the mouth of the Charles River. Across the river lived a recluse, an Anglican clergyman, William Blackstone. He learned that disease was rampant among the Puritans due to the scarcity of fresh drinking water, and invited them to move their settlement over the river. Winthrop and his followers were quick to accept. They first called this new land Trimountain, but soon renamed it Boston after the town in England they had left behind. In 1635 they established the Boston Latin School, the first public school in the British colonies. A year later the Puritans founded a university, named subsequently after John Harvard, who had bequeathed it his library.

Mary Dyer with other condemned Quakers, before being hanged in 1660

Although the Puritans had come to Massachusetts in pursuit of religious freedom, they often proved intolerant of others. Anne Hutchinson was driven out of Boston in 1638 for not conforming to the Puritan tradition. Many Quakers were also beaten, fined, or banished. The Quaker preacher Mary Dyer was hanged for religious unorthodoxy on June 1, 1660 on Boston Common. In 1692 after several girls in the town of Salem accused three women of witchcraft, mass hysteria broke out throughout Massachusetts, and many innocents were tried, and hanged. No one felt safe until Governor William Phips put an end to the trials in 1693.

Seeds of Rebellion

The British had passed the Navigation Acts to encourage the colonists to trade only with them, but when the colonists refused to obey, Charles II withdrew the Massachusetts Bay Charter in 1684, putting the colony under the control of the king. His successor James II appointed Sir Edmund Andros as royal governor. After James II lost power, the colonists arrested their governor and in 1689 established their own government. But in 1691 William and Mary granted a new charter to the Massachusetts Colony, combining the Massachusetts Bay and Plymouth colonies and recognizing a bicameral legislature. Later, the British and French started a long series of battles over New World territory. France finally ceded control of Canada and the American West, but the cost of war had taken its toll on the British, and the colonists were asked to pay their share in taxes. The seeds of rebellion were sown.

Painting of the commercial port of Boston in about 1730

1691 William and Mary grant new charter to Massachusetts Colony

Execution for witchcraft at Salem in 1692

1763 France cedes control of Canada and the West

1690   **1710**   **1730**   **1750**

1692 Women in Salem accused of witchcraft

1689 Colonists oust Governor Andros

1754 French and Indian War between the French and the British begins

Revolutionary Boston

It was in Boston, the most important city in the 13 British colonies, that ideas for independence were nurtured and the American Revolution born. The colonists' main quarrel with Britain lay in taxation. The Stamp Act of 1765, and the later Townshend Acts, which placed duties on imports, inflamed colonists because they had no vote. "No taxation without representation" became a common cry. The so-called "Sons of Liberty," led by Samuel Adams, demanded and received the repeal of the Stamp Act. However, attempts to enforce the Townshend Acts led to the Boston Massacre, a tragedy that signaled increasingly poor relations between Britain and its colonies.

The Boston Tea Party (1773)
In protest at taxation, Boston patriots boarded three British East India Company ships and threw their cargoes of tea into Boston Harbor (see p77).

The Boston Massacre (1770)
At the time of the Townshend Acts, British troops were sent to Boston to protect customs commissioners. Bostonians often scoffed at the soldiers and threw stones. On March 5, 1770 the jeering got out of hand. Shots were fired and five Americans fell.

Old State House
(see pp62–63)

Five Americans were killed when British troops shot into the crowd.

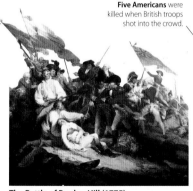

The Battle of Bunker Hill (1775)
In June 1775, militiamen from all over New England traveled to Boston to wrest control of the city from the British. The Americans lost the ensuing battle, the bloodiest of the Revolution.

1765 British Parliament passes the Stamp Act

British Revenue stamp

1773 Tea Act gives British East India Company monopoly. Boston Tea Party

1765

1770

1767 Townshend Acts place duties on imports

1770 Five Americans killed in Boston Massacre

1766 Repeal of the Stamp Act

Evacuation of Boston 1776
Following the Battle of Bunker Hill, Boston remained under British control. For almost a year American troops lay siege to the city, until in March 1776 George Washington masterminded a strategy that finally led the British to evacuate.

John Hancock
A key participant in the Revolution, Hancock was chosen as a delegate of Massachusetts to attend the first ever Continental Congress, held in 1774.

British soldiers were sent to protect customs commissioners.

Declaration of Independence (1776)
Events surrounding the Battle of Bunker Hill and the evacuation of Boston inspired insurrection throughout the 13 colonies. This led, in July 1776, to the signing of the Declaration of Independence. Freedom from Britain finally came in 1781.

Paul Revere's Ride

On April 18, 1775 the British planned to march to Lexington to capture Samuel Adams and John Hancock, and then on to Concord to seize arms. To signal the route of British troops, sexton Robert Newman hung lanterns in the tower of the Old North Church (*see p73*) and, so legend has it, Paul Revere undertook his "midnight ride." Revere's ride is immortalized in Longfellow's 1863 verse book *Tales of a Wayside Inn*. During the ensuing skirmish at Lexington Green, eight American militiamen were killed – the first battle of the American Revolution had been fought.

Warning lights in the Old North Church

1774 Intolerable Acts passed; Boston Harbor is closed

1776 Siege of Boston ends. Declaration of Independence adopted by Continental Congress

1781 General Cornwallis surrenders at Yorktown, Virginia

1775

1780

1775 Midnight ride of Paul Revere

Grand Union, America's first national flag

1783 U.S. and Britain sign Treaty of Paris

1777 U.S. victory at Battle of Saratoga is the turning point of the war

Athens of America

With the end of the Revolutionary War, Boston's population began to grow and its economy flourish. Its port boomed, and trade, with China in particular, flourished. Some Bostonians made their fortunes at sea; others started profitable textile mills. A number of old Boston families – the Cabots, the Lowells, the Lodges – rose to great prominence boasting of their lineage, their wealth, and their Yankee independence. The United States elected not one but two members of the Adams family (both Boston residents) to the presidency: John Adams (1797–1801) and his son John Quincy Adams (1825–1829). John Adams' wife Abigail, one of the nation's most revered first ladies, made an early call for women's rights when she admonished her husband to "remember the Ladies," for "we … will not hold ourselves bound by any law in which we have no voice, or representation."

Boston soon earned a reputation as the intellectual capital of the new United States. The Boston Athenaeum (see p51),

Abigail Smith Adams
(1744–1818)

both a museum and library, was first organized in 1807 "for the promotion of literary and scientific learning." Eminent Bostonians (see pp32–33) at this time included the essayist Ralph Waldo Emerson, who formed the Transcendental Club, naturalist Henry David Thoreau, novelist Nathaniel Hawthorne, poet Henry Wadsworth Longfellow, whose epic poem made famous the midnight ride of Paul Revere (see p23), James Russell Lowell, the first editor of the Atlantic Monthly, and poet, diarist and educational reformer Oliver Wendell Holmes (see p47) . The Boston Public Library, the oldest free library in the U.S., was founded in 1852.

Initially most of Boston's European settlers came from England, but from 1846 Boston attracted thousands of immigrants driven out of Ireland by the potato famine. When the Irish first arrived they settled in overcrowded tenements along the city's waterfront and faced discrimination from the city's residents, especially its social elite, the Boston Brahmins (see p47). Signs went

The Boston Athenaeum, first organized in 1807 but later housed in this building, which was designed in 1846

1787 Constitutional Convention held in Philadelphia

1789 Inauguration of George Washington as president

1812 War with England

1825 William Ellery Channing founds American Unitarian Association

1800

1820

1786 Daniel Shay's rebellion

1796 John Adams elected as second president

George Washington (1732–99)

1807 Boston Athenaeum is founded

Irish immigrants, who poured into mid 19th-century Boston

up around the city with the words "No Irish Need Apply." But despite these obstacles, the Irish rose in stature and by the end of the 19th century would dominate Boston politics and other areas of the city's life.

The Abolition Movement

Some of America's most vehement anti-slavery sentiment originated in Boston. William Lloyd Garrison *(see p32)* published the first issue of *The Liberator* on January 1, 1831 calling for the unconditional abolition of slavery: "I will not equivocate … I will not excuse … I will not retreat a single inch … and I will be heard." Not all Bostonians sympathized with his cause. To escape from angry mobs he once had to seek safety for the night in a Boston jail. Garrison and other abolitionists (Charles Sumner, Wendell Phillips, Frederick Douglass) gave rousing antislavery speeches in Faneuil Hall *(see p65)*, and accounts of their fiery oratory spread across the United States. The city also played an active role in the underground railroad. Fugitive slaves were assured a safe haven, and

popular stopping-off points were the Second African Meeting House, the home of Lewis Hayden (a former slave), and John J. Smith's barbershop on the corner of Howard and Bulfinch Streets. When the first shots of the Civil War were fired on Fort Sumter on April 12, 1861, President Abraham Lincoln immediately asked volunteers to enlist. The state of Massachusetts answered the call first, sending 1,500 men within four days. As soon as African Americans were admitted to the Union forces, black soldiers started training in Boston. The Boston Brahmin, Colonel Robert Gould Shaw *(see p32)* led these men (the 54th Regiment of the Massachusetts Volunteer Infantry) in an assault on Fort Wagner, South Carolina – Shaw and 62 members of the regiment lost their lives. The battle is still remembered for the role played by African Americans, and a monument *(see p49)* to it on Boston Common was dedicated on May 31, 1897.

Attack on Fort Wagner by black soldiers of the 54th Massachusetts

1846 First influx of Irish immigrants into Boston

1852 Boston Public Library founded

1861 First shots at Fort Sumter begin Civil War

1840

1860

Mural in the Boston Public Library

1831 First issue of William Lloyd Garrison's abolitionist newspaper, *The Liberator*

1863 The 54th Massachusetts leads assault on Fort Wagner

1865 General Robert E. Lee surrenders. The Union is preserved. President Abraham Lincoln is assassinated

Growth and Destruction

The end of the Civil War in 1865 led to a decline in shipping, but the Industrial Revolution, specifically in cotton and wool manufacturing, enabled Boston to thrive again and grow both in size and population. The Back Bay had been filled and some of the neighboring towns already annexed. However, on November 9, 1872, Boston suffered a terrible setback as flames from a fire that started in a dry goods store spread to warehouses downtown, destroying 765 buildings. Newspaper headlines declared a loss of $250 million with "rich men beggared in a day." The city recovered quickly, though, rebuilding and revitalizing textile and shoe manufacturing.

The Great Fire of Boston, November 9, 1872

Public institutions also continued to flourish. The Museum of Fine Arts, Boston (see pp106–9) was opened in 1876, and the Boston Symphony Orchestra (see p160) founded in 1881. The first subway in the United States, the "T," opened in 1897. In Boston and the surrounding areas educational establishments such as Harvard, Radcliffe, the Massachusetts Institute of Technology (MIT), the New England Conservatory of Music, and Boston University all played their part in making the city a mecca for young students. The renowned collector of art Isabella Stewart Gardner (see p105), a rich, famously outspoken, and well-connected woman, opened her house to the public on New Year's Day, 1903.

The Early 20th Century

Following World War I, changing political and cultural attitudes across the U.S. increasingly left government clashing violently with the wishes of the people. Life in Boston was no exception. The Boston Police Strike of 1919 marks one of the most dramatic chapters in the U.S. Labor movement. As many as 1,290 policemen filed complaints over low wages, unsanitary stations, and lack of overtime compensation and sought affiliation with the American Federation of Labor (A.F.L.). When the strike started, mobs smashed windows and looted stores. After a skirmish with state militia, in which two were wounded and nine killed, A.F.L. president Samuel Gompers persuaded the police to return to work.

However, this was not just a time of conflict, but also one when popular culture

Matthew James Dailey, a captain during the Boston Police Strike

1872 The Great Fire of Boston

1884 First Irish mayor, Hugh O'Brien, elected

1897 The "T," the U.S.'s first subway, opens.

1905 "Honey Fitz" elected mayor

1919 Boston Police Strike results in riots

1875

1900

1925

1876 Museum of Fine Arts, Boston opened

1881 Boston Symphony Orchestra formed

Museum of Fine Arts, Boston exhibit

1912 Fenway Park opens

1914 James Michael Curley elected mayor for the first time

1903 Isabella Stewart Gardner opens her house to the public

came to the fore. One way this manifested itself was in spectator sports, which began to enjoy unparalleled popularity. Fenway Park in Boston, home to the Boston Red Sox, had opened on April 20, 1912. The Boston Red Sox won the World Series four times before 1918. Supposedly cursed by the sale of slugger Babe Ruth to the New York Yankees, they did not win the World Series again until 2004.

Prominent politicians from this time included John F. Kennedy's grandfather, John F. Fitzgerald, or "Honey Fitz," as he was known, who was elected mayor in 1905. The flamboyant James Curley, son of Irish immigrants, who became mayor, congressman, and governor, and spent time in jail for fraud, became a legend in his own lifetime.

Babe Ruth (1895–1948) in an ad for chewing gum

U.S. President John F. Kennedy was born of Boston Irish stock

City Renaissance

In the late 20th and early 21st centuries, the face of central Boston was transformed. The Big Dig – a 20-year, $15-billion project to bury the I-93 highway – ended in 2005, providing new tunnels and bridges. A linear park, the Rose Fitzgerald Kennedy Greenway, replaced the surface highway. Adjacent land in South Boston was developed as the Seaport district, even as a Boston economy based on finance, education, biomedical research, and information technology soared.

Post-War Politics

The most famous Boston-born politician was John F. Kennedy, great-grandson of an Irish potato famine immigrant. In 1960 he became the United States' first Catholic, and youngest elected, president. His brother, Robert, served as attorney general and U.S. senator for New York. Another brother, Edward, became a U.S. senator for Massachusetts and a leading progressive figure in national politics. Michael Dukakis, the son of Greek immigrants, was elected governor in 1974, becoming the Democratic presidential candidate in 1988. The first mayor of Italian descent, Thomas Menino, presided over Boston from 1993 through 2014.

Boat tours on the Charles River, evidence that Boston is prospering

1960 John F. Kennedy elected president

1988 Governor Michael Dukakis becomes Democratic presidential candidate

1993 John F. Kennedy Library and Museum (see p104) opens

2006 Deval Patrick elected as first African-American governor of Massachusetts

2013 Terrorist bombings during Boston Marathon kill 3 and injure many

1950   1975   2000   2025

1962 Edward Kennedy elected to U.S. Senate

1963 John F. Kennedy assassinated

2004 Red Sox win World Series

Michael Dukakis, Democratic presidential candidate in 1988

2015 Edward M. Kennedy Institute for the U.S. Senate opens

2010 Museum of Fine Arts, Boston (see pp106–9) opens Art of the Americas wing

BOSTON AT A GLANCE

Although it is a small, compact city, Boston offers a wealth of attractions that draw visitors from all over the world. Indeed the range of attractions can exceed that of much larger cities in the U.S. The sights in the center and a little way out of Boston are covered in the *Area by Area* section of the book. There are historic neighborhoods, such as Beacon Hill and Back Bay; examples of some of the best Federal architecture in the U.S., such as the Massachusetts State House; and beautiful examples of late 19th-century opulence such as Trinity Church. The treasures of the Museum of Fine Arts and the Harvard museums are also shown. A selection of Boston's best is featured below.

Boston's Top Ten Attractions

Beacon Hill
See pp44–7

Old State House
See pp62–3

Massachusetts State House
See pp52–3

Museum of Fine Arts
See pp106–9

New England Aquarium
See pp78–9

Newbury Street
See p95

Trinity Church
See pp96–7

Old North Church
See p73

Harvard University
See pp112–16

Boston Common
See pp48–9

◀ Federal-style rowhouses on Beacon Hill, one of the wealthiest neighborhoods in Boston

Boston's Best: Museums

The city of Boston's Athenian self-image is manifested in dozens of museums, galleries, and archives. Wealthy 19th-century patrons stocked art museums that have now become world-class collections, the best example being the Museum of Fine Arts. Likewise, Boston's leadership in scientific inquiry has created first-rate natural history and science collections. Museums such as the John F. Kennedy Library and Museum provide insight into some of the city's most compelling and influential historical figures, while a strong architectural heritage means that some of the museum buildings are also very beautiful.

Museum of Science
A favorite family destination, this museum has more than 700 interactive exhibits, that explain the laws of nature and the science of computers.

Harvard University Museums
These museums house a diverse range of collections, including archaeology and natural history. The Harvard Art Museums *(right)* combine the holdings of three museums, displaying European, Asian, American, and Near Eastern art.

0 meters	500
0 yards	500

Isabella Stewart Gardner Museum
This Venetian-style *palazzo* stands as Isabella Gardner left it – filled to the brim with fine old masters and modern paintings. Her taste in art was considered by many to be impeccable.

CHARLES ST

BEACON STREET

ARLINGTON ST

COMMONWEALTH AVENUE

BOYLSTON STREET

BACK BAY AND SOUTH END

HUNTINGTON AVE

COLUMBUS AVENUE

WASHINGTON ST

Museum of Fine Arts
One of the largest museums in North America, the MFA is famous for its Greek, Roman, and Egyptian art, and French Impressionist paintings.

Otis House Museum

Designed by Charles Bulfinch *(see p55)*, this house ushered in the Federal style of architecture. It presents a snapshot of life in the early days of the American Republic.

New England Aquarium

This aquarium displays a huge array of creatures from the world's oceans. The researchers at the aquarium are also involved in key international fish and whale conservation programs.

NORTH END AND THE WATERFRONT

HANOVER ST

COMMERCIAL ST

BEACON HILL AND WEST END

OLD BOSTON AND THE FINANCIAL DISTRICT

ATLANTIC AVE

TREMONT STREET

SUMMER ST

CHINATOWN AND THE THEATER DISTRICT

WASHINGTON ST

Institute of Contemporary Art

Boston's first new major art museum building to open in nearly a century sits on a prime spot on the South Boston waterfront.

Nichols House Museum

An elegant Federal-style house on Beacon Hill, this museum offers a glimpse of the domestic life of the 19th-century social elite.

John F. Kennedy Library and Museum

The nation's 35th president is celebrated here – video clips of the first president to fully grasp the power of the media make this a compelling museum.

Eminent Bostonians

Founded as a refuge for religious idealists, Boston has always been obsessed with ideas and learning. Mark Twain once observed that "In New York they ask what a man is worth. In Boston they ask, 'What does he know?'" This insistence on the power of ideas has made Boston a magnet for thinkers and doers, and a hotbed of reform movements and social revolution. Education has always been one of the city's leading industries. Consequently, Boston is disproportionately represented in the honor roll of American intellectual life. Bostonians are generally considered to be liberal minded, and tend to occupy the left flank of American political thought.

Malcolm X (1925–65), one of Boston's famous residents and head of the Nation of Islam

Reformers, Rabble Rousers and Revolutionaries

Even while Boston was still in its infancy, Bostonians began to agitate to do things differently. Anne Hutchinson (1591–1643) was exiled for heresy in 1638 (she moved south to found Portsmouth, Rhode Island), while friend and fellow religious radical Mary Dyer died on the Boston Common gallows for Quakerism in 1660 (see p21). Spokesman for the Sons of Liberty and part-time brewer Samuel Adams (1722–1803) incited Boston to revolution in the "Boston Tea Party" (see p77). The city bubbled over with

Abolitionist William Lloyd Garrison (1805–79)

19th-century reformers, including Dorothea Dix (1802–87), who championed the welfare of the mentally ill, and William Lloyd Garrison (1805–79), publisher of *The Liberator*, who was one of America's most strident voices calling for the abolition of slavery. Malcolm Little (1925–65) spent his adolescence in Boston before converting to Islam in prison and emerging as the charismatic Black Muslim leader Malcolm X. Like Malcolm X, Nguyen Tat Thanh (1890–1969) spent part of his youth in Boston, working for a time in the restaurant of the Omni Parker House Hotel (see p60). Traveling much of the world in his 20s, he was later to assume the name Ho Chi Minh.

Boston Brahmins

In 1860 Oliver Wendell Holmes (1809–94) dubbed Boston's prosperous merchant class the "Boston Brahmins … a harmless, inoffensive, untitled aristocracy" (see p47). Any suggestion that the Brahmins were unaccomplished, however, could not be farther from the truth. Julia Ward Howe (1819–1910) was a prominent abolitionist and later a crusader for women's rights. She also penned the Unionists' Civil War marching song, "The Battle Hymn of the Republic." Brahmin Colonel Robert Gould Shaw (1837–63) led the all-Black 54th Massachusetts Regiment in the Civil War, and Major Henry Lee Higginson (1834–1919) survived the war to found the Boston Symphony Orchestra in 1881.

Many famous authors were also Brahmins, notably the Lowell clan: James Russell Lowell (1819–91) was the leading literary critic of his day, Amy Lowell (1874–1925) championed "free verse" and founded *Poetry* magazine, and Robert Lowell (1917–77) broke the barriers between formal and informal verse in American poetry. The Brahmins' greatest chronicler was the noted historian Samuel Eliot Morison (1887–1976).

The Brahmins persist through business partnerships, family trusts, and intermarriage, as highlighted in their ditty: "And this is good old Boston, The home of the bean and the cod, Where the Lowells talk to the Cabots, And the Cabots talk only to God."

Inventors and Entrepreneurs

Innovation has always been a way of life in Boston. Donald McKay's (1810–80) East Boston clipper ships revolutionized international sea trade in the

Edwin Land (1909–91), inventor of Polaroid instant photography

1850s. Working in his Cambridge workshop, Elias Howe (1819–67) created the modern sewing machine, radically altering both the clothing trade and the shoe industry. Alexander Graham Bell (1847–1922) had offices in Cambridge and Boston, and later joined the faculty of Boston University. Edwin H. Land (1909–91) experimented with polarized light in his Harvard lab before inventing Polaroid instant photography. The innovators Bolt, Beranek, and Newman also made academic affiliations with the Massachusetts Institute of Technology, and they also sent the world's first electronic mail message in the 1970s. Facebook was launched from a dorm room at Harvard University in 2004.

Thinkers

In addition to showing the world how to do things, Bostonians have always been adept at explaining why. In his many essays and poems, Ralph Waldo Emerson (1803–82) first laid the philosophical groundwork for an American school of transcendental religious thought. Meanwhile, his friend and fellow Harvard graduate Henry David Thoreau (1817–62) wrote many seminal works of natural philosophy. A professor at Harvard, William James (1842–1910) not only taught psychology and

physiology, but also promulgated philosophical pragmatism, the concept that the worth of an idea is based on its usefulness. His student, George Santayana (1863–1952) blossomed as the 20th-century's chief philosopher of aesthetics.

More pragmatically, the Harvard economist John Kenneth Galbraith (1908–2006) investigated the sources of societal affluence and advocated social policies to put that affluence to work for the common good.

Political Leaders

Boston's most infamous politician was the "rascal king" James Michael Curley (1874–1958), who served many terms as mayor and U.S. Congressman, winning his last election from a jail cell. His life was to serve as the model for the novel *The Last Hurrah*. Boston also gave the country four presidents: John Adams (1735–1826) and his son John Quincy Adams (1767–1848); the tight-lipped ex-governor Calvin Coolidge (1872–1933), who rose to prominence by crushing the Boston police strike in 1919; and John F. Kennedy, infamously assassinated in Dallas in 1963. Kennedy's brothers were also prominent on the national stage: Robert F. Kennedy (1925–1968) served as attorney general and then as senator, when he, too, was assassinated. Edward M. Kennedy (1932–2010) served for 46 years in the U.S. Senate as a leading advocate for social justice. His good friend, Thomas P. "Tip" O'Neill (1912–94), served as U.S. Speaker of the House.

John F. Kennedy campaign button

Authors

America's first published author was Boston's Anne Bradstreet (1612–72). The first published African American author was Phillis Wheatley (1753–84), born in Africa, enslaved, then freed in Boston. Her 1778 volume, *Poems on Various Subjects, Religious and Moral*, echoed Boston authors' moral concerns. Henry Wadsworth Longfellow (1807–82) made his fortune from best-selling verse epics such as *Evangeline* and *Hiawatha*, but made his mark translating Dante. Although associated with nearby Concord, popular novelist Louisa May Alcott (1832–88) also lived on Beacon Hill and was active in Boston reform movements. New York-born Henry James (1843–1916) was educated at Harvard and often returned to Boston from his London home, spending a lifetime contrasting American and European culture. Former U.S. poet laureate Robert Pinsky (born 1940) teaches at Boston University, as does novelist Leslie Epstein (born 1938). The popular Boston-based fictional detective Spenser was the creation of Robert Parker (1932–2010), and when not hanging out with Clint Eastwood, suspense novelist and screenwriter Dennis Lehane (born 1966) broods at Fort Point Channel.

Author Louisa May Alcott (1832–88), part of Boston's reform movement

Boston's Architecture

Buildings followed British styles through the 1790s, when the first American architect of note, Charles Bulfinch, defined the Federal style. In the 19th century, Bostonians evolved a local Victorian style, which first embraced Greek Classicism, then French and Italian styles. Two styles of the late 19th century, Renaissance Revival and Richardsonian Romanesque, remained influential through World War I. In the 20th century, Harvard University and Massachusetts Institute of Technology (MIT) attracted many leading modern and post-modern architects, all of whom left their mark.

Renaissance Revival interior of the Boston Public Library

Freestanding Federal-style Harrison Gray Otis House

Federal

Charles Bulfinch and his protégé Asher Benjamin adapted British Georgian styles to create Boston's first signature architectural style. Typical of this style are freestanding mansions and town houses, with symmetrical brick façades adorned by shuttered windows, and ground-floor windows set in recessed arches. Entrances are often cut from granite slabs, featuring gently fluted columns. The largest and most elegant rooms of Federal homes are usually found on the second floor.

Some of the grander examples of Federal domestic architecture, found mainly on Beacon Hill, feature ornamental ironwork and are often crowned with octagonal cupolas. Chestnut Street on Beacon Hill (see pp44–5) represents the greatest concentration of Federal-style row houses in Boston. Individual examples of the style include the Harrison Gray Otis House (see p54) and the Hepzibah Swan Houses (see p47).

Boston Granite

The granite outcrops found around Boston Harbor provided stone for the city's waterfront development in the early 19th century. Technological advances had made it possible to cut entire columns from single blocks of granite. Freed from the constraints of soft limestone or sandstone, Alexander Parris and other architects adopted granite as a principal material for markets and warehouses, as can be seen for example at Charlestown Navy Yard (see p117) and Quincy Market (see p66). Although the basic style is an adaptation of Greek Revival, it also includes modern innovations such as iron tension rods and laminated wooden ribs to support copper domes.

Granite Greek Revival façade of Quincy Market

Renaissance Revival

Charles McKim's 1887 design for the Boston Public Library (see p98), conceived as a "palace of the people," established Renaissance Revival architecture as a favorite American style for monumental public structures. Evenly spaced windows and arches, adorned by inscriptions and sculptural details, define the style. Soaring, barrel vaulted interiors are also featured. Boston's Renaissance Revival structures make extensive use of New England and Italian marbles, carved stucco ceilings, and carved wood in staircases and walls. Many of the Italian artisans who were brought over to execute this work stayed in Boston, forming an elite group within the Italian immigrant community by around 1900.

Richardsonian Romanesque

America is far too young to boast a true Romanesque style, but Henry Hobson Richardson effectively created one from European inspirations and American stone. By the 1870s, the wealthy city of Boston demanded more elaborate

Distinctive, multicolored, square tower of Trinity Church

churches than the existing sparsely designed "boxes with a spire." Gothic styles, however, were associated with medieval Catholicism and were unacceptable to the Protestant heirs of the Puritans. Richardson's churches provided a pleasing alternative. Often, the building's main components were massed around a central tower, as can be seen in Boston's most important example of the style, Trinity Church (see pp96–7), as well as in the First Baptist Church (see p94). In sharp contrast to the Boston Granite style, which used many similar materials and sharp angles, Richardson used stones of contrasting colors and rounded off virtually every square edge.

Romanesque-style front portico of the First Baptist Church

Victorian

Boston's Victorian style largely eschews the pointed Gothic lines of English Victorian in favor of French Academic, French Empire, and various Italianate influences. The variations are displayed in an almost chronological march of styles in the Back Bay and South End (see pp90–101), paralleling the decade-by-decade creation of filled land in those neighborhoods in the second half of the 19th century. Earlier buildings tend to reflect their stylistic influences more accurately; for example, the Italianate Gibson House Museum (see p94) on Beacon Street, which would have been among the first wave of Back Bay development. The later town houses of upper Newbury

Italianate interior detail of the Victorian Gibson House Museum

Street and Massachusetts Avenue reflect a more mature synthesis: raised granite entrances, slate-shingled mansard roofs, and dormer and bay windows. Nowhere is the transition from early to late Victorian styles so evident than on the walk westward, from the center of Boston, along Commonwealth Avenue (see p95).

Art Deco

Most of Boston's Art Deco buildings are clustered around Post Office Square in the Financial District, with the former Post Office (see p67) and the Verizon Building (see p67) being the finest examples. Essentially tall buildings of light gray granite, they are constructed with vertical strips and slit windows that elongate their forms. Elaborate geometric steps and surface ornament on the upper stories help relieve their mass. Boston

The Verizon Building, overlooking Post Office Square

Art Deco tends also to make great use of Greco-Roman geometric friezes and stylized, vegetable-inspired ornament. Some Financial District Art Deco buildings also feature bas-relief murals of historic and heroic themes. Back Bay was once the site of many Art Deco storefronts with stylized Parisian pilasters and grillwork, but only the former quarters of Shreve, Crump & Low Inc. on Boylston Street (see p98) remain intact.

Modernist interior of the Kresge Chapel, built in the 1950s

Modernism

The willing embrace of Modernism at Boston and Cambridge colleges has graced the Boston area with a wide range of outstanding 20th-century buildings where simplicity of form is favored over ornament, and expressive lines grow out of function. When Bauhaus director Walter Gropius fled the Nazis for the safety of Harvard University, he served as a magnet for some of the mid-century's great designers and architects. The range of styles in Boston's Modernist buildings is diverse: the poetic sculptural grace of Eero Saarinen's Kresge Auditorium and Chapel at MIT (see p111); Le Corbusier's Carpenter Center for the Visual Arts (see p113); and Josep Lluis Sert's International-style Smith Campus Center, both near Harvard Yard (see pp112–13).

BOSTON THROUGH THE YEAR

Perhaps more than in any other city in the U.S., Boston's cultural life tends to follow the academic calendar, with the "year" beginning when classes commence at its many colleges and universities in September, and winding down a little with the start of the summer recess in May and June. In between is so-called "ice cream" season, when the warm weather causes most activities to shift out of doors, and reading lists favor fiction over more scholarly texts. Though the cultural life of the city tends to flourish from fall to spring, the summer months do feature many of Boston's major carnivals, festivals, parades, and free outdoor concerts at the Hatch Shell *(see p94)*. After the students' return to their studies in the fall, the busy performing arts season begins, with symphony concerts, theater, and ballet continuing into the following spring.

Springtime tulips in full bloom, Public Garden

Spring

When the weather warms, Boston bursts into bloom. Thousands of tulips explode in the Public Garden, and the magnolia trees of Commonwealth Avenue are sheathed in pink and white. Spring is a season of remembrance, with commemorations of events leading up to the American Revolution. It also marks the start of the season for the Boston Red Sox.

March
Reenactment of Boston Massacre *(early Mar)*, Old State House. Marks watershed event that turned Bostonians against their British rulers.
Boston Flower & Garden Show *(mid-Mar)*, various venues. One of the oldest annual flower exhibitions in the United States.
St. Patrick's Day Parade *(mid-Mar)*, South Boston.

This annual parade also commemorates the British evacuation of Boston during the Revolutionary War.

April
Baseball *(early Apr)*, Fenway Park. Major league season starts for Boston Red Sox.
Annual Lantern Festival *(Patriots Day Eve)*, Old North Church. Commemorates hanging signal lanterns in the steeple to warn revolutionaries.
Patriots Day Parade *(third Mon)*, from City Hall Plaza to Paul Revere Mall, where the start of Paul Revere's Midnight Ride is reenacted.
Boston Marathon *(third Mon)*, Hopkinton to Back Bay. America's oldest marathon.

May
MayFair *(early May)*, Harvard Square. International street fair.
Walk for Hunger *(first Sun)*, 20-mile (32-km) walk, one of the oldest and largest pledge walks in the country, raises funds for food banks.
Duckling Day Parade *(second Sun)*, Boston Common. Parade retracing the route of the ducklings in Robert McCloskey's classic children's storybook, *Make Way for Ducklings*.
Arts First *(late Apr–early May)*, Cambridge. More than 200 free performances of music, theater, and dance – all on Harvard campus.
Hidden Gardens of Beacon Hill *(third Thu)*, Beacon Hill. Garden tours organized.
Lilac Sunday *(mid-May)*, Arnold Arboretum. More than 400 lilac bushes are in bloom.
Street Performers Festival *(late May)*, Faneuil Hall Marketplace. Street musicians, jugglers, acrobats, and others launch their season.
Boston Pops *(May–Jun)*, Symphony Hall. Season features light Classical repertory and American popular music.

Runners at the annual Boston Marathon, held in April

Average Daily Hours of Sunshine

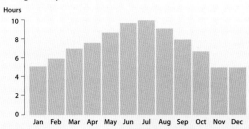

Hours

Jan Feb Mar Apr May Jun Jul Aug Sep Oct Nov Dec

Sunshine Chart
Boston enjoys long and light summer days from June to August, with July being the sunniest month. Fall has more sunshine than spring, but while spring is mild, fall becomes quite chilly. Winter days are shorter, but many are still clear and bright.

Summer

When summer's heat finally arrives, Bostonians head outdoors to relax on the grassy banks of the Charles River, along the harbor, and in the city's many parks. The Hatch Shell on the Esplanade becomes the scene of many free open-air concerts. The grandest celebration occurs on the Fourth of July, with one of the country's greatest fireworks displays, following an invariably rousing performance by the Boston Pops Orchestra.

Fourth of July fireworks lighting up the sky over the Charles River

Summer outdoor concert at Hatch Shell, Charles River Esplanade

June
Performing Arts Series at the Hatch Shell *(Jun–Sep)*, Hatch Shell, Esplanade. Free outdoor movies, and pop, rock, and classical concerts.
Cambridge River Festival *(early Jun)*. Multicultural festival on the banks of the Charles River.
Scooper Bowl *(early Jun)*, City Hall Plaza. One of the largest ice cream festivals in the U.S.
Boston Pride *(mid-Jun)*. New England's largest gay pride

parade and festival caps a week of celebrating diversity.
Bunker Hill Weekend *(weekend before Jun 17)*, Charlestown. Costumed reenactments, demonstrations, a parade, and guided tours at Bunker Hill Monument.
Dragon Boat Festival *(mid-Jun)*, Charles River. Traditional Asian dragon boat races.

July
Italian Feast Days *(Jul–Aug)*, North End. Religious processions with music and food take place almost every weekend.
Boston Harborfest *(week of Jul 4)*. Features children's events, concerts, harbor cruises, and a Chowderfest on City Hall Plaza.
Boston Pops Annual Fourth of July Concert and Fireworks *(Jul 4)*, Esplanade. The largest of the free Boston Pops concerts in July.
Bastille Day *(Fri before Jul 14)*, Back Bay. Annual celebration sponsored by the French Cultural Center.

Annual Festival Betances *(mid-Jul)*, South End. Annual Puerto Rican festival with music, dance, and food.

August
August Moon Festival *(mid-Aug)*, Chinatown. Lion dance, martial arts, Chinese opera.
Dine Out Boston *(late Mar and late Aug)*, Boston and Cambridge. Around 200 restaurants offer low fixed-price lunch and dinner menus.
Boston Caribbean Carnival *(late Aug)*, Franklin Park. Extravagant costumes, music, food, and dancing.

July 4th parade, Government Center

Average Monthly Temperature

°C
30
20
10
0
-5

☐ Maximum temperature
☐ Minimum temperature

°F
86
68
50
32
23

Jan Feb Mar Apr May Jun Jul Aug Sep Oct Nov Dec

Temperature Chart
This chart shows the average minimum and maximum temperatures for each month in Boston. The highest temperatures of the year are in July and August, when it is hot and humid. Winters are cold, and while they can be clear and bright, they are also often stormy, resulting in wind-chill temperatures well below freezing point.

Fall

After Labor Day, Boston's massive student community returns. This time also sees the start of seasons for the performing arts and for basketball and hockey. The vivid colors of New England's deciduous fall trees attract thousands of people to Boston, on their way to backcountry tours. Mid-November brings cold weather and the beginning of the holiday season.

Famous fiery colors of New England's fall foliage

September

Feast of Saints Cosma & Damiano (second weekend), East Cambridge. Italian festival with parade.
Cambridge Carnival (mid-Sep). Ethnic cuisine, music, crafts, and a colorful parade to celebrate African and Caribbean cultural heritage.
Berklee BeanTown Jazz Festival (late Sep), South End. This event features contemporary jazz, blues, and salsa.
Boston Fashion Week (late Sep), city-wide. A variety of events showcase Boston's established couturiers and rising fashionistas.

Outdoor musical performance

Boston Open Studios (Sep–early Dec). Art communities in Boston, including Fort Point and the South End, schedule studio tours.

October

Boston Symphony Orchestra Season (Oct–Apr). Orchestra performs in historic Symphony Hall.
Basketball (Oct–Apr), TD Garden. NBA (National Basketball Association) season begins for the Boston Celtics.
Hockey (Oct–Apr), TD Garden. NHL (National Hockey League) season begins for the Boston Bruins.
Columbus Day Parade (early Oct), parade alternates between East Boston (even years) and the North End.
Boston Ballet Season (mid-Oct–May), Opera House. Professional repertory company gives performances.
Head of the Charles Regatta (second to last Weekend Oct), Cambridge. Rowing event featuring 1,400 boats and 11,000 athletes.
Ellis Memorial Antiques Show (late Oct–early Nov), various locations.
Boston Jewish Film Festival (late Oct–mid-Nov), contemporary films on Jewish themes, lectures, and discussions.

November

Boston International Antiquarian Book Fair (early to mid-Nov), Hynes Convention Center. One of oldest and largest in the U.S.
Ice Skating on Frog Pond (mid-Nov–March), Boston Common.
Ski and Snowboard Expo (mid-Nov), Seaport World Trade Center. Sports enthusiasts prepare for the winter season.
Veterans Day Parade (Nov 11), Downtown. Marching and high school bands, and veterans' groups honor all those who served in the armed forces.

Average Monthly Precipitation

MM
300
240
180
120
60
0

Jan Feb Mar Apr May Jun Jul Aug Sep Oct Nov Dec

☐ Rainfall (from baseline)
☐ Snow (from baseline)

Inches
12
9
6
3
0

Rainfall Chart
This chart shows the average monthly rain and snowfall in Boston. Precipitation levels are fairly constant throughout the year, at around 3–4 inches (8–10 cm) per month, apart from during winter when much of this falls as snow, which stays on the ground until March.

Winter

Tree-lighting ceremonies and decorated store windows help make Boston's cityscape magical at Christmas. As the old year ends, the entire city joins in the downtown festivities that celebrate the joy of First Night, a worldwide institution launched in Boston. When the frigid weather arrives in mid-January, Bostonians get geared up for a busy season of performing arts and food and wine expositions.

December

CraftBoston Holiday *(early to mid-Dec)*, Boston Center for the Arts. Top-quality juried crafts exhibition for artistic gift-buying.
Reenactment of the Boston Tea Party *(mid-Dec)*. Begins at Old South Meeting House and proceeds to Boston Harbor, where this key historical event is replayed.
First Night *(Dec 31)*. The original

First Night ice sculpture

city-wide New Year's Eve celebration, now an international phenomenon.

January

Chinese New Year *(late Jan to Mar depending on lunar calendar)*, Chinatown. Celebration includes parade, dragon dances, and firecrackers.
Boston Wine Expo *(late Jan–early Feb)*, World Trade Center. Two arduous days of international wine tastings and cooking demonstrations.

February

Beanpot Tournament *(mid-Feb)*, TD Garden. Annual college hockey tournament between Boston College, Boston University, Northeastern University, and Harvard University *(see pp112–13)*.
Longfellow Birthday Celebration, *(late Feb)*, Cambridge. Poetry readings and wreath-laying at the illustrious poet's grave at Mt. Auburn Cemetery.
Harvard's Hasty Pudding Club Parades *(variable)*, Cambridge. Outrageous Harvard theatrical club presents Man and Woman of the Year Awards to Hollywood celebrities after cross-dressing parades through Harvard Square.

Public Holidays

New Year's Day (Jan 1)
Martin Luther King Day (3rd Mon, Jan)
Presidents Day (mid-Feb)
Evacuation Day (Mar 17) (Boston only)
Patriots Day (3rd Mon, Apr) (Middlesex and Suffolk counties, including Boston and Cambridge)
Memorial Day (end May)
Bunker Hill Day (Jun 17) (Boston only)
Independence Day (Jul 4)
Labor Day (1st Mon, Sep)
Columbus Day (2nd Mon, Oct)
Veterans Day (Nov 11)
Thanksgiving (4th Thu, Nov)
Christmas Day (Dec 25)

Christmas lights on a snowy Boston Common in December

Aerial view of Boston and the waterfront ▶

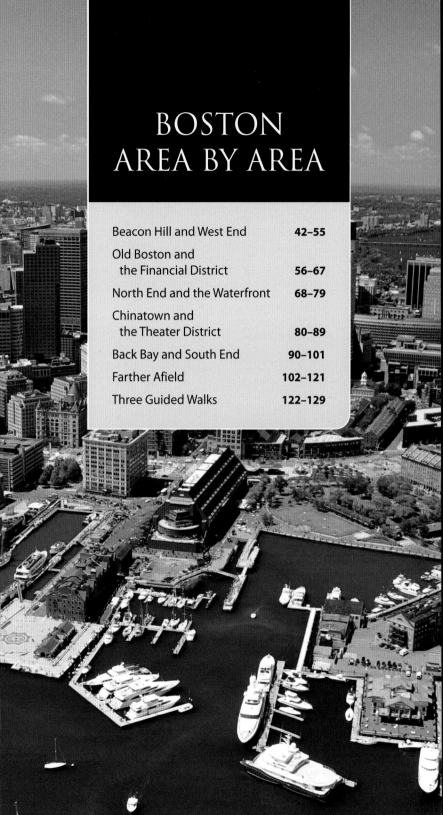

BOSTON
AREA BY AREA

BEACON HILL AND WEST END

Beacon Hill was developed from pasture-land in the 1790s. The south slope, facing Boston Common, became the main seat of Boston wealth and power, while the north slope and the land rolling down to the mouth of the Charles River, known as the West End, became populated by tradesmen, servants, and free blacks. South-slope Beacon Hill retained its cachet into the late 19th century, while the north slope and West End degenerated. Urban renewal in the 1950s and 1960s cleared away the slums and coherent neighborhood of the West End, while gentrification of the north slope made even the most modest homes on Beacon Hill highly desirable, and this neighborhood one of Boston's most picturesque.

Sights at a Glance

Historic Streets and Squares
- **1** Charles Street
- **2** Louisburg Square
- **3** Mount Vernon Street
- **6** Beacon Street

Historic Buildings, Churches, and Museums
- **4** Nichols House Museum
- **5** Hepzibah Swan Houses
- **8** Park Street Church
- **10** Boston Athenaeum
- **11** Massachusetts State House pp52–3
- **12** Museum of African American History
- **13** Otis House Museum
- **14** Old West Church
- **15** Massachusetts General Hospital
- **16** Museum of Science and Science Park

Parks and Cemeteries
- **7** Boston Common and Public Garden pp48–9
- **9** Old Granary Burying Ground

☐ Restaurants pp142–3
1. 75 Chestnut
2. Anna's Taqueria
3. Artú
4. Beacon Hill Bistro
5. Bin 26 Enoteca
6. Cheers
7. Figs
8. Grotto
9. Harvard Gardens
10. King and I
11. Lala Rokh
12. No. 9 Park
13. Panificio
14. Scampo
15. The Paramount
16. Tip Tap Room
17. Toscano Restaurant

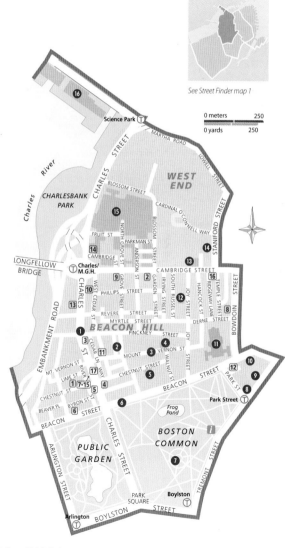

See Street Finder map 1

0 meters		250
0 yards		250

◀ Bronze statue of George Washington in Boston's Public Garden

For keys to symbols see back flap

Street-by-Street: Beacon Hill

From the 1790s to the 1870s, the south slope of Beacon Hill was Boston's most sought-after neighborhood – its wealthy elite decamped only when the more exclusive Back Bay (see pp90–101) was built. Many of the district's houses were designed by Charles Bulfinch (see p55) and his disciples, and the south slope evolved as a textbook example of Federal architecture. Elevation and view were all, and the finest homes are either on Boston Common or perched near the top of the hill. Early developers abided by a gentleman's agreement to set houses back from the street, but the economic depression of 1807–12 resulted in row houses being built right out to the street.

Cobbled street, once typical of Beacon Hill

❷ Louisburg Square
The crowning glory of the Beacon Hill district, this square was developed in the 1830s. Today, it is still Boston's most desirable address.

Charles Street Meeting House was built in the early 19th century to house a congregation of Baptists.

Key

— Suggested route

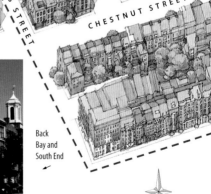

Back Bay and South End

| 0 meters | 50 |
| 0 yards | 50 |

❶ ★ Charles Street
This elegant street is the main shopping area for Beacon Hill. Lined with upscale grocers and antique stores, it also has some fine restaurants.

❹ ★ Nichols House Museum
This modest museum offers an insight into the life of Beacon Hill resident Rose Nichols, who lived here from 1885 to 1960.

Locator Map
See Street Finder map 1

❸ Mount Vernon Street
Described in the 19th century as the "most civilized street in America," this is where the developers of Beacon Hill (the Mount Vernon Proprietors) chose to build their own homes.

Massachusetts State House

SPRUCE STREET

WALNUT STREET

BEACON STREET

Boston Common

❺ Hepzibah Swan Houses
Elegant in their simplicity, these three Bulfinch-designed houses were wedding gifts for the daughters of a wealthy Beacon Hill proprietress.

❻ Beacon Street
The finest houses on Beacon Hill were invariably built on Beacon Street. Elegant, Federal-style mansions, some with ornate reliefs, overlook the city's most beautiful green space, Boston Common.

Charles Street, lined with shops catering to the residents of Beacon Hill

❶ Charles Street

Map 1 B4. ⓣ Charles/MGH.

This street originally ran along the bank of the Charles River, although subsequent landfill has removed it from the riverbank by several hundred feet. The main shopping and dining area of the Beacon Hill neighborhood, the curving line of Charles Street hugs the base of Beacon Hill, giving it a quaint, village-like air. Many of the houses remain residential on the upper stories, while street level and cellar levels were converted to commercial uses long ago. Though most of Charles Street dates from the 19th century, widening in the 1920s meant that some of the houses on the west side acquired new façades. The Charles Street Meeting House, designed by Asher Benjamin (see p34) in 1807, was built for a Baptist congregation that practiced immersion in the then adjacent river. It is now a commercial building. Two groups of striking Greek Revival row houses are

situated at the top of Charles Street, between Revere and Cambridge Streets. Charles Street was one of the birthplaces of the antique trade in the U.S. and now has more than a dozen antique dealers.

❷ Louisburg Square

Map 1 B4. ⓣ Charles/MGH, Park Street.

Home to millionaire politicians, best-selling authors, and corporate moguls, Louisburg Square is arguably Boston's most prestigious address. Developed in the 1830s as a shared private preserve on Beacon Hill, the square's tiny patch of greenery surrounded by a high iron fence sends a clear signal of the square's continued exclusivity. On the last private square in the city, the narrow Greek Revival

bow-fronted town houses sell for a premium over comparable homes elsewhere on Beacon Hill. Even the on-street parking spaces are deeded. The traditions of Christmas Eve carol singing and candlelit windows are said to have begun on Louisburg Square. A statue of Christopher Columbus, presented by a wealthy Greek merchant in 1850, stands at its center.

❸ Mount Vernon Street

Map 1 B4. ⓣ Charles/MGH, Park Street.

In the 1890s the novelist Henry James (see p33) called Mount Vernon Street "the most civilized street in America," and it still retains that air of urbane culture. Most of the developers of Beacon Hill, who called themselves the Mount Vernon Proprietors, chose to build their private homes along this street. Architect Charles Bulfinch (see p55) envisioned Beacon Hill as a district of large freestanding mansions on spacious landscaped grounds, but building costs ultimately dictated much denser development. The sole remaining example of Bulfinch's vision is the second Harrison Gray Otis House, built in 1800 at No. 85. The Greek Revival row houses next door (Nos. 59–83), graciously set back from the street by 30 ft (9 m), were built to replace the single mansion belonging to Otis's chief development partner, Jonathan Mason. The original mansion was torn down after Mason's death in 1836. The three Bulfinch-designed houses at Nos. 55, 57, and 59 Mount Vernon Street were built by Mason for his daughters. No. 55 was ultimately passed on to the Nichols family (see p47) in 1885.

Columbus Statue, Louisburg Square

Oliver Wendell Holmes and the Boston Brahmins

In 1860, Oliver Wendell Holmes *(see p32)* wrote that Boston's wealthy merchant class of the time constituted a Brahmin caste, a "harmless, inoffensive, untitled aristocracy" with "their houses by Bulfinch, their monopoly on Beacon Street, their ancestral portraits and Chinese porcelains, humanitarianism, Unitarian faith in the march of the mind, Yankee shrewdness, and New England exclusiveness." So keenly did he skewer the social class that the term has persisted. In casual usage today, a Brahmin is someone with an old family name, whose finances derive largely from trust funds, and whose politics blend conservatism with *noblesse oblige* toward those less fortunate. Boston's Brahmins founded most of the hospitals, performing arts bodies and museums of the greater metropolitan area.

Oliver Wendell Holmes (1809–94)

Drawing room of the Bulfinch-designed Nichols House Museum

❹ Nichols House Museum

55 Mount Vernon St. **Map** 1 B4. **Tel** (617) 227-6993. ⓣ Park Street. **Open** Apr–Oct: 11am–4pm Tue–Sat; Nov–Mar: 11am–4pm Thu–Sat. 🅿 ♿ 📷 🅦 nicholshousemuseum.org

The Nichols House Museum was designed by Charles Bulfinch in 1804 and offers a rare glimpse into the tradition-bound lifestyle of Beacon Hill. Modernized in 1830 by the addition of a Greek Revival portico, the house is nevertheless a superb example of Bulfinch's domestic architecture. It also offers an insight into the life of a true Beacon Hill character. Rose Standish Nichols moved into the house aged 13 when her father purchased it in 1885. She left it as a museum in her will in 1960. A woman ahead of her time, strong-willed and famously hospitable, Nichols was, among other things, a self-styled landscape designer who traveled extensively around the world to write about gardens.

❺ Hepzibah Swan Houses

13, 15 & 17 Chestnut St. **Map** 1 B4. ⓣ Park Street. **Closed** to the public.

The only woman who was ever a member of the Mount Vernon Proprietors *(see p46)*, Mrs. Swan had these houses built by Bulfinch as wedding presents for her daughters in 1806, 1807 and 1814. Some of the most elegant and distinguished houses on Chestnut Street, they are backed by Bulfinch-designed stables that face onto Mount Vernon Street. The deeds restrict the height of the stables to 13 ft (4 m) so that her daughters would still have a view over Mount Vernon Street. In 1863–65, No. 13 was home to Dr. Samuel Gridley Howe, abolitionist and educational pioneer who, in 1833, founded the first school for the blind in the U.S.

❻ Beacon Street

Map 1 B4. ⓣ Park Street.

Beacon Street is lined with urban mansions facing Boston Common. The 1808 **William Hickling Prescott House** at No. 55, designed by Asher Benjamin, offers tours of rooms decorated in Federal, Victorian, and Colonial Revival styles. The American Meteorological Society occupies No. 45, which was built as Harrison Gray Otis's last and finest house, with 11 bedrooms and an elliptical room behind the front parlor where the walls and doors are curved. The elite Somerset Club stands at Nos. 42–43 Beacon Street. In the 1920s to 1940s, Irish Catholic mayor James Michael Curley would lead election night victory marches to the State House, pausing at the Somerset to taunt the Boston Brahmins within. The Parkman House at No. 33 is now a city-owned meeting center. It was the home of Dr. George Parkman, who was murdered by Harvard professor and fellow socialite Dr. John Webster in 1849. Boston society was torn apart when Webster was sentenced to be hanged.

🏛 **William Hickling Prescott House** **Open** May–Sep: noon–4pm Wed & Sat. 🅿 ♿ 📷

Elegant Federal-style houses on Beacon Street, overlooking Boston Common

❼ Boston Common and Public Garden

Acquired by Boston in 1634 from first settler William Blackstone, the 48-acre (19-ha) Boston Common served for two centuries as common pasture, military drill ground, and gallows site. British troops camped here during the 1775–76 military occupation. As Boston grew in the 19th century, the Boston Common became a center for open-air civic activity and remains so to this day. By contrast, the 24-acre (10-ha) Public Garden is more formal. When the Charles River mudflats were first filled in the 1830s, a succession of landscape plans were plotted for the Public Garden before the city chose the English-style garden scheme of George F. Meacham in 1859. The lagoon was added to the garden two years later.

The Public Garden, a popular green space in the heart of the city

★ George Washington Statue
Cast by Thomas Ball from bronze, with a solid granite base, this is one the finest memorial statues in Boston. It was dedicated in 1869.

Lagoon Bridge
This miniature, ornamental bridge over the Public Garden lagoon was designed by William G. Preston in 1869 in a moment of whimsy. The lagoon it "spans" was constructed in 1861.

CHARLES STREET

0 metres   100
0 yards   100

★ Shaw Memorial
This relief immortalizes the Civil War's 54th regiment of Massachusetts Infantry, the first free black regiment in the Union Army, and their white colonel Robert Shaw.

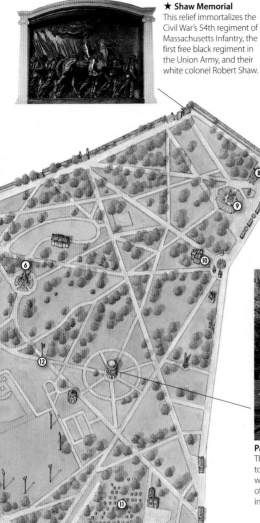

VISITORS' CHECKLIST

Practical Information
Map 1 B4.
Tel (617) 426-3115.
W swanboats.com
W bostonusa.com
Open 24 hrs. Visitors' Center:
139 Tremont St;
Open 8:30am–5pm Mon–Fri,
9am–5pm Sat & Sun. Times vary
in winter. **Tel** (617) 522-1966.
Swan Boats: Public Garden.
Open mid-Apr–mid-Sep:
10am–5pm daily. Times may
vary. 🎨

Transport
Ⓣ Park Street, Boylston Street,
Arlington.

Parkman Bandstand
This bandstand was built in 1912 to memorialize George F. Parkman, who bequeathed $5 million for the care of Boston Common and other parks in the city.

KEY

① **Statue of Edward Everett Hale**

② **The Swan Boats,** originally inspired by Wagner's *Lohengrin,* have been a feature of the Public Garden lagoon since 1877.

③ **Statue of Reverend William Ellery Channing**

④ **The Ether Monument** memorializes the first use of anaesthesia in 1846.

⑤ **Make Way for Ducklings** is the sculpture of a duck and her brood of ducklings, based on the classic children's story by Robert McCloskey.

⑥ **The Soldiers and Sailors Monument,** erected in 1877, features prominent Bostonians from the time of the Civil War.

⑦ **Blackstone Memorial Tablet** recalls the purchase of the common in 1634 and is cited as proof that it belongs to the people.

⑧ **Park Street subway**

⑨ **Brewer Fountain** was purchased at the 1867 Paris Expo.

⑩ **Visitors' Center**

⑪ **Central Burying Ground** dates from 1756 and holds the remains of many British and American casualties from the Battle of Bunker Hill *(see p22).* The portraitist Gilbert Stuart is also buried at this graveyard.

⑫ **The Flagstaff**

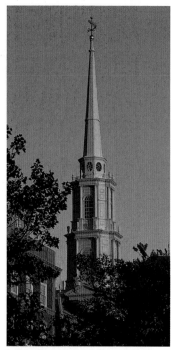

Park Street Church at the corner of Tremont and Park Streets, near Boston Common

❽ Park Street Church

1 Park St. **Map** 1 C4. **Tel** (617) 523-3383. Ⓣ Park Street. **Open** late Jun–Aug: 9:30am–3pm Tue–Sat; Sep–late Jun: by appointment. ✉ ♿

Ⓦ parkstreet.org

Park Street Church's 217-ft (65-m) steeple has punctuated the intersection of Park and Tremont Streets since its dedication in 1810. Designed by English architect Peter Banner, who adapted a design by the earlier English architect Christopher Wren, the church was commissioned by parishioners wanting to establish a Congregational church in the heart of Boston. The church was, and still remains, one of the city's most influential pulpits.

Contrary to popular belief, the sermons of Park Street ministers did not earn the intersection the nickname of "Brimstone Corner." Rather, the name came about during the War of 1812 when the U.S.

and Britain were in conflict over British restrictions on trade and freedom of the seas, as well as the U.S.'s ties with Napoleonic France. The U.S. militia, based in Boston, stored its gunpowder in the church basement as safekeeping against bombardment from the British navy, hence the nickname.

Park Street Church later became famous throughout the islands of the Pacific, when in 1819 the church sent a number of Congregational missionaries to carry the Gospel to Pacific islanders from a base in the Hawaiian Islands. In 1829, William Lloyd Garrison (1805–79), a firebrand of the movement to abolish slavery *(see p32)*, gave his first abolition speech from the Park Street pulpit, while in 1849 a speech called *The War System of Nations* was addressed to the American Peace Society by Senator Charles Sumner. Much later, in 1893, the anthem *America the Beautiful* by Katharine Lee Bates debuted at a Sunday service. Today the church continues to be involved in religious, political, cultural, and humanitarian activities.

❾ Old Granary Burying Ground

Tremont St. **Map** 1 C4. Ⓣ Park Street. **Open** 9am–5pm daily.

Named after the early colonial grain storage facility that once stood on the adjacent site of Park Street Church, the Granary Burying Ground dates from 1660. Buried here were three important signatories to the Declaration of Independence *(see p23)* – John Hancock, Samuel Adams, and Robert Treat Paine, along with Benjamin Franklin's parents, merchant-philanthropist Peter Faneuil, and some victims of the Boston Massacre.

The orderly array of gravestones, often featured in films and television shows set in Boston, is the result of modern groundskeeping. Few stones, if any, mark the actual burial site of the person memorialized. In fact, John Hancock may not be here at all. On the night he was buried in 1793, grave robbers cut off the hand with which he had signed his name to the Declaration of Independence, and some scholars believe that the rest of the body was later spirited away during 19th-century construction work. Although many heroes of the Revolution are still known to be buried here, Paul Revere, one of Boston's most famous sons, was nearly denied the honor because the cemetery was technically full when he died in 1818. The city made an exception, and he was able to join his comrades in perpetuity.

Old Granary Burying Ground, final resting place for Revolutionary heroes

Stone frieze decoration on the 19th-century, Renaissance Revival-style Athenaeum

⑩ Boston Athenaeum

10½ Beacon St. **Map** 1 C4. **Tel** (617) 227-0270. ⓣ Park Street. **Open** 9am–8pm Mon–Thu, 9am–5:30pm Fri, 9am–4pm Sat, noon–4pm Sun. Ⓒ
W bostonathenaeum.org

Organized in 1807, the collection of the Boston Athenaeum quickly became one of the country's leading private libraries. Sheep farmer Edward Clarke Cabot won the 1846 design competition to house the library, with plans for a gray sandstone building based on Palladio's Palazzo da Porta Festa in Vicenza, a building Cabot knew from a book in the Athenaeum's collection. The building

reopened in fall 2002 after extensive renovations. Among the Athenaeum's major holdings are the personal library that once belonged to George Washington and the theological library supplied by King William III of England to the King's Chapel *(see p60)*. In its early years the Athenaeum was Boston's chief art museum; when the Museum of Fine Arts was proposed, the Athenaeum graciously donated much of its art, including unfinished portraits of George and Martha Washington purchased in 1831 from the widow of the painter Gilbert Stuart. Non-members of the Athenaeum may visit only the first floor of the building, an area that includes the art gallery (with changing exhibitions) and several reading rooms.

⑪ Massachusetts State House

See pp52–3.

⑫ Museum of African American History

46 Joy St. **Map** 1 C3. **Tel** (617) 725-0022. ⓣ Park Street. **Open** 10am–4pm Mon–Sat. **Closed** public hols.
Ⓒ Ⓒ W afroammuseum.org

Built from town house plans by Asher Benjamin *(see p34)*, using salvaged materials, the African Meeting House was dedicated in 1806 and is the centerpiece of the museum. The U.S.'s oldest black church building, it was the political and religious center of Boston's African American society. Cato Gardner, a native African, raised $1,500 toward the eventual $7,700 to build the church and is honored with an inscription above the entrance. The interior is plain and simple but rang with the oratory of some of the 19th century's most fiery abolitionists: from Sojourner Truth and Frederick Douglass to William Lloyd Garrison *(see p32)*, who founded the New England Anti-Slavery Society in 1832. The meeting house basement was Boston's first school for African American children until the adjacent Abiel Smith School was built in 1831. When segregated education was barred in 1855, however, the Smith School closed. The meeting house became an Hasidic synagogue in the 1890s, as most of Boston's African American community moved to Roxbury and Dorchester. The synagogue closed in the 1960s, and in 1987 the building reopened as the linchpin site on the Black Heritage Trail.

Black Heritage Trail

Holmes Alley, once an escape route for slaves on the run

In the first U.S. census in 1790, Massachusetts was the only state to record no slaves. During the 19th century, Boston's substantial free African American community lived principally on the north slope of Beacon Hill and in the adjacent West End. The Black Heritage Trail links several key sites, ranging from the African Meeting House to private homes that are not open to visitors. Among them are the 1797 George Middleton House (Nos. 5–7 Pinckney Street), the oldest standing house built by African Americans on Beacon Hill, and the Lewis and Harriet Hayden House (No. 66 Phillips Street). The Haydens made their home a haven for runaways in the "Underground Railroad" of safe houses between the South and Canada. The walking tour also leads through mews and alleys, like Holmes Alley at the end of Smith Court, once used by fugitives to flee professional slave catchers.

Free tours of the Black Heritage Trail are led by National Park Service rangers – (617) 742-5415 – from Memorial Day weekend to Labor Day, 10am, noon, and 2pm Monday to Saturday, leaving from the Shaw Memorial. Tours are at 2pm Mon–Sat through late November and in May.

Abiel Smith School, where Boston's free blacks received an education

⓫ Massachusetts State House

The cornerstone of the Massachusetts State House was laid on July 4, 1795, by Samuel Adams and Paul Revere. Completed on January 11, 1798, the Charles Bulfinch-designed center of state government served as a model for the U.S. Capitol Building in Washington and as an inspiration for many of the state capitols around the country. Later additions were made, but the original building remains the archetype of American government buildings. Its dome, sheathed in copper and gold, serves as the zero mile marker for Massachusetts, making it, as Oliver Wendell Holmes *(see p47)* remarked, "the hub of the universe."

The State House, from Boston Common

★ **House of Representatives**
This elegant oval chamber was built for the House of Representatives in 1895. The Sacred Cod, which now hangs over the gallery, came to the State House when it first opened in 1798, and it has since hung over any place where the representatives have met.

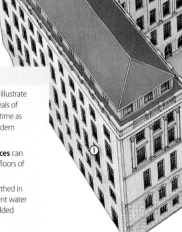

KEY

① **The wings** of the State House, thought by many to sit incongruously with the rest of the structure, were added in 1917.

② **The Great Hall** is the latest addition to the State House. Built in 1990, it is lined with marble and topped by a glass dome, and is used for state functions.

③ **The main staircase** is decorated with beautiful stained-glass windows. The windows illustrate the many varied state seals of Massachusetts: from its time as a colony through to modern statehood.

④ **Administrative offices** can be found on the upper floors of the building.

⑤ **The dome** was sheathed in copper in 1802 to prevent water leakage, and, in 1872, gilded in 23-carat gold.

Hall of Flags
Flags carried into battle by regiments from the state of Massachusetts are housed here. They are displayed beneath a stained-glass skylight depicting seals of the original 13 colonies.

VISITORS' CHECKLIST

Practical Information
Beacon Hill. **Map** 1 C4.
Tel (617) 727-3676.
W sec.state.ma.us/trs
Open 10am–3:30pm Mon–Fri
(reservations recommended).

Transport
Ⓣ Park Street.

★ **Nurses Hall**
This marble hall is lined with murals depicting critical events leading up to the American Revolution. The name derives from the statue of an army nurse here, erected to honor all the nurses who took part in the Civil War.

Entrance

Doric Hall
George Washington is among the historical figures represented here. The center doors of the hall are only ever opened for a state governor at the end of his term or for a visiting head of state.

Senate Chamber
Prior to 1895, this was the meeting chamber of the House of Representatives. Situated directly beneath the State House's magnificent dome, the chamber features a beautiful sunburst ceiling, also designed by Charles Bulfinch.

Flamboyantly decorated dining room of the Otis House Museum

⑬ Otis House Museum

141 Cambridge St. **Map** 1 C3. **Tel** (617) 994-5820. Ⓣ Charles/MGH, Government Center. **Open** 11am–4:30pm Wed–Sun (Dec–Feb: Fri–Sun). 🏛 ✉ 📷 🅦 **historicnewengland.org**

Designed by Charles Bulfinch for Harrison Gray Otis, co-developer of Beacon Hill (see pp44–5) and Boston's third mayor, this 1796 town mansion was built to serve the needs of a young man on the way up in Federal Boston. Descended from both British colonial administrators and Boston revolutionary patriots, Otis took a practical view of local government that paved the way for Boston's development as a powerhouse of international trade and finance. Having already made a fortune in the land development of Beacon Hill, Otis commissioned this home as a showpiece, where he could entertain. It was the first of three homes Bulfinch designed for him.

After Otis moved out, the house fell on hard times as the West End neighborhood around it absorbed successive waves of immigration, and tenements replaced single family homes. By the 1830s the Otis house was serving as a ladies' Turkish bath and later became a patent medicine shop before ending up as a

boarding house. Historic New England saved the building in 1916 and established its headquarters here. A gallery in the house depicts the time when the building was a boarding house in the 1950s.

Visitors who tour the Otis house, now restored to the way it looked in around 1800, are often surprised by the bright, even gaudy, style of decoration. Although the rooms were initially decorated

Red-brick façade of Asher Benjamin's Old West Church

in the muted Williamsburg Colonial style, subsequent art history detective work revealed that Bostonians had much more flamboyant taste than, for example, the wealthy Virginians. Thus, the house has been restored with touches typical of such upper-class aspirations. The wallpaper in the main entrance has a border of scenes from Pompeii and scores of lithographs showing views of European cities. The colors throughout the rest of the house are bright, and gilt detail flashes from moldings and furniture.

Inquire about the Beacon Hill and Haymarket walking tours that depart from Otis House Museum.

⑭ Old West Church

131 Cambridge St. **Map** 1 C3. **Tel** (617) 227-5088. Ⓣ Charles/ MGH, Bowdoin. **Open** for Sunday worship. 🔔 11am Sun. ✉ ♿ 🅦 **oldwestchurch.org**

A wood-frame church built on this site in 1737 was used as a barracks for British soldiers during the occupation of Boston (see pp22–3) in the period just prior to the American Revolution. The British later razed the original church in 1775, since they suspected revolutionary sympathizers of using the steeple to signal Continental Army troops across the Charles River. Many of the church's timbers were used to construct the African Meeting House (see p51). Asher Benjamin (see p34), a protégé of Charles Bulfinch, designed the current red-brick structure, erected in 1806. The swag-ornamented clocks on the sides of the tower are distinctive landmarks, while inside there is a superb Fisk tracker-action pipe organ. This organ is often played in classical organ concerts and in recordings.

⑮ Massachusetts General Hospital

Cambridge & Fruit Sts. **Map** 1 B2.
Tel (617) 726-8363. ⓣ Charles/MGH.
Open 24 hrs daily. Ether Dome and
Russell Museum: **Open** 9am–5pm
Mon–Fri (also mid-Apr–mid-Oct:
11am–5pm Sat). ♿ ◪ self-
guided tour brochure available
at information desk.
🌐 **massgeneral.org/vep**

The sprawling complex of
Massachusetts General
Hospital covers the original
site of Harvard Medical School.
The main hospital building,
the George R. White Memorial
Building, is a massive Art
Deco structure from 1939,
largely hidden from Cambridge
Street by other buildings.
The eye-catching Bulfinch
Pavilion and Ether Dome was
Charles Bulfinch's last Boston

commission (1818).
Alexander Parris,
who succeeded
Bulfinch as the
city's leading
architect, was
involved in
preparing the
drawings for this
"modern" hospital
built of local
Chelmsford granite.
The operating
theater, with
seating for observers, is set
beneath a skylit dome. In
1846, the use of ether as a
surgical general anesthetic
was first demonstrated here.
The Paul S. Russell, MD
Museum of Medical History
and Innovation explores the
evolution of healthcare and
medicine throughout the
hospital's history.

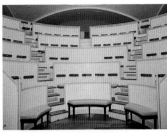
Charles Bulfinch's Ether Dome, part of Massachusetts
General Hospital

Charles Bulfinch

Born in 1763 in Boston, Charles Bulfinch *(see p34)* was among
America's first professional architects and one of the most influential.
He rose to prominence with his 1795 plan for the Massachusetts
State House *(see pp52–3)*, and went on to design many of the
neighboring mansions on Beacon Hill. His own forays into real estate
development cast him into bankruptcy, but he continued to enjoy
the steady patronage of Boston's wealthiest citizens for his elegant
yet boldly confident house designs. These patrons also helped him
secure many public commissions, including the renovation of
St. Stephen's Church in the North End *(see p74)* and the enlargement
of Faneuil Hall *(see p65)*. His application of local granite building
stone to the Massachusetts General Hospital surgical pavilion laid
out principles later followed by Alexander Parris and others as they
forged the Boston Granite style of architecture, exemplified by
Quincy Market *(see p66)* and Charlestown Navy Yard *(see p117)*.
Bulfinch left Boston in 1818 to assume direction of the construction
of the U.S. Capitol Building in Washington, DC.

19th-century view of Massachusetts State House from Boston Common

⑯ Museum of Science and Science Park

Science Park. **Map** 1 B2. **Tel** (617) 723-
2500. ⓣ Science Park. **Open** 9am–
5pm Mon–Thu & Sat–Sun (Jul–early
Sep: 9am–7pm), 9am–9pm Fri.
Closed Thanksgiving, Dec 25. 🍴 ♿
📷 🌐 **mos.org**

The Museum of Science
straddles the Charles River atop
the inactive flood control dam
that sits at the mouth of the
Charles River. The museum itself
was built in 1951, but Science
Park has taken shape around
it since, virtually obscuring the
dam structure with theater
and planetarium buildings and
a massive parking garage.
  With more than 700
interactive exhibits covering
natural history, medicine,
astronomy, and the wonders
of the physical sciences, the
Science Museum is oriented to
families with children. In 1999
the museum absorbed the
holdings of Boston's Computer
Museum, one of the first of its
kind in the world.
  The Mugar Omni Theater
contains a five-story domed
IMAX® screen with multi-
dimensional sound system
with wraparound sound, and
shows mostly educational
films, usually with a natural
science theme. The Charles
Hayden Planetarium offers
daily shows about stars,
planets, and other celestial
phenomena.
  An extensive array of
educational toys can be bought
from the museum's shop, while
the food court has a number
of concessions catering to
children's tastes.

OLD BOSTON AND THE FINANCIAL DISTRICT

This is an area of Boston where old and new sit one on top of the other. Some of its sights, situated in the older part of the district closest to Boston Common, predate the American Revolution *(see pp22–3)*. Much of what can be seen today, though, was built more recently. The north of the district is home to Boston's late 20th-century,

modernist-style City Hall and Government Center, while to the east is the city's bustling Financial District. This once formed part of Boston's harbor waterfront, a district built on mercantile wealth. Today, the wharves and warehouses have been replaced by skyscrapers belonging to banks, insurance companies, and high-tech industries.

Sights at a Glance

Historic Streets and Squares

🔟 Blackstone Block
⓫ Boston Public Market and Greenway
⓯ Post Office Square

Historic Buildings and Churches

❶ Omni Parker House
❷ King's Chapel and Burying Ground
❸ Old City Hall
❹ Old Corner Bookstore
❺ Old South Meeting House
❻ *Old State House pp62–3*
❼ Center Plaza
❽ Boston City Hall
❾ Government Center
⓬ Faneuil Hall
⓭ Quincy Market
⓮ Custom House
⓰ Verizon Building

🔲 Restaurants *pp143–4*

1 Anthem
2 The Black Rose
3 Boloco
4 Bond Restaurant and Lounge
5 Chacarero
6 Durgin Park
7 The Kinsale
8 Mooo...
9 The Oceanaire Seafood Room
10 Ruth's Chris Steakhouse
11 Sakura-Bana
12 Sam LaGrassa's
13 Silvertone
14 Society on High
15 Union Oyster House

See Street Finder maps 1 & 2

0 meters 300
0 yards 300

◀ The iconic Old State House in Boston's Financial District

For keys to symbols *see back flap*

Street-by-Street: Colonial Boston

An important part of Boston's Freedom Trail *(see pp126–9)* runs through this historic core of the city, the site of which predates American Independence. Naturally, the area is now dominated by 19th- and 20th-century development, but glimpses of a colonial past are prevalent here and there in the Old State House, King's Chapel and its adjacent burying ground, and the Old South Meeting House. Newer buildings of interest include the Omni Parker House, as well as the towering skyscrapers of Boston's financial district, located on the northwest edges of this area.

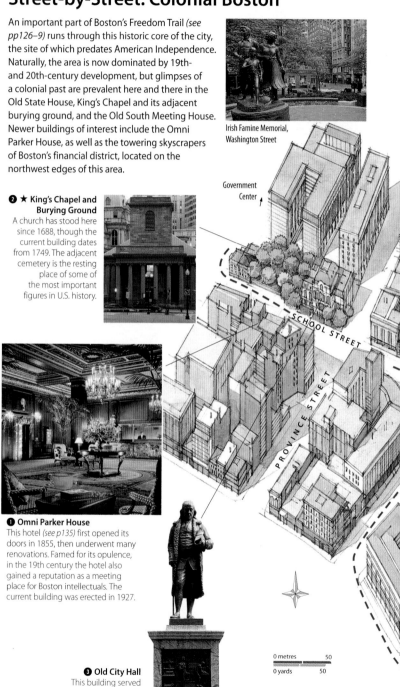

Irish Famine Memorial, Washington Street

Government Center

SCHOOL STREET

PROVINCE STREET

❷ ★ **King's Chapel and Burying Ground**
A church has stood here since 1688, though the current building dates from 1749. The adjacent cemetery is the resting place of some of the most important figures in U.S. history.

❶ **Omni Parker House**
This hotel *(see p135)* first opened its doors in 1855, then underwent many renovations. Famed for its opulence, in the 19th century the hotel also gained a reputation as a meeting place for Boston intellectuals. The current building was erected in 1927.

❸ **Old City Hall**
This building served as Boston's City Hall from 1865 to 1969. Today it is converted into a steak house.

0 metres   50
0 yards   50

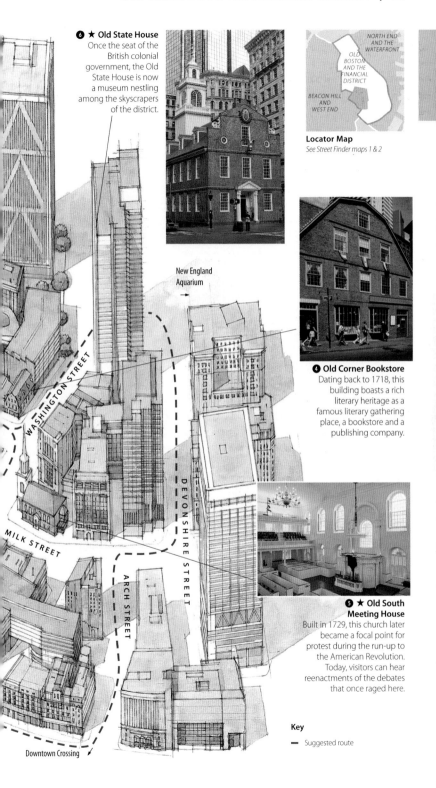

6 ★ Old State House
Once the seat of the British colonial government, the Old State House is now a museum nestling among the skyscrapers of the district.

Locator Map
See Street Finder maps 1 & 2

New England Aquarium →

4 Old Corner Bookstore
Dating back to 1718, this building boasts a rich literary heritage as a famous literary gathering place, a bookstore and a publishing company.

WASHINGTON STREET

DEVONSHIRE STREET

MILK STREET

ARCH STREET

5 ★ Old South Meeting House
Built in 1729, this church later became a focal point for protest during the run-up to the American Revolution. Today, visitors can hear reenactments of the debates that once raged here.

Downtown Crossing ↙

Key

— Suggested route

❶ Omni Parker House

60 School St. **Map** 1 C4.
Tel (617) 227-8600. Ⓣ Park Street,
State, Government Center.
W omnihotels.com

Harvey D. Parker, raised on a farm in Maine, became so successful as the proprietor of his Boston restaurant that he achieved his ambition of expanding the property into a first-class, grand hotel. His Parker House opened in 1855, with a façade clad in white marble, standing five stories high, and featuring the first passenger elevator ever seen in Boston. It underwent several, rapid transformations during its early years, with additions made to the main structure in the 1860s and a 10-story, French chateau-style annex completed later that century. The building saw many successive transform-ations, and its latest 14-story incarnation has stood across from King's Chapel on School Street since 1927.

This hotel attained an instant reputation for luxurious accom-modations and fine, even lavish, dining, typified by 11-course menus prepared by a French chef. Among Parker House's

Simply decorated, pure white interior of King's Chapel on Tremont Street

many claims to fame are its Boston Cream Pie, which was first created here, and the word "scrod," a uniquely Bostonian term for the day's freshest seafood, still in common usage. Two former Parker House employees later became recognized for quite different careers. Vietnamese revolu-tionary leader Ho Chi Minh worked in the hotel's kitchens around 1915, while black activist Malcolm X was a busboy in Parker's Restaurant in the 1940s.

Parker House Guests

Boston's reputation as the "Athens of America" was widely acknowledged when members of a distinguished social club began meeting for lengthy dinners and lively intellectual exchanges in 1857. Their get-togethers took place on the last Saturday of every month at Harvey Parker's fancy hotel. Regular participants included New England's literary elite *(see pp32–3)*: Henry Wadsworth Longfellow, Ralph Waldo Emerson, Nathaniel Hawthorne, and Henry David Thoreau, to name a few. Charles Dickens participated while staying

John Wilkes Booth, infamous Parker House guest

at the Parker House during his American speaking tours, and used his sitting-room mirror to rehearse the public readings he gave at Tremont Temple next door. The mirror now hangs on a mezzanine wall. In 1865, actor John Wilkes Booth, in town to see his brother, a fellow thespian, stayed at the hotel and took target practice at a nearby shooting gallery. Ten days later, at Ford's Theatre in Washington, he pulled a pistol and shot Abraham Lincoln.

❷ King's Chapel and Burying Ground

58 Tremont St. **Map** 1 C4.
Tel (617) 523-1749. Ⓣ Park Street,
State, Government Center. **Open**
10am–5pm Mon–Sat, 1:30–5pm Sun;
call for off-season opening hours.
Music Recitals: 12:15pm Tue.
✝ 11am Sun, 6pm Wed.
W kings-chapel.org

British crown officials were among those who attended Anglican services at the first chapel on this site, which was built in 1688. When New England's governor decided that a larger church was needed, the present granite edifice – on which work begun in 1749 – was constructed around the original wooden chapel, which was then dismantled and heaved out through the windows of its replacement. After the Revolution, the congregation's religious allegiance switched from Anglican to Unitarian. The sanctuary's raised pulpit – dating from 1717 and shaped like a wine glass – is one of the oldest in the United States. High ceilings, open arches, and clear glass windows enhance the interior's sense of spaciousness and light. The bell inside the King's Chapel is the largest ever cast by Paul Revere *(see p23)*.

The adjacent cemetery is the oldest in Boston.

❸ Old City Hall

45 School St. **Map** 2 D4. ⓣ Park Street, State, Government Center.

A fine example of French Second Empire architectural gaudiness, this was Boston's City Hall from 1865 to 1969 – it was superseded by the rakishly modern New City Hall structure at nearby Government Center (see p64). The renovated 19th-century building now features a steak house.

Previous occupants have included such flamboyant mayors as Honey "Fitz" Fitzgerald (see p27) and James Michael Curley. Statues here memorialize Josiah Quincy, Boston's second mayor and after whom Quincy Market is named, as well as Benjamin Franklin, who was born on nearby Milk Street.

19th-century French-style façade of Boston's Old City Hall

❹ Old Corner Bookstore

1 School St. **Map** 2 D4. ⓣ Park Street, State, Government Center.

A dormered gambrel roof crowns this brick landmark, which opened as Thomas Crease's apothecary shop in 1718 and was reestablished as the Old Corner Bookstore in 1829. Moving in 16 years later, the Ticknor & Fields publishing company became a gathering place for a notable roster of authors: Emerson, Hawthorne, Longfellow, Thoreau, early feminist writer Margaret Fuller, and *Uncle Tom's Cabin* novelist Harriet Beecher Stowe. The firm is often credited with carving out the first distinctively American literature. The earliest editions of the erudite *Atlantic Monthly* periodical were also printed here under editor James Russell Lowell, before he handed the reins over to William Dean Howells. Julia Ward Howe's rousing tribute to American Civil War bravado, *The Battle Hymn of the Republic*, first appeared in the *Atlantic*'s February 1862 issue. Although no publishing activities take place here, the Old Corner Bookstore remains a touchstone of American literary history.

Historic image of the Old Corner Bookstore, the hub of American literature

❺ Old South Meeting House

310 Washington St. **Map** 2 D4. **Tel** (617) 482-6439. ⓣ Park Street, State, Government Center. **Open** Apr–Oct: 9:30am–5pm daily; Nov–Mar: 10am–4pm daily. 🎭 ♿ 🛍 📷 ⓦ oldsouthmeetinghouse.org

Built in 1729 for Puritan religious services, this edifice, with a tall octagonal steeple, had colonial Boston's biggest capacity for town meetings – a fact capitalized upon by a group of rebellious rabble-rousers calling themselves the Sons of Liberty (see p22). Their outbursts against British taxation and other royal annoyances drew increasingly large and vociferous crowds to the pews and upstairs galleries.

During a candlelit protest rally on December 16, 1773, fiery speechmaker Samuel Adams flashed the signal that led to the Boston Tea Party (see p77) down at Griffin's Wharf several hours later. The British retaliated by turning Old South into an officers' tavern and stable for General John Burgoyne's 17th Lighthorse Regiment of Dragoons. In 1877, the budding Historic Preservation Movement saved the building from destruction and created a museum. Displays, exhibits, and a multimedia presentation entitled *Voices of Protest* relive those raucous days as well as more recent occurrences in the 20th century. The Meeting House offers a series of lectures covering a wide range of New England topics and also holds chamber music concerts and other musical performances.

There is a shop downstairs containing a broad selection of merchandise, which includes the ubiquitous tins of "Boston Tea Party" tea.

Directly across Washington Street, sculptor Robert Shure's memorial to the 1845–49 Irish Potato Famine was added to the small plaza here in 1998.

Old South Meeting House, in stark contrast to the modern city

❻ Old State House

Dwarfed by the towers of the Financial District, this was the seat of British colonial government between 1713 and 1776. The royal lion and unicorn still decorate each corner of the eastern façade. After independence, the Massachusetts legislature took possession of the building, and it has had many uses since, including produce market, merchants' exchange, Masonic lodge, and Boston City Hall. Its wine cellars now function as a downtown subway station. The Old State House houses two floors of Bostonian Society memorabilia and a sound and light show about the Boston Massacre *(see p22).*

Old State House amid the skyscrapers of the Financial District

West Façade
A Latin inscription, relating to the first Massachusetts Bay colony, runs around the outside of this crest. The relief in the center depicts a local Native American.

KEY

① **Keayne Hall** is named after Robert Keayne who, in 1658, gave £300 to the city so that the Town House, predating the Old State House, could be built. Exhibits in the room depict events from the Revolution.

② **A gold sculpture** of an eagle, symbol of America, can be seen on the west façade.

③ **The tower** is a classic example of Colonial style. In 18th-century paintings and engravings it can be seen clearly above the Boston skyline.

④ **The Declaration of Independence** was read from this balcony in 1776. In the 1830s, when the building was City Hall, the balcony was enlarged to two tiers.

Entrance

★ **Central Staircase**
A fine example of 19th-century workmanship, the central spiral staircase has two beautifully crafted wooden handrails. It is one of the few such staircases still in existence in the U.S.

Site of the Boston Massacre

A brass and stone marker below the balcony on the eastern façade of the Old State House indicates the site of the Boston Massacre *(see pp22–3)*. After the Boston Tea Party *(see p77)*, this was one of the most inflammatory events leading up to the American Revolution. On March 5, 1770, an unruly mob of colonists taunted British guardsmen with insults, rocks, and snowballs. The soldiers opened fire, killing five colonists. A number of articles relating to the Boston Massacre are exhibited inside the Old State House, including a musket found near the site and a coroner's report detailing the incident.

Marker on the site of the Boston Massacre

VISITORS' CHECKLIST

Practical Information
Washington & State Sts.
Map 2 D4.
Tel (617) 720-1713.
Ⓦ **bostonhistory.org**
Open 9am–5pm daily (to 6pm late May–early Sep). **Closed** Jan 1, Thanksgiving, Dec 25. 🚫 🚫 📷 ♿ 🏛

Transport
Ⓣ State.

British Unicorn and Lion
A royal symbol of Britain, the original lion and unicorn were pulled down when news of the Declaration of Independence reached Boston in 1776.

★ East Façade
This façade has seen many changes. An earlier clock from the 1820s was removed in 1957 and replaced with an 18th-century replica of the sundial that once hung here. The clock has now been reinstated.

Council Chamber
Once the chambers for the royal governors, and from 1780 chambers for the first governor of Massachusetts (John Hancock), this room has seen many key events. Among them were numerous impassioned speeches made by Boston patriots.

❼ Center Plaza

Cambridge St. **Map** 1 C3.
Ⓣ Government Center.

Downtown's old, irregular
street pattern has given rise
to some unusual buildings,
including the Center Plaza,
which was designed in the
mid-1960s by Welton Beckett
& Associates. It was designed
specifically to follow the long
curve of the existing Cambridge
Street, and the low-slung office
complex is often referred to
as a "skyscraper laid sideways."
Shops and restaurants run
at street level along Center
Plaza's sidewalk arcade, on
the Government Center side,
while the plaza behind incorporates some much older city
center buildings.

Curved, Modernist structure of Center
Plaza, on Cambridge Street

❽ Boston City Hall

City Hall Plaza. **Map** 2 D3. **Tel** (617)
635-4000. Ⓣ Government Center.
Open 8:30am–5pm Mon–Fri. ♿
Ⓦ ci.boston.ma.us

The firm of architects
Kallmann, McKinnell & Knowles
won a nationwide design
competition for their striking
city hall, a seemingly top-
heavy, cantilevered, Modernist
building. Completed in 1968,
the concrete-and-brick City
Hall combines the offices and
services of municipal government, with ample space for
holiday-season concerts,
school band and glee-club
performances, and community
art exhibits. An outdoor stage
on City Hall's north side is
often the venue for evening
rock and pop concerts during
the summer months.

Old-fashioned flower stall on the sidewalk
outside Center Plaza

❾ Government Center

Cambridge, Court, New Sudbury &
Congress Sts. **Map** 2 D3.
Ⓣ Government Center.

This city center development
was built on the site of what
was once Scollay Square,
demolished as part of the fad
for local urban renewal that
began in the early 1960s. Some
viewed the development as
controversial; others did not
lament what was essentially
a disreputable cluster of saloons,
burlesque theaters, tattoo
parlors, and scruffy hotels.
The overall master plan for
Government Center was
inspired by the alfresco vitality
and spaciousness of Italian

piazzas. Architects I.M. Pei &
Partners re-created some of
this feeling by surrounding
Boston's new City Hall with a
vast terraced plaza covering
56 acres (23 ha), paved with
1,800,000 bricks. Its spaciousness makes it an ideal venue
for events such as skateboard
contests, political and sports
rallies, food fairs, patriotic
military marches, and concerts.
    A remnant of old Boston
hangs from the Sears Block
at City Hall Plaza's Court
Street perimeter. This gilded,
227-gallon *Steaming Tea Kettle*
was made for the Oriental
Tea Company by a firm of
coppersmiths in 1873. Near
New Sudbury Street, the
John F. Kennedy Federal Office
Building features two pieces
of abstract art: Dmitry Hadzi's
15-ft (4.5-m) high *Thermopylae*
sculpture, and Robert
Motherwell's *New England
Elegy*, a mural recalling the
assassination of President
Kennedy in Dallas in 1963.

❿ Blackstone Block

Union, Hanover, North & Blackstone
Sts. **Map** 2 D3. Ⓣ Government
Center, Haymarket.

Cobblestones pave Boston's
only surviving web of
17th-century lanes and alleyways, a remnant of the
city's oldest neighborhood.

Boston City Hall and Government Center, one of Boston's main focal points

Benjamin Franklin grew up near Union and Hanover streets, where his father owned a candleworks. Prior to landfill programs, the block was close to the water's edge, and streets still bear names such as Marsh Lane, Creek Square, and Salt Lane.

The oldest surviving building dates from 1714; the Duke of Chartres, later to be crowned France's King Louis Philippe, lived here in 1798 and gave French lessons to support himself while waiting for funds. Since 1826, the building has housed the Union Oyster House *(see p143)*, renowned for its original mahogany and soapstone raw bar, its political clientele, and, of course, its oysters.

Across Union Street is the New England Holocaust Memorial, dedicated in 1995 to the Jewish victims of World War II. It is designed as a sculpture that visitors can walk through – a surreal, justly disquieting experience.

⓫ Boston Public Market & Greenway

100 Hanover St. **Map** 2 D3. Ⓣ Haymarket. **Open** 8am–8pm daily (winter: Wed–Sun). ♿
Ⓦ bostonpublicmarket.org

This indoor public market features about 40 regional growers and producers, grab-and-go dining options, and a demonstration kitchen. It also sponsors seasonal midweek farmers' markets on adjacent Blackstone Plaza, facing the Rose Fitzgerald Greenway linear park, and at Dewey Square on the Greenway, opposite South Station. The Greenway, which replaced the elevated highway buried by the Big Dig, contains walkways, fountains, pools, plazas, and even a children's carousel. It is a favorite location for midday food trucks.

Liberty and Union, Now and Forever by George Healy, Faneuil Hall

⓬ Faneuil Hall

Dock Sq. **Map** 2 D3. Ⓣ Government Center, Haymarket, State. Great Hall: **Open** 9am–5pm daily (may close for special events). ♿ 📷 📖
Ⓦ nps.gov/bost

A gift to Boston from the wealthy merchant Peter Faneuil in 1742, this Georgian, brick landmark has always functioned simultaneously as a public market and town meeting place. Master tinsmith Shem Drowne modeled the building's grasshopper weathervane after the one on top of the Royal Exchange in the City of London, England. Revolutionary gatherings packed the hall, and as early as 1763 Samuel Adams used the

The Union Oyster House, one of Boston's most famous restaurants, Blackstone Block

hall as a platform to suggest that the American colonies should unite against British oppression and fight to establish their independence *(see pp22–3)*; hence the building's nickname "Cradle of Liberty" and the bold posture of the statue of Samuel Adams at the front of the building.

Toward the end of the 18th century it became apparent that the existing Faneuil Hall could no longer house the capacity crowds that it regularly attracted. The commission to expand the building was undertaken by Charles Bulfinch *(see p55)*, who completed the work from 1805 to 1806. The building then remained unchanged until 1898, when it was expanded still farther according to long-standing Bulfinch stipulations.

Among the paintings upstairs in the Neoclassical Great Hall is George Healy's enormous canvas, *Liberty and Union, Now and Forever*, showing Massachusetts Senator Daniel Webster in full oratorical passion. The uppermost floor contains the headquarters and armory of the Ancient and Honorable Artillery Company, chartered in 1638 for defense of the Massachusetts Bay Colony and an occupant of Faneuil Hall since 1746. Displays include weapons, commendations, and medals.

Faneuil Hall also houses the visitor center of Boston National Historical Park.

Gallery of the Greek Revival main dome in Quincy Market's central hall

⑬ Quincy Market

Between Chatham & Clinton Sts.
Map 2 D3. **Tel** (617) 523-1300.
Ⓣ Government Center, State. **Open**
10am–9pm Mon–Sat, noon–6pm Sun
(restaurants and bars open later). ♿
Ⓦ faneuilhallmarketplace.com

This popular shopping and dining complex attracts in the region of 14 million people every year, and was developed from the buildings of the former Faneuil Hall produce and meat market, or Quincy Market. These buildings had fallen into disrepair before they underwent a widely acclaimed restoration by the architects Benjamin Thompson & Associates in the 1970s. The imposing center-piece, a granite Greek Revival structure *(see p34)* dating from

1825, was planned as an extension to the first Faneuil Hall Markets, which had become overstretched by Boston's rapid development. Originally called the New Faneuil Hall Market, the building came to be known as Quincy Market after the mayor, Josiah Quincy, whose original vision was responsible for the new market's creation. The façade's four Doric columns were, at the time of construction, the largest single pieces of granite ever to be quarried in the U.S. The 535-ft (163-m) long colonnaded hall is now filled with fast-food stalls and a large seating area, located in the spectacular Rotunda. Completing the ensemble are twin North and South Market buildings – these individual warehouses have been refurbished to accommodate boutiques, restaurants, pubs, stores, and upstairs offices.

⑭ Custom House

3 McKinley Square. **Map** 2 E3. **Tel** (617)
310-6300. Ⓣ Aquarium. Museum:
Open 8am–9pm daily. Tower: **Open**
2pm and 6pm Sat–Thu. 🎦
Ⓦ marriott.com

Before landfill altered downtown topography, early Boston's Custom House perched at the water's edge. A temple-like Greek Revival structure with fluted Doric columns, the granite building had a skylit dome upon completion in 1847. Since 1915, however, it has supported an

anachronistic tower rising 495 ft (150 m), which means that for the best part of the 20th century, the Custom House was Boston's only bona fide skyscraper. Four sculpted eagles and a four-sided illuminated clock add decorative flourishes. The public has free access to a small museum of maritime history in the 19th-century rotunda. It displays objects on loan from the Peabody Museum in Salem, including maritime paintings, nautical instruments, items that depict Boston's trade with China, and several pieces of decorative art. The observatory, which offers panoramic views, is also open to the public. The rest of the building, occupied by a Marriott hotel and timeshare apartments, is not open to the public.

Glass fountain on the Pearl Street side of Post Office Square

⑮ Post Office Square

Between Congress & Pearl Sts.
Map 2 D4. Ⓣ State, Aquarium.

This beautifully landscaped park, a small island of green situated amid the soaring skyscrapers of the financial district, replaced an ugly concrete garage that once stood here – it was demolished and rebuilt as an underground parking facility in 1990. Vines climb a 143-ft (44-m) long trellis along one side of the park, and a fountain made of green glass cascades on the square's Pearl Street side. On Angell Memorial Plaza across the road, a fountain dating from 1912 commemorates George Thorndike Angell,

Greek Revival Custom House tower, one of Boston's most striking sights

Alexander Graham Bell (1847–1922)

A native of Edinburgh, Scotland, and son of a deaf mother, Bell moved to Boston in 1871 to embark on a career of teaching speech to the deaf. It led to his appointment, two years later, as professor of vocal physiology at Boston University. In a rented fifth-floor garret assisted by young repair mechanic and model maker Thomas Watson, Bell worked in his spare time on an apparatus for transmitting sound by electrical current. Initial success came on June 3, 1875, when the barely intelligible utterings of a human voice (his own) traveled over a laboratory wire. History was made on March 17, 1876, when Bell, while experimenting on voice transmission, upset a battery, spilling acid on his clothing. He called to another room: "Mr. Watson, come here. I want you." With each of those seven words reaching Watson clearly and distinctly, the "electrical speech machine" was invented. In August that year, Bell proved its practical value by sending messages over Canadian telegraph wires. By 1878, he had set up the first public telephone exchange in New Haven, Connecticut. Six years later, long-distance calls were being made between Boston and New York City.

Distinctive, Art Deco-style Verizon Building, a landmark of Boston

founder of the Massachusetts' Society for the Prevention of Cruelty to Animals. Some of the most important buildings overlooking the square and plaza include the New England Telephone Building and the John W. McCormack courthouse building, which formerly housed downtown's main post office. Other important buildings include the Langham Boston hotel *(see p137)* – this classic Renaissance Revival showpiece was completed in 1922 and was originally the Federal Reserve Bank – and

One Post Office Square, which offers great views over Boston Harbor and Downtown. These views can be seen from the atrium at the top of the building, which, not strictly open to the public, may be accessible through polite inquiry. A focal point for the whole district, the grassy space of the square comes into its own during the warmer months of the year, when office workers can be seen sprawling across its well-kept lawns – a great place for visitors to rest their weary feet and watch Bostonians take a few minutes out.

⓰ Verizon Building

185 Franklin St. **Map** 2 D4. **Tel** (617) 743-9340. Ⓣ State, Aquarium. Museum: **Closed** to the public. ♿

Dating from 1947 and overlooking the south side of Post Office Square, this Art Deco building, formerly the New England Telephone Building, is still in use today. Dean Cornwell's monumental 160-ft (49-m) long *Telephone Men and Women at Work* mural – populated by 197 life-size figures – encircled the lobby for over five decades, a truly remarkable work of art. Unfortunately, the mural has now been removed and the building is closed to the public. Despite this the building remains an iconic Boston landmark in light of its impressive history.

The building, one of the best examples of Art Deco remaining in the city, provides an attractive backdrop for area workers having lunch on Post Office Square. Some of the interior's original elements – high ceilings and stately hallways made from Marine granite – remain in place, while others (floral drapes and orange carpeting) became dated and were removed over time.

Post Office Square is a popular lunchtime spot for Financial District workers

NORTH END AND THE WATERFRONT

This was Boston's first neighborhood, and one that has been key to the city's fortunes. Fringed by numerous wharves, the area prospered initially through shipping and shipbuilding, with much of America's early trade passing through its warehouses. The more recent importance of finance and high-tech industries, however, has seen the waterfront evolve; its old warehouses

transformed into luxury apartment blocks and offices. Away from the waterfront, the narrow streets of the North End have historically been home to European immigrants, drawn by the availability of work. An Italian immigrant neighborhood through much of the 20th century, it retains an Italian-American flavor in its many cafés, restaurants, and specialty shops.

See Street Finder map 2

🔲 **Restaurants** *pp144–5*

1   Antico Forno
2   Barking Crab
3   Bricco
4   Carmen
5   Dino's Café
6   Ernesto's Pizzeria
7   Giacomo's Ristorante
8   James Hook & Co.
9   La Famiglia Giorgio
10 Legal Harborside
11 Maurizio's Ristorante Italiano
12 Menton
13 Meritage
14 Neptune Oyster
15 Pizzeria Regina
16 Prezza
17 Scopa
18 Sportello
19 State Street Provisions
20 Terramia
21 Trade
22 Yankee Lobster Company

Sights at a Glance

Historic Sites and Churches

❶ Copp's Hill Burying Ground
❷ Clough House
❸ Old North Church *p73*
❹ Paul Revere Mall
❺ St. Stephen's Church
❻ Paul Revere House

Waterfront Sights

❼ Christopher Columbus Park
❽ Long Wharf
❾ New England Aquarium *pp78–9*
❿ Rowes Wharf
⓫ Institute of Contemporary Art
⓬ Boston Tea Party Ships & Museum
⓭ Children's Museum

◀ The redeveloped Rowes Wharf with the iconic archway

For keys to symbols *see back flap*

Street-by-Street: North End

The main arteries of this area are Hanover and Salem Streets. Topped by the Old North Church, Salem Street is indicative of this area's historical connections – indeed the Old North Church is one of Boston's premier Revolutionary sights. In general the area consists of narrow streets and alleys, with four- and five-story tenements, many of which are now expensive condominiums. Hanover Street, like much of the area, has a distinctly Italian feel, while just south of here is North Square, site of the famous Paul Revere House *(see p75)*.

❷ Clough House
This 18th century home has a replica colonial printing press and functions as a "historic" chocolate shop.

HULL STREET

SHEAFE STREET

NORTH BENNET

SALEM STREET

PRINCE STREET

Charlestown

❶ Copp's Hill Burying Ground
During the American Revolution, the British used this low hilltop to fire cannon at American positions across Boston Harbor. Created in 1659 it is the city's second oldest graveyard.

❸ ★ Old North Church
Built in 1723 and famous for the part it played in Paul Revere's midnight ride *(see p23)*, this is Boston's oldest religious building. On festive occasions, the North End still rings with the sound of its bells.

Key

— Suggested route

Government Center

0 meters		50
0 yards		50

4 ★ Paul Revere Mall
Linking the Old North Church to Hanover Street, this tree-lined mall dates only from 1933. Its antique feel is enhanced by a statue of Paul Revere, which was modeled in 1885.

Locator Map
See Street Finder map 2

5 St. Stephen's Church
North End's Italian theme continues in this church, though only by chance. Long before the first Italians arrived, Charles Bulfinch *(see p55)* incorporated Italian Renaissance features and a bell tower into his refit of an earlier church building.

Hanover Street is the most Italian of Boston's streets, brought to life by Italian restaurants and cafés, as well as the day-to-day activities of its ethnic community.

The waterfront

6 ★ Paul Revere House
This is the house where Paul Revere began his midnight ride *(see p23)*. Revere's home from 1770 to 1800, it is now a museum.

Slate tombstones of Boston's early settlers, Copp's Hill Burying Ground

❶ Copp's Hill Burying Ground

Entrances at Charter & Hull Sts.
Map 2 D2. Ⓣ Government Center,
North Station. **Open** 9am–5pm daily.

Established in 1659, this is Boston's second-oldest cemetery after the one by King's Chapel *(see p60)*. Nicknamed "Corpse Hill," the real name of the hill occupied by the cemetery derives from a local man by the name of William Copp. He owned a farm on its southeastern slope from 1643, and much of the cemetery's land was purchased from him. His children can be found buried here. Other more famous people interred here include Robert Newman, the sexton

who hung Paul Revere's signal lanterns in the belfry of Old North Church *(see p73)*, and Edmund Hartt, builder of the *U.S.S. Constitution (see p117)*. Increase, Cotton, and Samuel Mather, three generations of a family of highly influential colonial period Puritan ministers, are also buried here. Hundreds of Boston's Colonial-era black slaves and freedmen are also buried here, including Prince Hall, a free black man who founded the African Free-masonry Order in Massachusetts.

During the British occupation of Boston, the site was used by British commanders who had an artillery position here. They would later exploit the prominent hilltop location during the Revolution, when they directed cannon fire from here across Boston harbor toward American positions in Charlestown. King George III's troops were said to have used the slate headstones for target practice, and pockmarks from their musket balls are still visible on some of them.

Copp's Hill Terrace, directly across Charter Street, is a prime observation point for views over to Charlestown and

Quiet, leafy street, typical of the area around Copp's Hill

Bunker Hill. It is also the site where, in 1919, a 2.3-million-gallon molasses tank exploded, creating a huge, syrupy tidal wave that killed 21 people.

❷ Clough House

21 Unity St. **Map** 2 E2. **Tel** (617) 523-6676. Ⓣ Haymarket, Aquarium.
Open Jun–Oct: 11am–5:30pm daily (call for winter hours).

Ebenezer Clough was a master mason and one of the Sons of Liberty who participated in the Boston Tea Party *(see p77)*. One of two masons who helped to build the neighboring Old North Church *(see p73)*, he was also the head of a syndicate that laid out Unity Street in 1710 and built a series of six town houses here. The only building to survive is the one at No. 21 Unity Street, which was built in 1712, and was the house in which Ebenezer Clough himself lived. In a bad state of decay for many years, and in danger of demolition,

Decorative column, Copp's Hill

the house was only saved when Reverend P. Kellet, vicar of Christ Church, launched a fund-raising campaign in 1962. A rather austere three-story building, it is typical of much of Boston's colonial architecture. Now fully restored to its former condition, the house has finely executed window and door lintels, decorated with raised brick panels over the first-floor windows and simple, carved-brick detailing over the door. Now part of the Old North Church campus, the house illustrates life in the late colonial era through two businesses. Costumed interpreters at the printing office of Edes & Gill demon-strate newspaper and broadside printing of the 18th century, while interpreters at Captain Jackson's Historic Chocolate Shop discuss how colonial Americans prepared and consumed chocolate.

❸ Old North Church

Christ Episcopal Church is the official name of this, Boston's oldest surviving religious edifice, which dates from 1723. It was built of brick in the Georgian style similar to that of St. Andrew's-by-the-Wardrobe in Blackfriars, London, designed by Sir Christopher Wren. The church was made famous on April 18, 1775, when sexton Robert Newman, aiding Paul Revere *(see p23),* hung a pair of signal lanterns in the belfry. These were to warn the patriots in Charlestown of the westward departure of British troops, on their way to engage the revolutionaries.

VISITORS' CHECKLIST

Practical Information
193 Salem St.
Map 2 E2.
Tel (617) 523-6676.
🅦 **oldnorth.com**
Open Jan, Feb: 10am–4pm Tue–
Sun; Mar–May: 9am–5pm daily
Jun–Oct: to 6pm; Nov–Mar:
10am–5pm daily. **Closed** Jan,
Feb: Mon. 🔂 9 & 11am. 📷 ♿
📷 📷 call for details.

Transport
Ⓣ Haymarket, Aquarium,
North Station.

Tower
The tower of the Old North Church contains the first set of church bells in North America, cast in 1745.

★ Box Pews
The unusual, high-sided box pews in the church were designed to enclose footwarmers, which were filled with hot coals or bricks during wintry weather.

Chandeliers
The distinctive chandeliers were brought from England in January 1724 for the first Christmas season.

Entrance

★ Bust of George Washington
This marble bust of the first U.S. president, modeled on an earlier one by Christian Gullager, was presented to the church in 1815.

❹ Paul Revere Mall

Hanover St. **Map** 2 E2. Ⓣ Haymarket, Aquarium. ♿

This brick-paved plaza gives the crowded neighborhood of the North End a precious stretch of open space between Hanover and Unity Streets. A well-utilized municipal resource, the Mall is always full of local people: children, teenagers, young mothers, and older residents chatting in Italian and playing cards or checkers. Laid out in 1933, and originally called the Prado, its focal point is Cyrus Dallin's equestrian statue of local hero Paul Revere, which was originally modeled in 1885. However, it was only sculpted and placed here in 1940. Bronze bas-relief plaques on the mall's side walls commemorate a number of North End residents who have played an important role in the history of

Equestrian statue by Cyrus Dallin, Paul Revere Mall

Boston. Benches, a fountain, and twin rows of linden trees complete the space, which has a distinctly European feel.

❺ St. Stephen's Church

401 Hanover St. **Map** 2 E2. **Tel** (617) 523-1230. Ⓣ Haymarket, Aquarium. **Open** 8:30am–4:30pm Mon–Sat. ✝ 11am Sun, 4:30pm Sat, 7:30am Tue–Fri.

Opened in 1714 as a humble Congregationalist meeting house, St. Stephen's Church was extensively enlarged and embellished by the architect Charles Bulfinch (see p55) in 1802–04. Bulfinch incorporated a range of harmonious Italian Renaissance motifs in his redesign, adding a number of decorative pediments and pedestals, tall arched windows, as well as an ornate bell tower that is topped by a gilded cap. One

St. Stephen's Church, with its Renaissance-style bell tower

year after that project's completion, the first-ever bell cast by the famous revolutionary and master metalworker, Paul Revere (see p23), was hung in the belfry.

The church's present name dates from 1862, when it became Roman Catholic to accommodate the North End's increasing numbers of Irish immigrants. When Hanover Street was widened in 1869, the entire structure was moved back 16 ft (5 m) and, a year later, it was raised 6 ft (2 m) to accommodate a basement chapel. Damaged by fires in 1897 and 1929, and redecorated each time, the church was restored to its Bulfinch design in 1965.

The church's interior features include a gracefully curved ceiling, original white-painted pine columns, and a pair of pewter chandeliers, which are copies of those hanging in the Doric Hall of the Massachusetts State House. The church's pews were donated in honor of the numerous Irish, Italian, and Portuguese parishioners who live in the neighborhood, while the Italian mahogany Stations of the Cross are part of the 1965 refit. St. Stephen's is listed on the National Register of Historic Places.

The Great Brinks Robbery

Masterminded by Tony Pino, this infamous event took place on the night of January 17, 1950 on North End's Commercial Street. Disguised as Brinks guards, seven of Pino's men made off with $2,775,395.12 in payroll money – including cash totaling $1,218,211.29 – from the headquarters of the Brinks Armored Car Company. Nationwide headlines trumpeted the robbery as the biggest heist in U.S. history. Even though all members of the Brinks gang were eventually caught and imprisoned, only $60,000 of the loot has been recovered almost 70 years after the event.

Members of the infamous Brinks gang, in police custody

➏ Paul Revere House

19 North Sq. **Map** 2 E2. **Tel** (617) 523-2338. Ⓣ Haymarket, Aquarium. **Open** mid-Apr–Oct: 9:30am–5:15pm daily; Nov–mid-Apr: 9:30am–4:15pm daily (Pierce-Hichborn House call for tour hours). **Closed** Jan–Mar: Mon. 🅿 ♿ ✉ 🅿 🅦 paulreverehouse.org

The city's oldest surviving clapboard frame house is historically significant, for it was here in 1775 that Paul Revere began his legendary horseback ride to warn his compatriots in Lexington of the impending arrival of British troops *(see p23)*. This historic event was later immortalized in a boldly patriotic, epic poem by Henry Wadsworth Longfellow *(see p110)*. It begins "Listen, my children, and you shall hear of the midnight ride of Paul Revere."

Revere, a Huguenot descendent, was by trade a versatile gold- and silversmith, copper engraver, and maker of church bells, cannons, and false teeth. He and his second wife Rachel, mother of eight of his 16 children, owned the house

Colonial banknotes, exhibited in the Paul Revere House

from 1770 to 1800. Small leaded casement windows, an overhanging upper story, and nail-studded front door all contribute to make it a fine example of 17th-century Early American architecture. In the courtyard along one side of the house is a large bronze bell, cast by Paul Revere for a church in 1804 – Revere made nearly 200 church bells. Three rooms in the house contain period artifacts, including original pieces of family furniture, items made in Revere's workshop, and colonial banknotes. The house, which by the mid-19th century had become a decrepit tenement fronted by stores, was saved from demolition by preservationists' efforts led by a great-grandson of Revere.

Next door, the early 18th-century Pierce-Hichborn House is the earliest brick town house remaining in New England. It features Georgian English motifs such as shallow arches over the doors and windows, and twin chimneys. It is open for guided tours only.

The famous Paul Revere House built in the 17th century

➐ Christopher Columbus Park

Atlantic Avenue, between Long & Commercial Wharves. **Map** 2 E3. Ⓣ Aquarium.

Extensive urban renewal along the Inner Harbor resulted in the completion of this handsome park in 1976. It covers 4.5 acres (2 ha) with wisteria clinging to a 340-ft (104-m) long arched trellis, and is a superlative spot for views of the waterfront and the Financial District. The commemorative Rose Kennedy Garden was added to the park's layout in 1987.

Boston Harbor as seen from Christopher Columbus Park

Rowes Wharf development, typical of Boston's waterfront regeneration

❽ Long Wharf

Atlantic Avenue. **Map** 2 E3.
Ⓣ Aquarium.

The nation's oldest continuously operated wharf was built in 1710 to accommodate the boom in early maritime commerce. The following century was to be Boston's international maritime heyday; it was the busiest port in North America and one of the most important in the colonies, surpassed only by London and Bristol in the amount of cargo that it handled. Once extending 2,000 ft (610 m) into Boston harbor, and lined with shops and warehouses, Long Wharf provided secure mooring for the largest ships of the time.

Today, Long Wharf is used by boat services to Provincetown, Charlestown Navy Yard, and the Harbor Islands. The attractive esplanade at the end also offers good views across the city's waterfront. Running along the waterfront, Harbor Walk connects Long Wharf with other adjacent wharves, such as Union, Lewis, and Commercial wharves. Dating from the early 1800s, most are now converted to fashionable harborside apartments and condominiums.

❾ New England Aquarium

See pp78–9.

❿ Rowes Wharf

Atlantic Avenue. **Map** 2 E4.
Ⓣ Aquarium.

Completed in 1987, this fine example of waterfront revitalization replaced the two-part India wharf dating from the 1760s. Built of Bostonian red brick and designed by Skidmore, Owings & Merrill, the complex houses the luxury Boston Harbor Hotel (see p135), condominiums, offices, and a marina. A large archway links the city to the harbor.

⓫ Institute of Contemporary Art

25 Harbor Shore Drive. **Map** 2 F5.
Tel (617) 478-3100. Ⓣ Courthouse.
Open 10am–5pm Tue, Wed, Sat, Sun, 10am–9pm Thu, Fri. 📷 ♿
Ⓦ icaboston.org

In 2006 the Institute of Contemporary Art moved to a dramatic wood, steel, and glass landmark building on Fan Pier. Light-flooded galleries, a performance space open to harbor views, and a cutting-edge media center mean that the ICA can extend its eight-decade history of innovation well into the 21st century. Its exhibitions typically break the mold of convention and it is building its first permanent collection of avant-garde work.

⓬ Boston Tea Party Ships & Museum

306 Congress St. **Map** 2 E5.
Tel (617) 338-1773. Ⓣ South Station.
📷 Ⓦ bostonteapartyship.com

Griffin's Wharf, where the Boston Tea Party took place on December 16, 1773 (see p77), was buried beneath landfill many years ago. Today, visitors can enjoy interactive exhibits, including actors in period clothing, a traditional tea room, and Tavern Night shows. Floating in Fort Point Channel are perfect replicas of the *Beaver* and *Dartmouth*, two of the three ships that took part in the original Boston Tea Party, built by master builder Leon Poindexter. With its wraparound movie screen,

View down Long Wharf toward the waterfront and Custom House

the state-of-the-art Minute-man Theatre plays a multi-sensory film that dramatically recreates one of the most important events in the history of United States.

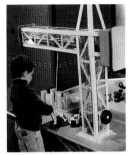

Playing on the mini-construction site at Boston's Children's Museum

⑬ Children's Museum

300 Congress St. **Map** 2 E5.
Tel (617) 426-6500. Ⓣ South Station.
Open 10am–5pm daily (to 9pm Fri).
📷 ♿ ⓦ **bostonkids.org**

Overlooking Fort Point Channel, a pair of rejuvenated 19th-century wool warehouses contain one of the country's best children's museums, which underwent an extensive expansion in 2007. There are many interesting exhibits, and youngsters are able to participate in games and learning activities, and hoist themselves up a climbing structure in the New Balance Center.

The Art Studio provides a hands-on recycling area with barrels of materials that children can use in self-instructive creative projects, while the KidPower exhibition is designed to encourage active, healthy lifestyles. An international flavor is injected into the proceedings by a visit to the silk merchant's house, which has been transplanted from the city of Kyoto in Japan (Boston's sister city).

A towering milk bottle from a local dairy stands outside in front of the museum building and is used as an ice-cream stand in summer. An outdoor park features mazes, giant boulders, and spaces for outdoor performances.

The Boston Tea Party

In 1767, when Britain decided to tax its American colonies, there was outrage. Boycotts were placed on British goods, and protesters took to the streets. One such protest in 1773 culminated in the Boston Massacre (see p22).

Despite a subsequent reduction in taxation, tax on tea remained. Parliament then granted the British East India Company sole rights to sell tea in the colonies, which caused prices to rise further. In November 1773, ships arrived in Boston Harbor loaded with tea, and merchants, who refused to buy the tea, came under pressure from Thomas Hutchinson, the Monarchist governor. On the night of December 16, however, around 7,000 rebels, gathered by Samuel Adams, marched to the wharf declaring "Tonight Boston Harbor is a teapot!" Fifty men, dressed as Mohawks, boarded the ships and dumped their cargoes into the water.

Britain reacted strongly, closing the port and putting Massachusetts under martial law. This retribution unified patriots across America, and the "Boston Tea Party," as the protest was soon known, became the spark that ignited the Revolutionary War.

Thomas Hutchinson
Governor of Boston and staunch monarchist, Thomas Hutchinson tried to force the rebels to comply with British colonial law.

342 bales of tea were thrown into the sea.

Many of the rebels were dressed as Mohawks.

A crowd of about 7,000 watched the events from the quayside.

The Boston Tea Party, depicted in a 19th-century engraving

⑨ New England Aquarium

The waterfront's prime attraction dominates Central Wharf. Designed by a consortium of architects in 1969, the aquarium's core encloses a vast four-story ocean tank, which contains a wide array of marine animals. A curving walkway runs around the outside of the tank from top to bottom and provides viewpoints of the interior of the tank from different levels. Also resident are colonies of penguins, playful harbor and fur seals, anacondas, rays, and mesmerizing seadragons. An IMAX® Theatre rounds out the facility.

★ Penguin Pool
One of the main attractions of the aquarium, the penguin pool runs around the base of the giant tank. It contains African, rockhopper, and little blue penguins.

Shark and Ray Touch Tank
The biggest shark and ray touch tank on the East Coast lets visitors handle some of the sea's oldest and most mysterious creatures.

★ Whale Watch
This marine safari from Boston to Stellwagen Bank lets city visitors see the largest mammals on earth. Naturalists lead viewing of humpback, finback, and minke whales.

①

Main entrance

Harbor Seals
Harbor seals cavort in a glass-sided outdoor tank that is always open for free viewing.

New Balance Foundation Marine Mammal Center
Northern fur seals frolic in this open-air exhibit where the aquarium meets the harbor. Shallow pools and large decks allow visitors to interact and learn about marine mammals up close.

VISITORS' CHECKLIST

Practical Information
Central Wharf. **Map** 2 E3.
Tel (617) 973-5200.
W neaq.org
Open Sep–Jun: 9am–5pm Mon–Fri, 9am–6pm Sat & Sun; Jul–Aug: 9am–6pm Sun–Thu, 9am–7pm Fri & Sat.

Transport
T Aquarium.

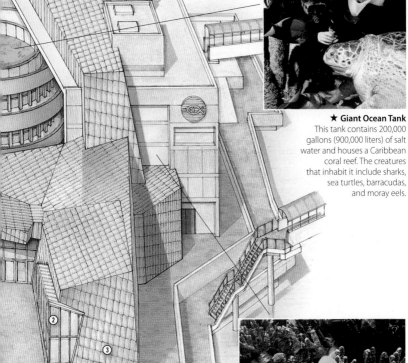

★ **Giant Ocean Tank**
This tank contains 200,000 gallons (900,000 liters) of salt water and houses a Caribbean coral reef. The creatures that inhabit it include sharks, sea turtles, barracudas, and moray eels.

↓ IMAX® Theatre

KEY

① Ticket booth

② Harbor View Café

③ Gift Shop

Tropical Gallery
This exhibit provides an account of the many types of environment manifested in reefs: starting with a darkened exhibit of deep-water reef fishes and ending with a brightly lit, Pacific coral reef.

CHINATOWN AND THE THEATER DISTRICT

Located south of Boston Common *(see pp48–9)* and west of the Financial District, this part of town has a noticeably gritty, more down-to-earth ambience. The area around Washington Street, with Downtown Crossing at its center *(see pp82–3)*, is the city's main shopping district. South of here is Chinatown, one of the largest in the United States, but a more manageable, less intimidating version of similar areas in San Francisco and New York. West of Chinatown is the Theater District, featuring touring Broadway shows and local productions. The former "Combat Zone," located at the lower end of Washington Street, between Chinatown and Boston Common, has rebounded as an extension of the Theater District following the restoration of two historic theaters.

Sights at a Glance

Historic Streets, Buildings, and Churches

1 St. Paul's Cathedral
2 Downtown Crossing
3 Ladder District
4 Brattle Book Shop
6 Massachusetts State Transportation Building
8 Chinatown
9 Jacob Wirth
10 Bay Village

Theaters

5 Boston Opera House
7 Colonial Theatre
11 Shubert Theatre
12 Wang Theatre

Restaurants pp145–6

1 Bristol Lounge
2 Chau Chow City
3 Dong Khanh
4 Doretta Taverna & Raw Bar
5 East Ocean City
6 Erbaluce
7 Gourmet Dumpling House
8 Jacob Wirth Restaurant
9 Legal Sea Foods
10 My Thai Vegan Cafe
11 Peach Farm
12 Penang
13 Pho Pasteur
14 Shabu-Zen
15 Taiwan Café
16 Teatro
17 Troquet
18 Winsor Dim Sum Cafe

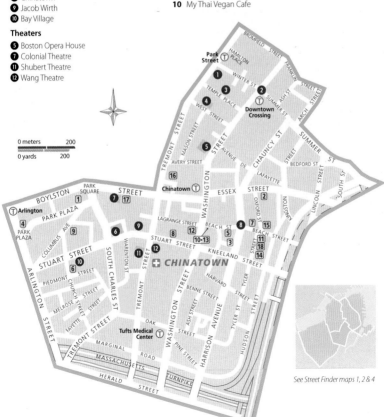

See Street Finder maps 1, 2 & 4

◄ Traditional decorative gate at the entrance of Chinatown

For keys to symbols *see back flap*

Street-by-Street: Around Washington Street

Running northeast from the Theater District, Washington Street lies at the heart of Boston's longtime main shopping area. Its focal point, Downtown Crossing, lies at its intersection with Winter and Summer Streets. Saturday afternoons, in particular, offer visitors a glimpse of Boston's sophisticated, and often multi-ethnic population, as they go about their shopping. Macy's is the main department store, though Washington Street and the streets off it offer a range of outlets such as bookstores, camera stores, and jewelers. Just to the south, the Theater District and Chinatown are only a few minutes away on foot. Note that incidences of petty crime sometimes occur in this crowded area.

Sidewalk café on Summer Street

Boston Common

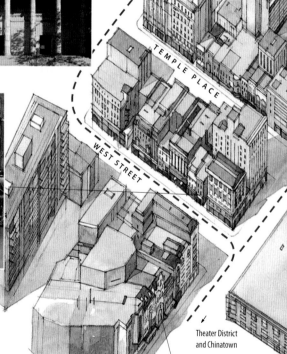

TEMPLE PLACE

WEST STREET

Theater District and Chinatown

AVE DE

❶ **St. Paul's Cathedral**
Dating from around 1820, this was one of the first Greek Revival granite buildings to go up in Boston. Today it is still used to broadcast Sunday morning religious programs.

❹ ★ **Brattle Book Shop**
At first glance, there is not a lot to recommend a second look at this Boston literary landmark. Inside, however, are more than 250,000 rare books and magazines, a treat for any lover of the printed word.

❺ ★ **Boston Opera House**
This building was opened as a theater in 1928. In 2004, it was completely restored and remains the focus of the revitalized lower Washington Street.

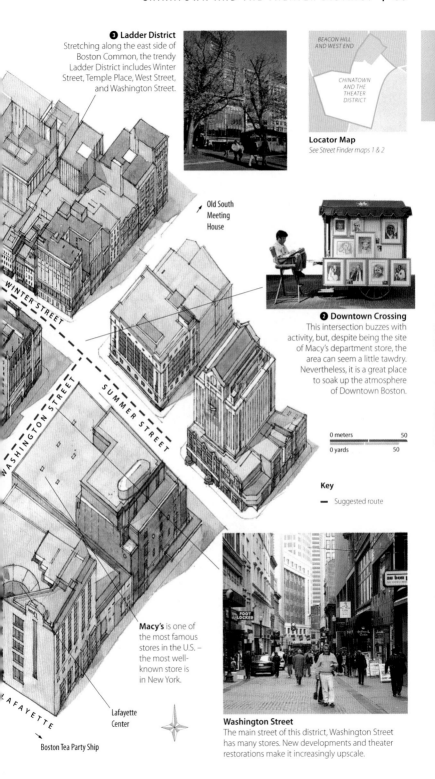

❸ Ladder District
Stretching along the east side of Boston Common, the trendy Ladder District includes Winter Street, Temple Place, West Street, and Washington Street.

BEACON HILL AND WEST END

CHINATOWN AND THE THEATER DISTRICT

Locator Map
See Street Finder maps 1 & 2

Old South Meeting House

❷ Downtown Crossing
This intersection buzzes with activity, but, despite being the site of Macy's department store, the area can seem a little tawdry. Nevertheless, it is a great place to soak up the atmosphere of Downtown Boston.

WINTER STREET

WASHINGTON STREET

SUMMER STREET

| 0 meters | 50 |
| 0 yards | 50 |

Key
— Suggested route

Macy's is one of the most famous stores in the U.S. – the most well-known store is in New York.

LAFAYETTE

Lafayette Center

Boston Tea Party Ship

Washington Street
The main street of this district, Washington Street has many stores. New developments and theater restorations make it increasingly upscale.

Classical chancel and box pews of the interior of St. Paul's Cathedral, typically austere in style

❶ St. Paul's Cathedral

138 Tremont St. **Map** 4 E1.
Tel (617) 482-5800. Ⓣ Park Street.
🕆 8am, 10am & 12:30pm Sun; 1pm Mon, 12:15pm Tue & Fri. ♿
Ⓦ stpaulboston.org

Consecrated in 1820, Boston's second example of Greek Revival architecture was designed by Alexander Parris, five years before the completion of his Quincy Market hall *(see p66)*, which also has the outward appearance of a Greek temple. The first Greek Revival

Church in Boston came about with Charles Bulfinch's design for the façade of the original New South Church, which was subsequently demolished.

The stone work on St. Paul's Cathedral is by Solomon Willard, who gave the church a portico of six unfluted stone columns with Ionic capitals. The building's pediment was initially intended to feature a frieze depicting St. Paul preaching before King Agrippa, but this was never constructed due to considerations of the cost involved.

The interior of the church, dominated by a classical chancel, curved apse, and box pews, is spacious and austere, typical of a style found in New England churches.

In 1908 the church became the cathedral of Massachusetts' Episcopal diocese. It also represents Boston's changing populations, offering a 12:30pm Sunday service in Chinese and 12:30pm Jum'ah Friday Muslim prayers.

❷ Downtown Crossing

Washington, Winter & Summer Sts.
Map 4 F1. Ⓣ Downtown Crossing.

This shopping-district crossroads was laid out as a pedestrian zone between 1975 and 1978. The area is anchored by a Beaux Arts building (now housing a market and luxury residences) that once held Filene's, and Modern-style Macy's. Smaller retail outlets, some in restored buildings with terracotta and cast-iron façades, are plentiful in the streets radiating from Downtown Crossing and Washington Street. Lively push-cart vendors and sparkling diamonds in the jeweler's district can also be found here. South of Downtown Crossing, the area recaptures an earlier era when it was part of Boston's original Theater Row.

❸ Ladder District

Connecting streets and rear alleys between Washington & Tremont Sts.
Map 4 E1–F2. Ⓣ Downtown Crossing & Chinatown.

Once a rather rundown part of Downtown, the web of small streets connecting Washington and Tremont Streets, along the east side of Boston Common, came into its own at the start of the new millennium. Soaring buildings were erected on vacant parking lots and old architectural treasures on the dark streets were refurbished and brought back to life. Today they house restaurants, bars, and nightclubs.

Along with upmarket condos came the Ritz-Carlton Boston Common hotel *(see p136)*, housed in a building that stretches the length of Avery Street. This building played a central role in the renaissance of what used to be a no man's land between the Theater District and Downtown Crossing. In addition to the luxury hotel, a bar and restaurant, and a fashionable gym, the Equinox Sports Club, the structure also

Beaux Arts façade of former Filene's department store, Downtown Crossing

houses the AMC Loews Boston Common (see p161). Boston's first premier cinema has 19 screens, stadium seating, child-friendly matinees and multiple dining concessions.

The nightclubs and restaurants of the Ladder District are often indistinguishable, although if a long line is standing outside, the establishment probably serves more liquor than food. Club names also tend to change frequently as owners tweak the themes to attract different crowds. Many maps do not show all the small streets in the district, such as Pi Alley, so it is best to take a leisurely stroll and discover the area for yourself.

Carts of second-hand books outside the Brattle Book Shop

❹ Brattle Book Shop

9 West St. **Map** 4 E1. **Tel** (617) 542-0210. Ⓣ Park Street, Downtown Crossing. **Open** 9am–5:30pm Mon–Sat. ♿ ⓦ brattlebookshop.com

Founded in 1825 and located at various sites around Boston since, this bibliophiles' treasure house is packed with more than 250,000 used, rare, and out-of-print books. Proprietor Kenneth Gloss also stocks back issues of periodicals, *Life*, *Look*, and *Collier's* magazines among them, along with antiquarian ephemera such as maps, prints, postcards, greeting cards, and autographed manuscripts. In front of and alongside the three-story building, passersby browse through bins and carts full of discounted bargain books priced in the range of $1 to $5.

Spanish Baroque, terracotta ornamentation on the façade of the Boston Opera House

❺ Boston Opera House

539 Washington St. **Map** 4 E1. **Tel** (617) 259-3400. Ⓣ Downtown Crossing, Chinatown, Boylston. ♿ ⓦ bostonoperahouse.com

The building that is now the Boston Opera House has been known by many names. Built on the site of the original Boston Theater, and designed by Thomas Lamb, it opened in 1928 as the B. F. Keith Memorial Theater, named after the late 19th-century showman who added the term "vaudeville" to show business vocabulary. It was renamed the Savoy Theater in the 1940s and served as home for the Opera Company of Boston from the late 1950s until 1991. The venue became internationally recognized for Sarah Caldwell's daringly innovative productions. With its white Spanish Baroque, terracotta façade, high ceilings, and three-tier horseshoe balconies, the theater represents the apogee of early 20th century hall design. A $54-million renovation completed in 2004 restored the theater's original opulence with gilded surfaces and exquisite ceiling murals, while installing modern climate control, technical systems, and seating. Primarily used for large touring Broadway musicals, the Boston Opera House is also the performance venue for the Boston Ballet.

Liberty Tree

At the corner of Washington Street and Boylston Street, a low relief of a tree marks the exact site of the famous Liberty Tree, where the Sons of Liberty would meet during the prelude to the American Revolution. The tree's fame first became widespread when it became a focal point for opposition to the Stamp Act (see p22). The British stamp master, Andrew Oliver, was hung in effigy from its branches, an incident that caused people from all over the region to gather around it. The tree was also a meeting place in the days running up to the Boston Tea Party (see p77). In August 1775, during the early part of the Revolution when Boston was still occupied by the British, a mob of Redcoats vented their anger on the tree and chopped it down.

Bostonians protest the Stamp Act of 1765, around the Liberty Tree

❻ Massachusetts State Transportation Building

8–10 Park Plaza, Stuart & Charles Sts.
Map 4 E2. ⓣ Boylston. Atrium
restaurants: **Open** 11am–8pm Mon–
Fri, noon–6pm Sat. ♿

The main feature of the
Massachusetts State
Transportation Building,
constructed in 1983, is its }
seven-story-high, skylit City
Place atrium, which is directly
accessible to the public.
Covering most of a sizeable city
block, this red-brick and glass
cantilevered building has won
several prestigious design
awards. It incorporates offices
and public-service facilities,
maintained by the state's
transportation administrators,
around a central mall of wide-
ranging shops and restaurants.
Lunchtime concerts, pop
or light-classical music, are
frequently scheduled in the
central mall, while gallery
showings are often held on the
upper levels overlooking the
atrium. Other facilities in the
building include a bank,
newsstand, and several
fast-food eateries.

The City Place atrium in the Massachusetts State Transportation Building

Gilt ornamentation from the lavishly decorated interior of the Colonial Theatre

❼ Colonial Theatre

106 Boylston St. **Map** 4 E2.
Tel (617) 426-9366. ⓣ Boylston.
Open phone to check. ♿
Ⓦ artsemerson.org

Clarence H. Blackall designed
14 Boston theaters during his
architectural career, among
them the Colonial, which is
the city's oldest theater to
have been in continuous
operation under the same
name. A two-story loggia sits
atop Blackall's structure, which
is otherwise quite plain. The
interior, on the other hand,
is an impressively opulent
showpiece by H.B. Pennell: his
Rococo lobby boasts gilded
trim, chandeliers, and lofty
arched ceilings. The 1,658-
seat auditorium is decorated
with allegorical figures,
frescoes, and friezes.
The theater opened on
December 20, 1900 with a
suitably extravagant performance of the melodrama
Ben Hur, featuring a cast of
350 and an on-stage chariot
race involving a dozen
horses pulling Roman
chariots on treadmills.
It was also the venue
for productions by
directors such as
Irving Berlin, Sigmund
Romberg, and Rodgers
and Hammerstein, and is where
Ziegfeld premiered his *Follies*
(*see p89*). The theater is now
owned by Emerson College.

❽ Chinatown

Bounded by Kingston, Kneeland,
Washington & Essex Sts.
Map 4 E2. ⓣ Chinatown.

Although smaller than those
in San Fransisco and New York,
this area remains one of the
largest Chinatowns in the U.S.
It covers blocks of filled land
that had been the South Cove
tidal backwater until the early
19th century. Pagoda-topped
telephone booths, as well as a
three-story gateway guarded
by four marble lions, set the
neighborhood's Asian tone.
The first 200 Chinese to settle
in New England came by ship
from San Francisco in 1870.
Mostly unskilled, they were
recruited to break a labor
strike at a shoe factory in
Massachusetts, but were jobless
by 1874. At this time, some
drifted to Boston, at first
pitching their tents on Oliver

Colorful, contemporary street mural in Chinatown

Place, which they renamed Ping On Alley – "the Street of Peace and Security." In the 1880s another wave of Chinese immigration from California was prompted by an economic boom that led to job openings in construction, on the railroad, and the laying of telephone lines. Boston's Chinese colony was fully established by the turn of the 19th century, and with it came the ubiquitous garment and textile industries.

Political turmoil in China immediately following World War II, and more recent arrivals from Vietnam, Laos, Korea, Thailand, and Cambodia, have swelled Chinatown's population, which now stands at around 8,000. Restaurants, bakeries, food markets, curio shops, and dispensers of Chinese medicine are especially numerous along the main thoroughfare of Beach Street, as well as on Tyler, Oxford, and Harrison Streets.

Typical store and restaurant façades in Boston's Chinatown

9 Jacob Wirth

31–37 Stuart St. **Map** 4 E2.**Tel** (617) 338-8586. Ⓣ Boylston, Chinatown. **Open** 11:30am–9pm Sun & Mon, 11:30am–10pm Tue & Wed, 11:30am – midnight Thu, 11:30am–1am Fri & Sat. ♿ Ⓦ jacobwirth.com

Occupying a 19th-century row house, Jacob Wirth (see p146) has been in business since 1868. It is Boston's second oldest restaurant after the Union Oyster House (see p143). Restaurateur Jacob Wirth had the majestic mahogany restaurant bar shipped in small pieces from Russia. The beer-hall, with its globe lighting, ceiling fans, dark paneling, bare wood floors, and brass railings, has barely changed since it first opened. Sausage-and-sauerkraut menu staples, combined with draft beers and German wines, make this the only authentic German restaurant in a city that is famous for its Irish and Italian heritage. Friday night piano sing-alongs are very popular.

10 Bay Village

Bounded by Tremont, Arlington & South Charles Sts. **Map** 4 D2. Ⓣ New England Medical Center, Boylston.

Originally an expanse of mud flats, the Bay Village area was drained in the early 1800s and initially became habitable with the construction of a dam in 1825. Many carpenters, cabinetmakers, artisans, and house painters involved in the construction of Beacon Hill's pricier town houses built their own modest but well-crafted residences here. As a result there are many similarities between the two neighborhoods, including plenty of red brick, arched doorways, window boxes and shutters, courtyards, tidy gardens, and antique gas lamps. Fayette Street was laid out in 1824 to coincide with the triumphant U.S. visit of the Marquis de Lafayette, the French general who allied himself with George Washington for some of the campaigns of the Revolutionary War.

Bay Street, located just off Fayette Street, features a single dwelling and is generally regarded as the city's shortest street. In 1809, poet and short-

Bay Village doorway, similar to those of Beacon Hill

story writer Edgar Allen Poe was born in a boarding house on Carver Street, where his thespian parents were staying while in Boston on tour with a traveling theatrical company. Although Poe was never fond of Boston (he called residents "Frogpondians"), the city honored him with a statue. Erected in October 2014 on the corner of Boylston Street and Charles Street South, it depicts Poe in mid-stride with a flowing cape and a suitcase filled with manuscripts. His signature raven is at his side.

In the 1920s, at the height of the Prohibition era, clandestine speakeasies gave Bay Village its still-prevalent bohemian ambience. More recently, the neighborhood has become a center for Boston's gay community.

The Coconut Grove nightclub fire of 1942, when 491 of the club's patrons died, remains one of the United States' highest fire death tolls. This devastating occurrence resulted in infamy for the area but, ultimately, to more stringent fire-safety codes throughout the United States.

The vast Grand Lobby of the Wang Theatre

⓫ Shubert Theatre

265 Tremont St. **Map** 4 E2. **Tel** (617) 482-9393. Ⓣ Boylston, New England Medical Center. **Open** phone for details. ♿ 🆆 **citicenter.org**

The 1,650-seat Shubert Theatre rivals the Colonial Theatre (see p86) for its long history of staging major pre-Broadway musical productions. Designed by the architects Charles Bond and Thomas James, the theater first

Palladian-style window over the entrance to the Shubert Theatre

opened its doors in 1910, and during its heyday many famous stars walked the boards here. Among them were Sarah Bernhardt, W.C. Fields, Cary Grant, Mae West, Humphrey Bogart, Ingrid Bergman, Henry Ford, and Rex Harrison.

The Shubert Theatre is listed on the National Register of Historic Places, and features a white, Neo-Classical façade with a pair of Ionic columns flanking a monumental, Palladian-style window that sits over the entrance. The entrance also boasts an ornate, wrought-iron canopy.

The theater closed for some years but in 1997 it reopened to premiere the pre-Broadway hit *Rent*. Local companies also stage performances here.

A plaque to the side of the main entrance recounts the history of the theater.

⓬ Wang Theatre

270 Tremont St. **Map** 4 E2. **Tel** (617) 482-9393. Ⓣ Boylston, New England Medical Center. **Open** phone for details. ♿ 🆆 **citicenter.org**

Opened in 1925 as the Metropolitan Theatre and later named the Music Hall, New England's most ornate variety theater was inspired by the Paris Opera House, and was originally intended to be a movie theater. Like the nearby Colonial Theatre, the Metropolitan was designed by Clarence Blackall. When it was first built the auditorium had over 4,000 seats, which made it one of the largest in the world. It was so big that at its opening, which over 20,000 people attended, one Hollywood magnate described it as a theater of "mountainous splendour, a movie palace of fabulous grandeur and stupendous stage presentations." Another observer described it as a "cathedral of the movies."

The theater was restored and renamed in 1983. The five-story Grand Lobby and seven-story auditorium are designed in a magnificent and ornate Renaissance Revival style: gold-plated chandeliers, bronze detailing, stained glass, florid ceiling murals, rose jasper pillars, and marble-framed doorways. There are also three sumptuous lobbies, which visitors must pass through before finally arriving at the awesome Grand Lobby.

Ornate, gilt decoration at the Wang

Today, the theater hosts a wide variety of events, including Broadway road shows, touring national and international dance and opera productions, celebrity concert appearances, and motion-picture revivals. It is also a popular performance venue for local dance and theater companies. Both the Wang and Shubert theaters are operated by Citi Performing Arts Center.

The History of Boston's Theater District

Boston's first theater opened in 1793 on Federal Street. Fifty years later Boston had become a major tryout town and boasted a number of lavish theaters. The U.S. premiere of Handel's *Messiah* opened in 1839, the U.S. premiere of Gilbert and Sullivan's *H.M.S. Pinafore* in 1877, and the world premiere of Tchaikovsky's *First Piano Concerto* in 1875. In the late 19th century theaters came under fire from the censorious Watch and Ward Society. In the 20th century, now celebrated dramas such as Tennessee Williams' *A Streetcar Named Desire* and Eugene O'Neill's *Long Day's Journey into Night* debuted here. Premieres included *Ziegfeld Follies*, Gershwin's *Porgy and Bess*, and musicals by Rodgers and Hammerstein.

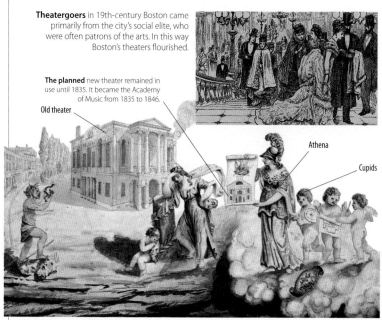

Theatergoers in 19th-century Boston came primarily from the city's social elite, who were often patrons of the arts. In this way Boston's theaters flourished.

The planned new theater remained in use until 1835. It became the Academy of Music from 1835 to 1846.

Old theater

Athena

Cupids

The Federal Street Theater

Designed by Charles Bulfinch, the Federal Street Theater was burned down in 1798. The old and new theaters are depicted in this allegorical painting, possibly a set design, which also shows characters from Greek mythology. Other Bulfinch buildings are also shown.

Tennessee Williams' *A Streetcar Named Desire* premiered at Boston's Wilbur Theatre. It starred a young Marlon Brando and Jessica Tandy.

Ziegfeld Follies, produced in the 1920s, had eight pre-Broadway "try-outs" at the Colonial Theatre *(see p86).*

The Rodgers and Hammerstein musical *Oklahoma!* premiered in Boston as a production entitled *Away We Go!* It was refined in Boston before hitting Broadway.

BACK BAY AND SOUTH END

Until the 19th century Boston was situated on a narrow peninsula surrounded by tidal marshes. Projects to fill Back Bay began in the 1850s and were made possible by new inventions such as the steam shovel. The Back Bay was filled by 1880 and developers soon moved in. Planned along French lines, with elegant boulevards, Back Bay is now one of Boston's most exclusive neighborhoods. The more bohemian South End, laid out on an English model of town houses clustered around squares, is home to many artists and Boston's gay community.

Sights at a Glance

Historic Streets and Squares

1 The Esplanade
4 Commonwealth Avenue
5 Newbury Street
7 Copley Square
8 Boylston Street
14 Copley Place
16 Union Park

Historic Buildings, Churches, and Museums

2 Gibson House Museum
3 First Baptist Church
6 Trinity Church pp96–7
9 Boston Public Library
10 John Hancock Tower

11 Berklee Performance Center
12 Prudential Center
13 Christian Science Center
15 Boston Center for the Arts

Restaurants pp146–8

1 B&G Oysters
2 Brasserie Jo
3 Coppa
4 Deuxave
5 L'Espalier
6 Grill 23
7 Mike's City Diner
8 Oishii
9 Orinoco
10 Parish Café
11 Post 390
12 Scoozi
13 Sonsie
14 Sorellina
15 Stephanie's on Newbury
16 Tapeo
17 Tico
18 Top of the Hub
19 Toro
20 Tremont 647
21 Trident Booksellers & Café
22 UNI

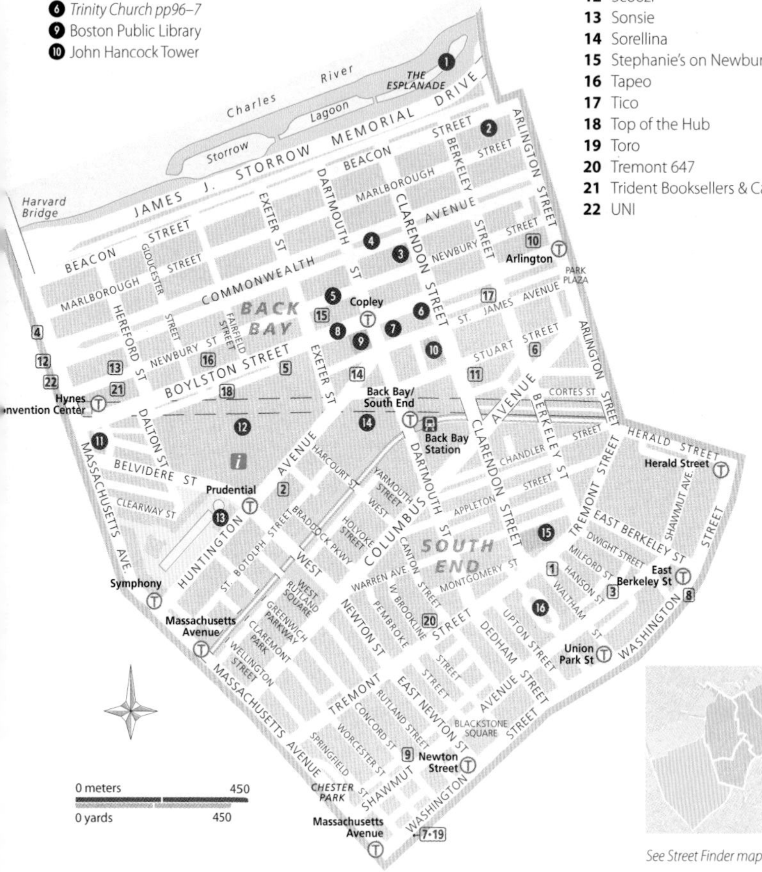

See Street Finder maps 3 & 4

◀ Grand arches and murals adorn the interior of Boston Public Library

For keys to symbols *see back flap*

Street-by-Street: Back Bay

This fashionable district unfolds westward from the
Public Garden *(see pp48–9)* in a grid that departs
radically from the twisting streets found elsewhere
in Boston. Commonwealth Avenue, with its grand
19th-century mansions and parkland, and Newbury
and Boylston Streets are its main arteries. Newbury
Street is a magnet for all of Boston wanting to
indulge in some upscale shopping, whereas the
more somber Boylston Street bustles with office
workers. Copley Square anchors the entire area
and is the site of Henry Hobson Richardson's
magnificent Trinity Church *(see pp96–7)* and
the 60-story John Hancock Tower *(see p99)*,
the tallest building in New England.

Weekly summer and fall farmers'
market, Copley Square

❼ Copley Square
This square was a marsh until
1870. It took on its present
form only in the late 20th
century as buildings around
its edges were completed. A
farmers' market, concerts, and
folk-dancing feature regularly.

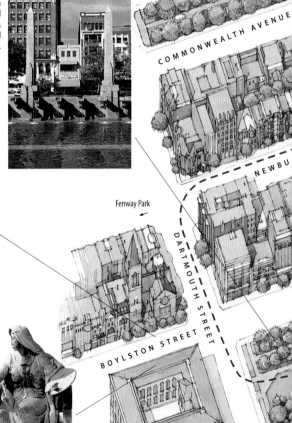

COMMONWEALTH AVENUE

NEWBU

Fenway Park

DARTMOUTH STREET

BOYLSTON STREET

South
End

❽ Boylston Street
The site of the Prudential
Center *(see p100)* and the
Boston Public Library *(see p98)*,
Boylston Street is also the
location of the fabulous New
Old South Church *(see p98)*.

**❾ ★ Boston
Public Library**
One of the first free
public libraries in the
world, this building
was designed by
Charles McKim. Inside
are murals by John
Singer Sargent.

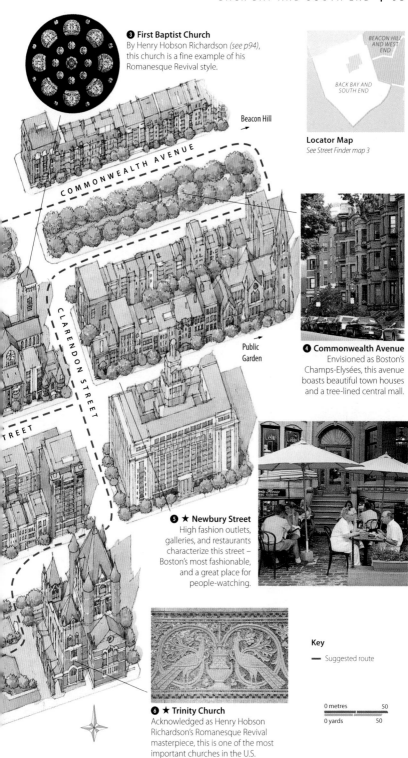

❸ First Baptist Church
By Henry Hobson Richardson *(see p94)*, this church is a fine example of his Romanesque Revival style.

Beacon Hill →

COMMONWEALTH AVENUE

CLARENDON STREET

TREET

Public Garden →

Locator Map
See Street Finder map 3

BEACON HILL AND WEST END

BACK BAY AND SOUTH END

❹ Commonwealth Avenue
Envisioned as Boston's Champs-Elysées, this avenue boasts beautiful town houses and a tree-lined central mall.

❺ ★ Newbury Street
High fashion outlets, galleries, and restaurants characterize this street – Boston's most fashionable, and a great place for people-watching.

Key

— Suggested route

❻ ★ Trinity Church
Acknowledged as Henry Hobson Richardson's Romanesque Revival masterpiece, this is one of the most important churches in the U.S.

0 metres	50
0 yards	50

① The Esplanade

Map 1 A4. ⓣ Charles/MGH.
Open 24 hrs daily. ♿

Running along the Boston side of the Charles River, between Longfellow Bridge and Dartmouth Street, are the parkland, lagoons, and islands known collectively as the Esplanade. The park is used extensively for in-line skating, cycling, and strolling and it is also the access point for boating on the river, including gondola rides. It is also the site of the city's leading outdoor concert venue.

In 1929, Arthur Fiedler, then the young conductor of the Boston Pops Orchestra, chose the Esplanade for a summer concert series that became a tradition. The Hatch Memorial Shell was constructed in 1939, and its stage is widely used by musical ensembles and other groups throughout the summer. Fourth of July concerts by the Boston Pops, which are followed by fireworks, can attract upward of 500,000 spectators *(see p37)*.

Fountains at the Esplanade, next to the Charles River

② Gibson House Museum

137 Beacon St. **Map** 1 A4.
Tel (617) 267-6338. ⓣ Arlington.
Open obligatory tours at 1pm, 2pm, 3pm Wed–Sun. 📷 📹 📁
🅦 thegibsonhouse.org

Among the first houses built in the Back Bay, the Gibson House preserves its original Victorian decor and furnishings through-out all six stories. The 1860 brownstone and red-brick structure was designed in the

The original Victorian-style library of the Gibson House Museum

popular Italian Renaissance Revival style for the widow Catherine Hammond Gibson, who was one of the few women to own property in this part of the city. Her grandson Charles Hammond Gibson, Jr., a noted eccentric, poet, travel writer, horticulturalist, and bon vivant, arranged for the house to become a museum after his death in 1954. As a prelude to this, Gibson began to rope off the furniture in the 1930s, instead inviting his guests to sit on the stairs to drink martinis made with his own bathtub gin.

One of the most modern houses of its day, the Gibson House boasted such technical advancements as gas lighting, indoor plumbing in the basement, and coal-fired central heating. Visitors can see a full dinner setting in the dining room or admire the whimsical Turkish pet pavilion. But it is Gibson's preservation of the 1860s decor (with some modi-fications in 1888) that makes the museum a true time capsule of Victorian life in Boston.

③ First Baptist Church

110 Commonwealth Ave. **Map** 3 C2.
Tel (617) 267-3148. ⓣ Arlington.
Open for Sunday worship.
🕇 11am Sun. 📷 ♿
🅦 firstbaptistboston.com

The Romanesque-style First Baptist Church on the corner of Commonwealth Avenue and Clarendon Street was Henry Hobson Richardson's *(see p34)* first major architectural commission and became an instant landmark when it was finished in 1872. Viewed from Commonwealth Avenue, it is one of the most distinctive buildings of the city skyline.

Richardson considered the nearly freestanding bell tower, which he modeled roughly on Italian campaniles, to be the church's most innovative structure. The square tower is topped with a decorative frieze and arches protected by an overhanging roof. The frieze was modeled in Paris by Bartholdi, the sculptor who created the Statue of Liberty, and was carved in place by Italian artisans after the stones were set. The faces in the frieze, which depict the sacraments, are likenesses of prominent Bostonians of that time, among them Henry Wadsworth Longfellow and Ralph Waldo Emerson *(see p33)*.

Detail of Bartholdi's frieze atop the distinctive square tower of the First Baptist Church

The trumpeting angels at the corners of the tower gave the building its nickname, "Church of the Holy Bean Blowers."

Four years after the church was completed, the Unitarian congregation dissolved because it was unable to bear the expense of the building. The church stood vacant until 1881, when the First Baptist congregation from the South End took it over.

❹ Commonwealth Avenue

Map 3 B2. Ⓣ Arlington, Copley, Hynes Convention Center/ICA.

Back Bay was Boston's first fully planned neighborhood, and architect Arthur Gilman made Commonwealth Avenue, modeled on the elegant boulevards of Paris, the centerpiece of the design. At 200 ft (61 m) wide, with a 10 ft (3 m) setback from the sidewalks to encourage small gardens in front of the buildings, Commonwealth became an arena for America's leading domestic architects in the second half of the 19th century. A walk from the Public Garden to Massachusetts Avenue is like flicking through a catalog of architectural styles.

Few of the grand buildings on either side of the avenue are open to the public, but strollers on the central mall of the avenue encounter a number of historic figures in the form of bronze statues. Some have only tangential relationships to the city, like Alexander Hamilton, the first secretary of the U.S. Treasury. The end of the mall features an heroic bronze of Leif Erikson, erected as a historically unsupported flight of fancy that the Norse explorer landed at Boston.

William Garrison statue on Commonwealth Avenue

The patrician statue of abolitionist William Garrison is said to capture exactly the man's air of moral superiority. The best-loved memorial depicts sailor and historian Samuel Eliot Morison dangling his feet from a rock.

❺ Newbury Street

Map 3 C2. Ⓣ Arlington, Copley, Hynes Convention Center/ICA.

Newbury Street is a Boston synonym for "stylish." The Taj Boston, formerly the Ritz-Carlton Hotel, at Arlington Street sets an elegant tone for the street that continues with a mix of prestigious and often well-hidden art galleries, stylish boutiques, and some

of the city's most *au courant* restaurants. Churches provide vestiges of a more decorous era. The Church of the Covenant at No. 67 Newbury contains the world's largest collection of Louis Comfort Tiffany stained-glass windows and an elaborate Tiffany lantern. A choir and musicians perform sacred music each Sunday at Emmanuel Church on the corner of Newbury and Berkeley Streets.

Most of Newbury Street was constructed as town house residences, but the desirability of these spaces for retail operations has pushed residents to the upper floors, while ground and underground levels are devoted to chic boutiques and eateries. Fashionable sidewalk dining gives great buzz to enduring classic bistro spots, such as Stephanie's on Newbury and Sonsie (see p147).

🏛 Church of the Covenant
67 Newbury St. **Tel** (617) 266-7480. **Open** 10:30am Sun for church service. ☒ 👣 🎧 📷
W cotcboston.org

Stylish Newbury Street, with its elegant shops, galleries, and restaurants, is the epitome of Boston style

❻ Trinity Church

Routinely voted one of America's finest churches, this masterpiece by Henry Hobson Richardson dates from 1877. Trinity Church was founded in 1733 near Downtown Crossing, but the congregation moved the church to this site in 1871. The church is a granite and sandstone Romanesque structure standing on wooden piles driven through mud into bedrock, surmounted with granite pyramids. John LaFarge designed the interior, while some of the windows are designed by Edward Burne-Jones and executed by William Morris.

KEY

① **The pulpit** is covered with carved scenes from the life of Christ, as well as portraits of great preachers through the ages.

② **Gold bas-reliefs** adorn the wall of the chancel, behind the altar. A series of such bas-reliefs can be seen in the church.

③ **The bell tower** was inspired by the Renaissance cathedral at Salamanca, central Spain.

④ **John LaFarge's** lancet windows show Christ in the act of blessing. They were designed at the request of Phillips Brooks – he wanted LaFarge to create an inspirational design for the west nave, which he could look at while preaching.

Parish House

★ North Transept Windows
Designed by Edward Burne-Jones and executed by William Morris, the three stained-glass windows above the choir relate the story of Christmas.

Chancel
Designed by Charles Maginnis, the present-day chancel was not dedicated until 1938. The seven windows by Clayton & Bell, of London, show the life of Christ.

David's Charge to Solomon

Located in the baptistry, to the right of the chancel, this also beautiful window is also the result of a partnership between Edward Burne-Jones and William Morris. The story shown is one of the few in the church from the Old Testament.

★ **West Portico**
Richardson disliked the original flat façade of Trinity Church, and so modeled the deeply sculpted west portico after St. Trophime in Arles, France. It was added after his death.

Carving of Phillips Brooks and Christ

Phillips Brooks

Born in Boston in 1835 and educated at Harvard, Brooks was a towering charismatic figure. Rector of Trinity Church from 1869, he gained a reputation for powerful sermons. From 1872 Brooks worked closely with Henry Hobson Richardson on the design of the new Trinity Church – at least five sculpted likenesses of him can be seen in and around the building.

Main entrance

The New Old South Church, which looks across Copley Square

➐ Copley Square

Map 3 C2. Ⓣ Copley.

Named after John Singleton Copley, the great Boston painter born nearby in 1737, Copley Square is a hive of civic activity surrounded by some of Boston's most striking architecture. Summer activities include weekly farmers' markets, concerts, and even folk-dancing.

The inviting green plaza took years to develop; when Copley was born it was just a marshy riverbank, which remained unfilled until 1870. Construction of the John Hancock Tower in 1975 anchored the southeastern side of Copley Square, and Copley Place *(see p101)* completed the square on the southwestern corner in 1984. Today's Copley Square, a wide open space of trees, grass, and fountains, took shape in the heart of the city in the 1990s, after various plans to utilize this hitherto wasted space were tendered.

A large plaque honoring the Boston Marathon, which ends at the Boston Public Library, was set in the sidewalk in 1996 to coincide with the 100th race. As well as pushcart vendors, the plaza has a booth for discounted theater, music, and dance tickets.

➑ Boylston Street

Map 3 C2. Ⓣ Boylston, Arlington, Copley, Hynes Convention Center/ICA.

The corners of Boylston and Berkeley streets represent Boston architecture at its most diverse. The stately French Academic-style structure on the west side was erected for the Museum of Natural History, a forerunner of the Museum of Science *(see p55)*. The east side spouts a Robert A.M. Stern tower and a Philip Johnson office building that resembles a table radio. Boston's finest jeweler, Shreve, Crump & Low, occupied the Art Deco building at the corner of Arlington Street until relocating around the corner to 39 Newbury Street.

Some notable office buildings stand on Boylston Street. The lobby of the New England building at No. 501 features large historical murals and dioramas depicting the process of filling Back Bay during the late 19th century. The towers of the Prudential Center *(see p100)* dominate the skyline on upper Boylston Street. Adjoining the Prudential is the Hynes Convention Center. It was enlarged in 1988 to accommodate the

city's burgeoning convention business and added upscale public dining.

The Italian Gothic-style **New Old South Church**, at the corner of Dartmouth and Boylston Streets, was built in 1874–5 by the congregation that had met previously at the Old South Meeting House *(see p61)*.

🔝 **New Old South Church** 645 Boylston St. **Map** 3 C2. **Tel** (617) 536-1970. **Open** 8am–7pm Mon–Fri, 10am–4pm Sat, 8:30am–4pm Sun. 🔔 9am, 11am Sun, 6pm Thu. 🚻 ♿ 📷 🔍 📧 oldsouth.org

➒ Boston Public Library

Copley Square. **Map** 3 C2. **Tel** (617) 536-5400. Ⓣ Copley. General Library: **Open** 9am–9pm Mon–Thu, 9am–5pm Fri–Sat, 1–5pm Sun. **Closed** public hols; Jun–Sep: Sun. 📷 2:30pm Mon, 6pm Tue & Thu, 11am Wed, Fri & Sat, 2pm Sun. ♿ 🔍 📧 bpl.org

Founded in 1848, the Boston Public Library was America's first metropolitan library for the public. It quickly outgrew its original building, hence the construction of the Italian *palazzo*-style Copley Square building in 1887–95, with "Free to All" emblazoned above the entrance. The architect Charles McKim drew on the highly skilled force of mostly Italian construction workers and artisans who had come to Boston to build mansions in the Back Bay and South End. Sculptor Daniel Chester French fashioned the huge bronze doors that represent Music and Poetry, Knowledge and Wisdom, and Truth and Romance. French painter Puvis de Chavannes executed the murals that wind up the staircase and along the second-floor corridor. Edward Abbey's Pre-Raphaelite murals of the Quest for the Holy Grail line the

The vast Bates Hall in the Boston Public Library, noted for its high barrel-vaulted ceiling

book request room, and John Singer Sargent's murals of Judaism and Christianity cover a third-floor gallery.

The McKim building, largely restored for its 1995 centennial, is a marvel of wood and marble. Bates Hall, on the second floor, is particularly noted for the soaring barrel-vaulted ceiling. A café and restaurant offer breakfast, lunch, and afternoon tea.

The library's circulating collection is housed in the 1971 Boylston Street addition, a modernist structure by architect Philip Johnson.

⑩ John Hancock Tower

200 Clarendon St. **Map** 3 C2.
Ⓣ Copley. **Closed** to the public.

The tallest building in New England, the 790-ft (240-m) rhomboid that is the John Hancock Tower cuts into Copley Square with its slimmest edge, its mirrored façade reflecting the surroundings and sky. The innovative design has created a 60-story office building that shares the square with its neighbors, the Romanesque Trinity Church and the Italian Renaissance Revival Copley Plaza Hotel, without dwarfing them. When the tower was under construction, 65 windows, each weighing 500lb (1,100 kg), came crashing to the ground. All 10,344 panes were replaced at a cost of almost $7 million before the building could be occupied in 1975.

Designed by Henry Cobb of I.M. Pei & Partners, the magnificent building inspired Massachusetts author John Updike to observe: "All art, all beauty, is reflection." From one angle viewers can see the reflections of Trinity Church and the original (1947) Hancock Building, topped by a weather beacon.

The observatory on the 60th floor of the tower closed for safety reasons following the tragic events in September 2001 at the World Trade Center in New York.

View over Back Bay and the Charles River

⑪ Berklee Performance Center

136 Massachusetts Ave.
Map 3 A3. **Tel** (617) 747-2261.
Ⓣ Hynes. Ⓦ berklee.edu/bpc

The largest independent music college in the world, Berklee was founded in 1945 and has produced a number of stars in jazz, rock, and pop music in the ensuing decades. Included in the list of well-known talents are the likes of producer and arranger Quincy Jones, singer and songwriter Melissa Etheridge, jazz saxophonist and composer Branford Marsalis, drummer

Joey Kramer of Aerosmith, and jazz pianist Diana Krall.

The school's students and distinguished faculty enliven the Boston music scene, performing primarily at the on-site Berklee Performance Center. The college purchased the 1915 Fenway Theatre movie palace in 1972 and transformed it into a top-rate, 1,215-seat concert hall for live performances, with rehearsal space and recording studios on the lower level. The center boasts extraordinary acoustics and a state-of-the-art light and sound system. Highlights of the approximately 200 events presented here each year include concerts by students, faculty members, and renowned visiting artists. The college also makes the facility available to other community organizations and arts presenters, which guarantees a lively and often surprising schedule of events.

Musicians playing at the state-of-the-art Berklee Performance Center

⓬ Prudential Center

800 Boylston St. **Map** 3 B3. **Tel** (617) 859-0648. Ⓣ Prudential, Hynes Convention Center/ICA. Skywalk: **Open** Mar–Oct: 10am–10pm daily; Nov–Feb: 10am–8pm daily. **Closed** Thanksgiving, Dec 25. ⬚ ⬚ ⬚

When it was erected in 1965, the Prudential Tower was the first skyscraper in the Back Bay, rising 52 floors. Office buildings and a shopping center now girdle its base, and the "Pru" is linked through indoor walkways with the Hynes Convention Center and the Sheraton Boston Hotel in one unified complex. An enclosed walkway even links

Inside the beautiful, stained-glass Mapparium, Christian Science Center

Prudential Tower viewed across the Christian Science reflecting pool

its shops to the more glamorous Copley Place across busy Huntington Avenue. Apart from the shops and food courts, the principal attraction of the "Pru" is the Skywalk on the 50th floor. The Skywalk is the only 360-degree aerial observatory in Boston, and its location near the top of Boylston Street hill provides striking views of the Emerald Necklace (see p105) as well as downtown and the waterfront. Signs on the windows assist in identifying the landmarks below. A similar view, which visitors do not need to pay for, is available at the Top of the Hub restaurant on the 52nd floor. Some of the bar windows here face west, so those having a drink can enjoy spectacular sunset views over Boston.

⓭ Christian Science Center

175 Huntington Ave. **Map** 3 B3. Ⓣ Symphony. Mother Church: **Tel** (617) 450-2000. **Open** free tours noon–4pm Tue, 1–4pm Wed, noon–5pm Thu–Sat. Library: **Tel** (617) 450-7000. **Open** 10am–4pm Tue–Sun (last entry to Mapparium 3:40pm). ⬚ ⬚ 10am & 5pm Sun, noon & 7:30pm Wed (no evening service Jul–Aug). ⬚ ⬚ ⬚ **marybakereddylibrary.org**

The world headquarters of the First Church of Christ, Scientist, occupies 14 acres on the corner of Huntington and Massachusetts Avenues. Known also as the Christian Science Church, this religious body was formed in 1879 by Mary Baker Eddy. The granite, Romanesque-style Mother Church dates from 1894, but it serves only as a chapel at the rear of a grander basilica, which was built in 1906 to seat 5,000 worshipers. The basilica houses the western hemisphere's largest pipe organ, manufactured in Boston by the Aeolian-Skinner Company. Between 1968 and 1973 the Christian Science complex expanded to its present design, which includes an elegant office tower, a reflecting pool, and a monumental plaza.

The Mary Baker Eddy Library for the Betterment of Humanity, on the Massachusetts Ave side of the complex, emphasizes Eddy's inspiration rather than church doctrine. Visitors can peer through a glass wall into the newsroom of the Christian Science Monitor. The most popular exhibit is the

Mary Baker Eddy

Born in Concord, New Hampshire in 1821, Mary Baker was plagued with poor health for much of her early life. Fearing death after a severe fall in 1866, she sought comfort in her Bible, where she found an account of how Jesus had healed a palsied man. Her own miraculous recovery led her to the principle of Christian Science, a doctrine which emphasizes spiritual regeneration and healing through prayer alone. In 1875 she published her ideas in Science and Health with Key to the Scriptures, the textbook of Christian Science, and gathered students around her, including Asa Gilbert Eddy, whom she married in 1877. Two years later she organized the First Church of Christ, Scientist, in Boston, from which Christian Science churches spread across the world. Mrs. Eddy remained the active leader of the Christian Science movement until her death in 1910. She is buried at Mount Auburn Cemetery in Cambridge.

Mapparium, where visitors literally walk through the globe viewing the planet from the inside. The different colors represent the world's political boundaries of 1935.

⓮ Copley Place

Huntington Ave & Dartmouth St. **Map** 3 C3. **Tel** (617) 262-6600. Ⓣ Back Bay/South End, Copley. **Open** 10am–8pm Mon–Sat, noon–6pm Sun. ♿

Copley Place is a creation of late 20th-century urban development, with hotels, an upscale shopping center, and restaurants. Offices and luxury apartments are also part of the development, which rises on land created above the Massachusetts Turnpike. Copley Place bears little relation to Copley Square, but the shopping mall was a success from the day it opened in 1984 and still ranks as Boston's most luxurious indoor shopping mall. Its stores include the jeweler Tiffany & Co. and the status-conscious department store Neiman Marcus *(see p153)*.

⓯ Boston Center for the Arts

539 Tremont St. **Map** 4 D3. **Tel** (617) 426-5000. Ⓣ Back Bay/ South End. Cyclorama: **Open** call for hours. Mills Gallery: **Open** noon–5pm Wed & Sun, noon–9pm Thu–Sat. **Closed** public hols. 🎭 for performances. 🎫 ♿ 🅦 bcaonline.org

The centerpiece of a resurgent South End, the BCA complex includes four stages, an art gallery, and artists' studios as well as the Boston Ballet Building, home to the company's educational programs, rehearsal space, and administrative offices.
  The Tremont Estates Building at the corner of Tremont Street, an organ factory in the years after the Civil War, now houses artists' studios, rehearsal space, and an art gallery.
  The largest of the BCA buildings is the circular, domed Cyclorama, which opened in 1884 to exhibit the 50-ft (15-m)

Bow-fronted, red-brick houses, typical of South End's Union Park

by 400-ft (121-m) painting *The Battle of Gettysburg* by the French artist Paul Philippoteaux. The painting was removed in 1889 and is now displayed at Gettysburg National Military Park. The Cyclorama now serves as a performance and exhibition space.
  The Stanford Calderwood Pavilion, with a 360-seat and a 200-seat theater, opened in 2004 as the first new theater built in Boston in 75 years.
  The Mills Gallery houses exhibitions focusing on emerging contemporary artists, with the emphasis on multimedia installations and shows with confrontational, often provocative, themes.

⓰ Union Park

Tremont & Shawmut Sts. **Map** 4 D4. Ⓣ Back Bay/South End. ♿

Union Park is the green gem of the South End, built from 1857 to 1859 when the neighborhood was still fashionable. South End property values crashed in the Panic of 1873, and the entire district, Union Park included, became tenement housing for immigrants arriving from eastern Europe and the Middle East. The South End remains broadly mixed by ethnicity, race, and sexual orientation. The handsome town houses along Union Park led the South End's economic resurgence in the 1970s, and it has become, once again, a coveted address. A pair of fountains, an iron fence, and large shade trees present a truly parklike setting for the beautifully restored brick row houses. The 19th-century ornamental ironwork on and around these houses is particularly prized by architecture buffs. Union Park is strictly residential, although there are a few small shops, and restaurants which have become very popular for Saturday and Sunday brunch.

Red-brick façade of the Boston Center for the Arts, site of theaters and exhibition spaces

FARTHER AFIELD

The late 19th and 20th centuries saw Boston expand out of the central colonial and Victorian city into the surrounding area. The old marshlands of the Fenway now house two of Boston's most important art museums, the Museum of Fine Arts and the Isabella Stewart Gardner Museum. Southeast of the city center, Columbia Point was developed in the mid-20th century and is home to the John F. Kennedy Library and Museum. West of central Boston, across the Charles River, lies Cambridge, sometimes referred to as the "People's Democratic Republic of Cambridge," a reference to the politics of Harvard and the Massachusetts Institute of Technology, its two major colleges. Harvard Square is a lively area of bookstores, cafés, and street entertainers. Charlestown is the site of the Bunker Hill Monument and the Charlestown Navy Yard, where the U.S.'s most famous warship, the U.S.S. *Constitution*, is moored. Farther northwest lie historic Concord and Lexington, where the first major battles of the Revolutionary War took place in 1775.

Sights at a Glance

Towns
7 Cambridge
8 Charlestown
9 Concord
10 Lexington

Museums and Historic Sites
1 John F. Kennedy Library and Museum
4 John F. Kennedy National Historic Site

5 Isabella Stewart Gardner Museum
6 *Museum of Fine Arts, Boston pp106–9*

Gardens and Zoos
2 Franklin Park Zoo
3 Arnold Arboretum

Key

▨ Main sightseeing area
▨ Urban area
━ Highway
━ Major road
═ Minor road
─ Railroad

0 kilometers 4
0 miles 2

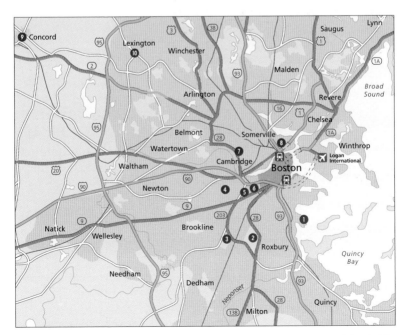

◀ The Harvard University campus in Cambridge

For keys to symbols *see back flap*

❶ John F. Kennedy Library and Museum

Columbia Point, Dorchester. **Tel** (617) 514-1600. Ⓣ JFK/U Mass. **Open** 9am–5pm daily. **Closed** Jan 1, Thanksgiving, Dec 25. 🅿️ ♿ 📷 📱
🅦 jfklibrary.org

The soaring white concrete and glass building of the John F. Kennedy Library stands sentinel on Columbia Point, near the mouth of the Boston Harbor. Exhibitions chronicle the 1,000 days of the Kennedy presidency and include a re-creation of the Oval Office. Kennedy was among the first politicians to grasp the power of media. The museum takes full advantage of film and video footage to let the president's own words and images tell his story, including his campaign for the Democratic Party nomination and landmark television debates with Republican opponent Richard M. Nixon. Gripping film clips capture the anxiety of nuclear brinksmanship during the Cuban Missile Crisis, as well as the inspirational spirit of the space program and the founding of the Peace Corps. The combination of artifacts, displays, and television footage evoke both the euphoria of "Camelot" and the numb horror of the assassination.

Two of the president's brothers are also recognized for their contributions to American history. Within the Kennedy Library, the re-created office of Attorney General Robert F. Kennedy touches on both his deft handling of race relations and his key advisory role to his brother. Adjacent to the library, the Edward M. Kennedy Institute for the United States Senate opened in 2015. Tours, exhibits, and a full-scale re-creation of the U.S. Senate Chamber in Washington, D.C., promote understanding of the legislative process and celebrate Kennedy's 46 years as senator.

Lowland gorilla with her baby in the simulated natural environment of Franklin Park Zoo

❷ Franklin Park Zoo

1 Franklin Park Rd. **Tel** (617) 541-5466. Ⓣ Forest Hills. 🚌 16 from Forest Hills subway. **Open** Apr–Sep: 10am–5pm Mon–Fri, 10am–6pm Sat–Sun; Oct–Mar: 10am–4pm daily. **Closed** Jan 1, Thanksgiving, Dec 25. 🅿️ ♿
🅦 zoonewengland.com

The zoo, originally planned as a small menagerie, has expanded dramatically over the past century and long ago discarded caged enclosures in favor of simulated natural environments. Lowland gorillas roam a forest edge with caves for privacy, lions lounge around a rocky kingdom while zebras, ostriches, and giraffes are free to graze on open grassland. Bird's World, a structure dating from the zoo's 1913 opening, features a free-flight cage with dozens of species of birds. Youngsters can interact with farm animals in a small petting zoo. A new children's zoo is scheduled to open in 2017.

❸ Arnold Arboretum

125 Arborway, Jamaica Plain. **Tel** (617) 524-1718. Ⓣ Forest Hills. 🚌 39. **Open** sunrise–sunset daily. Visitors Center: **Open** 10am–5pm Thu–Tue. **Closed** public hols. ♿ 📷
🅦 arboretum.harvard.edu

Founded by Harvard University in 1872 as a living catalog of all the indigenous and exotic trees and shrubs adaptable to New England's climate, the Arboretum is planted with more than 15,000 labeled specimens. It is the oldest

Dramatic, modern structure of the John F. Kennedy Library and Museum

arboretum in the U.S. and a key resource for botanical and horticultural research. The Arboretum also serves as a park where people jog, stroll, read, and paint.

The park's busiest time is on Lilac Sunday in May, when tens of thousands come to revel in the sight and fragrance of the lilac collection, one of the largest in the world. The range of the Arboretum's collections guarantees flowers from late March into November, beginning with cornelian cherry and forsythia. Blooms shift in late May to azalea, magnolia, and wisteria, then to mountain laurel and roses in June. Sweet autumn clematis bursts forth in September, and native witch hazel blooms in October and November. The Arboretum also has fine fall foliage in September and October.

A large scale model of the Arboretum can be seen in the Visitors' Information Center, which is just inside the main gate.

❹ John F. Kennedy National Historic Site

83 Beals St, Brookline. **Tel** (617) 566-7937. Ⓣ Coolidge Corner. **Open** late May–Oct: 9:30am–5pm Wed–Sun. **Closed** Thanksgiving. 🅿 ♿ ⬛ 🏛
🆆 nps.gov/jofi

The first home of the late president's parents, this Brookline house saw the birth of four of nine Kennedy children, including J.F.K. on May 29, 1917. Although the Kennedys moved to a larger house in 1921, the Beals Street residence held special memories for the family, who repurchased the house in 1966 and furnished it with their belongings circa 1917 as a memorial to John F. Kennedy. The guided tour includes reminiscences of J.F.K.'s mother Rose. A walking tour takes in other neighborhood sites relevant to the Kennedy family's early years.

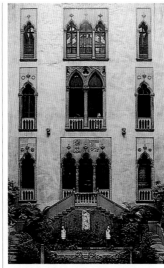

Central courtyard of the *palazzo*-style Isabella Stewart Gardner Museum

❺ Isabella Stewart Gardner Museum

25 Evans Way. **Tel** (617) 566-1401. Ⓣ MFA. **Open** 11am–5pm Wed–Mon (to 9pm Thu). **Closed** Jan 1, Thanksgiving, Dec 25. 🅿 ✉
🎵 Call for concert schedule.
🆆 gardnermuseum.org

The only thing more surprising than a Venetian *palazzo* on The Fenway is the collection of more than 2,500 works of art inside. Advised by scholar Bernard Berenson, the strong-willed Isabella Stewart Gardner turned her wealth to collecting art in the late 19th century, acquiring a notable collection of Old Masters and Italian Renaissance pieces. Titian's *Rape of Europa*, for example, is considered his best painting in a U.S. museum. The eccentric "Mrs. Jack" had an eye for her contemporaries, as well. She purchased the first Matisse to enter an American collection and was an ardent patron of James McNeill Whistler and John Singer Sargent. The paintings, sculptures, and tapestries are displayed on three levels around a stunning skylit courtyard. Mrs. Gardner's will stipulates the collection should remain assembled in the manner she originally intended. However, today, blank spaces can be seen where thieves stole 13 priceless works in 1990. Amongst the stolen art was a rare Rembrandt, *Storm on the Sea of Galilee*, then conservatively valued at $200 million. A $120 million expansion designed by Renzo Piano opened in 2012, providing space for special exhibitions, concerts, educational programs, and landscape classes.

The Emerald Necklace

Best known as designer of New York's Central Park, Frederick Law Olmsted based himself in Boston, where he created parks to solve environmental problems and provide a green refuge for inhabitants of the 19th-century industrial city. The Emerald Necklace includes the green spaces of Boston Common and the Public Garden (*see pp48–9*) and Commonwealth Avenue (*see p95*). To create a ring of parks, Olmsted added the Back Bay Fens (site of beautiful rose gardens and gateway to the Museum of Fine Arts and the

Jamaica Pond, part of Boston's fine parklands

Isabella Stewart Gardner Museum), the rustic Riverway, Jamaica Pond (sailing and picnicking), Arnold Arboretum, and Franklin Park (a golf course, zoo, and cross-country ski trails). The 7-mile (11-km) swath of parkland makes an excellent bicycle tour or ambitious walk.

❻ Museum of Fine Arts, Boston

The largest art museum in New England and one of the largest in the United States, its collection includes around 450,000 items, ranging from Egyptian artifacts to paintings by John Singer Sargent. The original 1909 Beaux Arts-style MFA building was augmented in 1981 by the addition of the Linde Family wing, designed by I.M. Pei. The $500 million Art of the Americas wing, designed by architect Norman Foster, has given new life to the museum housing 53 galleries and displaying over 5,000 works of art.

American Silver
The revolutionary Paul Revere *(see p23)* was also a noted silversmith and produced many beautiful objects, such as this ornate teapot.

★ Japanese Temple Room
This room was created in 1909 to provide a space in which to contemplate Buddhist art. The MFA has one of the finest Japanese collections outside Japan.

★ Egyptian Mummies
Among the museum's Egyptian and Nubian art is this tomb group of Nes-mut-aat-neru (767–656 BC) of Thebes.

Fenway
Entrance

Calderwood
Courtyard

Shapiro
Courtyard

Huntington
Entrance

★ Copley Portraits
John Singleton Copley (1738–1815) painted the celebrities of his day, hence this portrait of a dandyish John Hancock *(see p23)*.

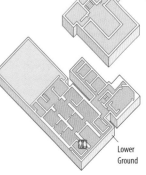

Lower
Ground

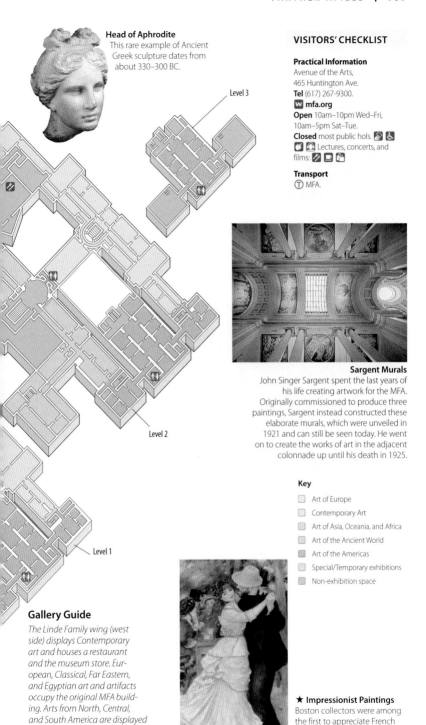

Head of Aphrodite
This rare example of Ancient Greek sculpture dates from about 330–300 BC.

Level 3

VISITORS' CHECKLIST

Practical Information
Avenue of the Arts,
465 Huntington Ave.
Tel (617) 267-9300.
w mfa.org
Open 10am–10pm Wed–Fri,
10am–5pm Sat–Tue.
Closed most public hols. 🎫 🚻
📷 🏛 Lectures, concerts, and
films: 📹 🖥 🏛

Transport
Ⓣ MFA.

Sargent Murals
John Singer Sargent spent the last years of his life creating artwork for the MFA. Originally commissioned to produce three paintings, Sargent instead constructed these elaborate murals, which were unveiled in 1921 and can still be seen today. He went on to create the works of art in the adjacent colonnade up until his death in 1925.

Level 2

Key

⬜	Art of Europe
⬜	Contemporary Art
⬜	Art of Asia, Oceania, and Africa
⬜	Art of the Ancient World
⬜	Art of the Americas
⬜	Special/Temporary exhibitions
⬜	Non-exhibition space

Level 1

Gallery Guide

The Linde Family wing (west side) displays Contemporary art and houses a restaurant and the museum store. European, Classical, Far Eastern, and Egyptian art and artifacts occupy the original MFA building. Arts from North, Central, and South America are displayed over four levels of the Art of the Americas wing. Works on display are subject to change.

★ Impressionist Paintings
Boston collectors were among the first to appreciate French Impressionism. *Dance at Bougival* (1883) by Renoir is typical of the MFA collection.

Exploring the Museum of Fine Arts, Boston

In addition to the major collections noted below, the Museum of Fine Arts has important holdings in the arts of Africa, Oceania, and the ancient Americas. The museum also houses collections of works on paper, contemporary art, and musical instruments. Several galleries are devoted to temporary thematic exhibitions. Other features of the museum include a seminar room, lecture hall, and well-stocked bookstore. There are regular talks, artist demonstrations, and events at the museum; check the website for the latest information.

Boston Harbor by the Luminist painter Fitz Henry Lane (1804–65)

Art of the America's Collection

The MFA's Art of the Americas wing features work from the birth of the United States through to the third quarter of the 20th century. The collection includes masterpieces of both ancient and contemporary Native American art. Designed by the English architect Norman Foster, the wing showcases approximately 5,000 works produced in North, Central, and South America.

The Colonial period in U.S. art is well represented, with more than 60 portraits by John Singleton Copley, perhaps America's most talented 18th-century painter, as well as works by Charles Wilson Peale. Other works on display are 19th-century landscapes, including harbor scenes by Fitz Henry Lane, an early Luminist painter; lush society portraits by John Singer Sargent; and paintings by other late 19th-century artists who constituted the "Boston School." Other notable highlights include seascapes by Winslow Homer and the muscular figure portraiture of Thomas Eakins. The MFA also exhibits works by 20th-century masters such as Stuart Davis, Jackson Pollock, Georgia O'Keeffe, and Arthur Dove.

The museum's holdings of American silver are superb. In addition to works by John Coney, there are two cases containing tea services and other pieces by Paul Revere *(see p75)*. The MFA also traces the development of the Boston style of 18th-century furniture through a definitive collection of desks, high chests, and tall clocks. Its famed period rooms display decorative arts in a historical context.

European Paintings, Decorative Arts and Sculpture

This collection of European paintings and sculpture ranges from the 7th to the late 20th century. It showcases numerous masterpieces by English, Dutch, French, Italian, and Spanish artists, including various portraits by the 17th-century Dutch painter Rembrandt. The collection of works from 1550 to 1700 is impressive both for the quality of art and for its size, which includes Francisco de Zurbarán, El Greco, Paolo Veronese, Titian, and Peter Paul Rubens.

Boston's 19th-century collectors enriched the MFA with wonderful French painting: the museum features several paintings by Jean-François Millet (the MFA has, in fact, the largest collection of his work in the world) as well as by other well-known 19th-century French artists, such as Edouard Manet, Pierre-Auguste Renoir, and Edgar Degas. Among this collection are the hugely popular and infamous *Waterlilies* (1905) by Claude Monet and *Dance at Bougival* (1883) by Renoir. The MFA's Monet holdings are among the world's largest, and there is also a good collection of paintings by the Dutch artist Vincent van Gogh. Early 20th-century European art is also exhibited.

La Berceuse by the Dutch painter Vincent Van Gogh (1853–90)

Part of the Processional Way of Ancient Babylonia (6th century BC)

The MFA is well known for its extensive collection of European decorative arts. Tableware, ceramics, and glass clustered by period from the early 17th to early 20th centuries are some examples of the works exhibited. Painstakingly transferred medieval stained-glass windows, beautifully illuminated bibles, and delicate French tapestries are displayed alongside works by Old Masters.

Some of the museum's most prized decorative arts include the opulent displays of 18th-century French silver housed in the Louis XVI-style gallery, and some of the world's most extensive holdings of Chinese export porcelain.

Ancient Egyptian, Nubian and Near Eastern Art

The MFA's collection of Egyptian and Nubian materials is unparalleled outside of Africa, and derives primarily from MFA-Harvard University excavations along the Nile, which began in 1905. One of the highlights is a 1998 installation showing Egyptian Funerary Arts, which uses the MFA's superb collection of mummies from nearly three millennia to illustrate the technical and art historical aspects of Egyptian burial practices. Also on display are some exceptional Babylonian, Assyrian, and Sumerian reliefs. Works from ancient Nubia, the cultural region around the Nile stretching roughly between the modern African cities of Aswan and Khartoum,

encompass gold and silver artifacts, ceramics, and jewels.

Other highlights from the Egyptian and Nubian collections include two monumental sculptures of Nubian kings from the Great Temple of Amen at Napata (620–586 BC and 600–580 BC). A few of the galleries are set up to re-create Nubian burial chambers, which allows cuneiform wall carvings to be displayed in something akin to an original setting; a superb example is the offering chapel of Sekhem-ankh-Ptah from Sakkara (2450–2350 BC).

Tang Dynasty Chinese Horse (8th century)

Classical Art

The MFA boasts one of America's top collections of Greek ceramics. In particular the red-and black-figured vases dating from the 6th and 5th centuries BC are exceptional. The Classical galleries of the museum are intended to thematically

Roman fresco, excavated from a Pompeian villa (1st century AD)

highlight the influence of Greek arts on both Etruscan and Roman art. The Etruscan collection has several carved sarcophagi, gold jewelry, bronze mirrors, and colorful terracottas, while the Roman collection features grave markers, portrait busts, and a series of wall panel paintings unearthed in Pompeii on an MFA expedition in 1900–1901.

Asian Art

The Asian collection is one of the most extensive that can be found under one roof. A range of works from India, the Near East and Central Asia are exhibited. Among the highlights are Indian sculpture and changing exhibitions of Islamic miniature paintings and Indian narrative paintings. Elsewhere, works from Korea feature some Buddhist paintings and sculptures, jewelry, and ornaments. The museum also boasts calligraphy, ceramics, and stone sculptures from China and the largest collection of Japanese prints outside Japan. Extensive holdings and limited display space mean that specific exhibitions change often, but the MFA's exhibitions of Japanese and Chinese scroll and screen paintings are, nevertheless, unmatched in the West. The strength of the MFA's Japanese art collection is largely due to the efforts of collectors such as Ernest Fenollosa and William Sturgis Bigelow. In the 19th century they encouraged the Japanese to maintain their traditions, and salvaged Buddhist temple art when the Japanese imperial government had withdrawn subsidies from these institutions. This collection is considered to contain some of the finest examples of Asian temple art in the world.

❼ Cambridge

Part of the greater Boston metropolitan area, Cambridge is, nonetheless, a city in its own right, and has the mood and feel of such. Principally a college town, it is dominated by Harvard University and other college campuses. It also boasts a number of important historic sights, such as Christ Church and Cambridge Common, which have associations back to the American Revolution. Harvard Square is the area's main entertainment and shopping district.

Site of the Washington Elm, on Cambridge Common

🏠 **Longfellow National Historic Site**

105 Brattle St. Tel (617) 876-4491. **Open** Jun–Oct: 9:30am–5pm Wed– Sun. 🅿 📧 ♿ 🎫 **W** nps.gov/long

This house on Brattle Street, like many around it, was built by Colonial-era merchants loyal to the British Crown during the Revolution. It was seized by American revolutionaries and served as George Washington's headquarters during the Siege of Boston.

The poet Henry Wadsworth Longfellow boarded here in 1837, was given the house as a wedding present in 1843, and lived here until his death in 1882. He wrote his most famous poems here, including *Tales of a Wayside Inn* and *The Song of Hiawatha*. Longfellow's status as literary dean of Boston meant that Nathaniel Hawthorne and Charles Sumner, among others, were regular visitors.

🏠 **Harvard Square**

Tel (617) 491-3434. ♿ **W** harvardsquare.com

Even Bostonians think of Harvard Square as a stand-in for Cambridge – the square was the original site of Cambridge from around 1630. Dominating the square is the Harvard Cooperative Society ("the Coop"), a Harvard institution, that sells inexpensive clothes, posters, and books. Harvard's large student population is very much in evidence here, adding color to the character of the square. Many trendy boutiques, inexpensive restaurants, and numerous cafés

Street musician, Harvard Square

cater to their needs. Street performers abound, especially on the weekends, and the square has long been a place where pop trends begin. Club Passim *(see p162)*, for example, has incubated many successful singer-songwriters since Joan Baez first debuted here in 1959.

🏠 **Cambridge Common**

Set aside as common pasture and military drill ground in 1631, Cambridge Common has served as a center for religious, social, and political activity ever since. George Washington took command of the Continental Army here on July 3, 1775, beneath the Washington Elm, now marked by a stone. The common served as the army's encampment from 1775 to 1776. Today the ball fields and playgrounds are popular with families. In 1997 the first monument in the U.S. to the victims of the Irish Famine was unveiled on the common.

⛪ **Christ Church**

Garden St. Tel (617) 876-0200. **Open** 8am–6pm Sun–Fri, 8am– 3pm Sat. ⛪ 7:45am, 10:15am Sun; 12:10pm Wed; 8am Thu. 📧 ♿ **W** cccambridge.org

With its square bell tower and plain, gray shingled edifice, Christ Church is a restrained example of an Anglican church. Designed in 1761 by Peter Harrison, the architect of Boston's King's Chapel *(see p60)*, Christ Church came in for rough treatment as a barracks for Continental Army troops in 1775 – British loyalists had almost all fled Cambridge by this time. The army even melted down the organ pipes to cast musket balls. The church was restored on New Year's Eve, 1775, when George Washington and his wife Martha were among the worshipers. Anti-Anglican sentiment remained strong in Cambridge, and Christ Church did not have its own rector again until the 19th century.

Simple interior of Christ Church, designed prior to the Revolution in 1761

🖼 Radcliffe Institute for Advanced Study

Brattle St. Tel (617) 495-8601. 🚹
🌐 **radcliffe.edu**

Radcliffe College was founded in 1879 as the Collegiate Institution for Women, when 27 women began to study by private arrangement with Harvard professors. By 1943, members of Harvard's faculty no longer taught separate undergraduate courses to the women of Radcliffe, and in 1999 Radcliffe ceased its official existence as an independent college. It is now an institute for advanced study promoting scholarship of women's culture. The first Radcliffe building was the 1806 Federal-style mansion, Fay House, on the northern corner of what became Radcliffe Yard. Schlesinger Library, on the west side of the yard, is considered a significant example of Colonial Revival

Stained glass, Radcliffe Institute

architecture. The library's most famous holdings are an extensive collection of cookbooks and reference works on gastronomy.

🖼 MIT

77 Massachusetts Ave. Tel (617) 253-4795. MIT Museum: **Open** 10am–5pm daily. 🖼 Hart Nautical Gallery: **Open** 10am–5pm daily. List Visual Arts Center **Open** noon–6pm Tue–Sun (to 8pm Thu). 🚻🚹🅿
🌐 **mit.edu**

Chartered in 1861 to teach students "exactly and thoroughly the fundamental principles of positive science with application to the industrial arts," the Massachusetts Institute of Technology has evolved into one of the world's leading universities in engineering and the sciences. Several architectural masterpieces dot MIT's 135-acre (55-ha) campus along the Charles River. Finnish Modernism is represented by Alvar Aalto's seminal Baker House dormitory (1949). Eero Saarinen's compressed arches make Kresge Auditorium (1955) seem poised for flight. The spare lines of Kresge Chapel (1955) embody ascetic faith. The Wiesner building houses the **List Visual Arts Center**, noted for its avant-garde art.

The **Hart Nautical Gallery** in the Rogers Building focuses on marine engineering, with models of ships and exhibits of the latest advances in underwater research. The **MIT Museum** blends art and science, with exhibits such as Harold Edgerton's ground-breaking stroboscopic flash photographs, and the latest holographic art.

Harvard University Environs

① Cambridge Common
② Christ Church
③ Harvard Square
④ Harvard University Museums (see pp114–15)
⑤ Harvard Yard (see pp112–13)
⑥ Longfellow National Historic Site
⑦ Radcliffe Institute for Advanced Study

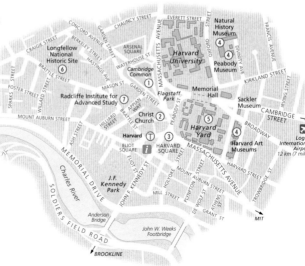

0 meters 400
0 yards 400

Harvard Yard

In 1636 Boston's well-educated Puritan leaders founded a college in Newtowne. Two years later cleric John Harvard died and bequeathed half his estate and all his books to the fledgling college. The colony's leaders bestowed his name on the school and rechristened the surrounding community Cambridge after the English city where they had been educated. The oldest university in the U.S., Harvard is now one of the world's most prestigious centers of learning. The university has expanded to encompass more than 400 buildings, but Harvard Yard is still at its heart.

Holden Chapel
Built in 1742, the chapel was the scene of revolutionary speeches and was later used as a demonstration hall for human dissections.

★ Old Harvard Yard
This leafy yard dates from the founding of the college in 1636. Freshman dormitories are around the yard, and throughout the year it is a focal point for students.

Harvard University
Information Center ↗

★ John Harvard Statue
This statue celebrates Harvard's most famous benefactor. Almost a place of pilgrimage, graduates and visitors invariably pose for photographs here.

★ Widener Library
This library memorializes Harry Elkins Widener who died on the *Titanic* in 1912. With more than 3 million volumes, it is the third largest library in the U.S.

★ **Memorial Church**
This church was built in 1931 and copies earlier styles. For example, the steeple is modeled on that of the Old North Church *(see p73)* in Boston's North End.

VISITORS' CHECKLIST

Practical Information
Massachusetts Ave.
🖿 harvard.edu
Open 24 hrs. ♿ 📷 🚻 Mon–Sat (call for details.) Harvard Information Center: **Tel** (617) 495-1573. Harvard Box Office: **Tel** (617) 496-2222. Harvard Film Archive: **Tel** (617) 495 4700.

Transport
Ⓣ Harvard.

④

Peabody Museum and Harvard Museum of Natural History *(see pp116–17)*

Sever Hall
One of the most distinctive of Harvard's Halls, this Romanesque style-building was designed by Henry Hobson Richardson *(see p34)*.

0 metres		50
0 yards		50

⑤

⑥

⑦

KEY

① **University Hall**, designed by Charles Bulfinch, was built in 1816.

② **Massachusetts Hall**, built in 1720, is Harvard's oldest building.

③ **Hollis Hall** was used as a barracks by George Washington's troops during the American Revolution.

④ **Memorial Hall**, a Ruskin Gothic building, memorializes Harvard's

Union casualties from the Civil War.

⑤ **Harvard Art Museums** *(see pp114–15)*

⑥ **Carpenter Center for Visual Arts** was opened in 1963. This is the only building in the U.S. designed by the avant-garde Swiss architect Le Corbusier.

⑦ **Tercentenary Theater**

Harvard University Museums

Harvard's museums were originally conceived to revolutionize the process of education; students were to be taught by allowing them access to artifacts from around the world. Today, this tradition continues, with the museums housing some of the world's finest university collections: art from Europe and America in the Fogg, Sackler, and Busch-Reisinger Museums; archaeological finds in the Peabody Museum; Asian, Islamic and Indian art in the Sackler Museum, and a vast collection of artifacts in the Harvard Museum of Natural History.

Exterior view of the renovated Harvard Art Museums

Harvard Art Museums
32 Quincy St. **Tel** (617) 495-9400.
Open 10am–5pm daily. 🎨 ♿ 📷
🌐 artmuseums.harvard.edu

Formerly housed in separate buildings, the Fogg, Busch-Reisinger, and Arthur Sackler Museums now occupy a single expanded facility designed by renowned Italian architect, Renzo Piano.

The stunning, eco-friendly complex was designed to provide greater access to the museums' collections. New resources have been created for study, teaching, conservation, and exhibition. The heart of the facility is the Calderwood Courtyard, from which the guests can access the various collections. The space has been modeled after the façade of the 15th-century Church of San Biagio in Montepulciano, Italy. It is open to the public free of charge, as are the adjoining museum shop and cafe.

Harvard's strong relationship with the arts dates back to 1874, when the school appointed Charles Eliot Norton as the first professor of art history in America. The Fogg

Art Museum was created in 1895 when Harvard began to build its own art collection in order to teach art history more effectively. Both the Fogg and the Busch-Reisinger have select collections of art from Europe and America.

The collections, which focus on Western art from the late Middle Ages to the present, are among the most lauded to be found on a university campus anywhere in the

Light-Space Modulator (1923–30) by the Hungarian Moholy-Nagy

world. Keep an eye out for stunning 12th-century capitals from Moutiers St-Jean in Burgundy, France.

Aficionados revel in the Fogg's extensive collection, some of which prefigure the Italian Renaissance. The massive altarpieces and suspended crucifix are particularly impressive.

Highlights include galleries devoted to 17th-century Dutch, Flemish, French, and Italian paintings, including four studies for Francesco Trevisiani's *Massacre of the Innocents*, a masterpiece destroyed in Dresden during World War II. Art students carefully examine Gian Lorenzo Bernini's use of clay models for his large-scale marble and bronze sculpture. The museum also features several works that examine the emergence of landscape as a subject in French 19th-century painting.

To many observers, one of the Fogg's most outstanding features is the Maurice Wertheim collection of Impressionist and Post-Impressionist art, most of it collected in the late 1930s. With a number of important paintings by Renoir, Manet, and Degas, the Wertheim gallery is the Fogg's most popular.

Also of note is the Grenville L. Winthrop Collection, which was donated to Harvard in 1943 and includes more than 4,000 items. Visitors and students carefully study paintings, sculpture, and drawings by some of the most important names of the 19th century such as William Blake, Jacques-Louis David, Honoré Daumier, Winslow Homer, Auguste Rodin, John Singer Sargent, Henri de Toulouse-Lautrec, and James Abbott McNeill Whistler.

Surprises lurk in a gallery of art made in France 1885–1960, often by expatriate artists. Edvard Munch's 1891 painting of *Rue de Rivoli*, for example, is both bright and impressionistic, in contrast with his bleak Expressionism.

Gian Lorenzo Bernini's clay model of a kneeling angel (1674–75)

The Fogg Art Museum also houses rotating displays from its collection of 19th- and 20th-century African art. In addition special exhibitions are frequently held, often focusing on drawings and graphic arts.

The Busch-Reisinger Museum, which was founded in 1903 as the school's Germanic Museum, focuses on the country's art and design from after 1880, with an emphasis on German Expressionism. In fact, the Busch-Reisinger is North America's only facility devoted solely to the art of the German-speaking regions of central and northern Europe. One of the chief exhibits of the museum is the *Light-Space Modulator* (1923-30) created by Hungarian painter and sculptor Moholy-Nagy. Harvard was a safe haven for many Bauhaus artists, architects, and designers who fled Nazi Germany, and both Walter Gropius and Lyonel Feininger chose the Busch-Reisinger as the depository of their personal papers and drawings.

Periodic exhibitions explore aspects of the work and philosophy of the Bauhaus movement. Although it doesn't offer the largest collection, this museum owns major paintings and sculptures by 20th-century masters such as Max Beckmann, Wassily Kandinsky, Moholy-Nagy, Paul Klee, Oskar Kokoschka, Emil Nolde, and Franz Marc.

The Busch-Reisinger impresses scholars and serious collectors with its significant examples of German Expressionism, Austrian Secession art, 1920s abstraction, and medieval sculpture. Also noteworthy is the variety of renowned post-war and contemporary art from the likes of Georg Baselitz, Anselm Kiefer, Gerhard Richter, and Joseph Beuys.

Named after a famous philanthropist, physician, and art collector, the Arthur M. Sackler Museum is home to Harvard's amazing collection of ancient, Asian, Islamic, and later Indian art.

The Sackler holds the largest collection of archaic Chinese jades outside of China. Also on display are Japanese *surimono* (woodblock print) and works on paper, Chinese bronzes, ceremonial weapons, Buddhist cave-temple sculptures, and ceramics from China and Korea. Notable works in various forms, such as vases, bronzes, and coins from Greece, Rome, Egypt, and the Near East and be found in the ancient Mediterranean and Byzantine collections. Also of note are works on paper (e.g. paintings, drawings, calligraphy, and manuscript illustrations) from Islamic lands and India, including important Islamic ceramics from the 8th through 19th century.

At the top level of the Harvard Art Museums complex, visitors

Skating (1877) by French Impressionist painter Edouard Manet

encounter the Lightbox Gallery. The new facility, which show-cases the intersection of art and technology, gives visitors a view into conservation labs. Another notable aspect of the new building is the Art Study Center, which provides students, faculty, and the public with various opportunities to examine original works of art from the museums' collections. A 300-seat lecture hall serves as a modern space in which to hold various events, presen-tations, and performances, many of which are open to the public.

The museum complex also houses the Straus Center for Conservation and Technical Studies – the first fine arts conservation, research, and training facility established in America. The center's glass walls allow visitors to observe various conservation and research activities.

Glass-roofed Calderwood Courtyard, the center stage of the museums

Peabody Museum of Archaeology and Ethnology

11 Divinity Ave. **Tel** (617) 496-1027.
Open 9am–5pm daily. **Closed** Jan 1, Thanksgiving, Dec 24, 25. 🅿 ♿ 📷
Ⓦ peabody.harvard.edu

The Peabody Museum of Archaeology and Ethnology was founded in 1866 as the first museum in the Americas devoted solely to anthropology. The many collections, which include several million artifacts and more than 500,000 photographic images, come from all around the world. The Peabody's pioneering investigations began with excavations of Mayan sites in Central America, research on the precontact Anasazi people of the American Southwest, and on the cultural history of the later Pueblo tribes of the same region. Joint expeditions sponsored by the Peabody Museum and the Museum of Fine Arts *(see pp106–9)* also uncovered some of the richest finds of dynastic and predynastic Egypt. Later research embraced the cultures of the islands of the South Pacific.

Native American totem pole, Peabody Museum

The Native American tribes of North America are represented in considerable detail in "Change and Continuity: Hall of the American Indian." Exhibits outline the distinct and different ways of life in indigenous culture areas of the Northeast, Southeast, Southwest, Plains, California/Plateau, Northwest Coast, Arctic, and Subarctic. Emphasis is placed on Native life during the 19th century, when each group came in contact – and sometimes conflict – with European culture. The exhibits, which include masterful totem-pole carvings, also highlight aspects of contemporary Native American culture.

Harvard Museum of Natural History

26 Oxford St. **Tel** (617) 495-3045.
Open 9am–5pm daily.
Closed Jul 4, Thanksgiving, Dec 24, 25. 🅿 ♿ 📷
Ⓦ hmnh.harvard.edu

The Harvard Museum of Natural History is actually three museums rolled into one, with collections from the Mineralogical and Geological Museum, the Museum of Comparative Zoology, and the Botanical Museum.

The mineralogical galleries include some of Harvard University's oldest specimen collections. Virtually every New England mineral, rock, and gem type is represented, including rough and cut gemstones and one of the world's premier meteorite collections. The zoological galleries owe their inception to the great 19th-century biologist Louis Agassiz and include his personal arachnid collection. The collection of taxidermied bird, mammal, and reptile specimens is comprehensive, and there is also a collection of dinosaur skeletons. The Birds of the World gallery features hundreds of rare specimens, representing more than 200

Triceratops skull in the Harvard Museum of Natural History

different bird families. Bird watchers greatly enjoy informative exhibits detailing the latest breakthroughs and scientific discoveries in the world of ornithology.

The collections in the botanical galleries include the Ware Collection of Blaschka Glass Models of Plants, popularly known as the "glass flowers." Between 1887 and 1936, father and son artisans Leopold and Rudolph Blaschka created these 4,000 exacting models of 830 plant species. Each species is illustrated with a scientifically accurate lifesize model and magnified parts.

The museum offers an array of free public lectures and presentations by leading · biologists, conservationists, and authors. Also of note is the museum's travel program, in which Harvard science faculty leads small groups of visitors to experience global centers of biodiversity.

Visitors at the botanical gallery of Harvard Museum of Natural History

❽ Charlestown

Situated on the north bank of the Charles River, directly opposite the North End, Charlestown exudes history. The site of the infamous Battle of Bunker Hill, when American troops suffered huge losses in their fight for independence, today the district forms a major part of Boston's Freedom Trail (see pp126–9).

Granite obelisk of the Bunker Hill Monument, erected in 1843

🏛 Bunker Hill Monument

Monument Square. **Tel** (617) 242-5641. **Open** mid-Mar–Nov: 9am–5pm daily; Dec–mid-Mar: 1–5pm Mon–Fri, 9am–5pm Sat & Sun; last climb: 4:30pm. **Closed** Jan 1, Thanksgiving, Dec 25. 🆆 **nps.gov/bost**

In the Revolution's first pitched battle between British and colonial troops, the British won but failed to escape from Boston. Following the June 17, 1775 battle, American irregulars were joined by other militia to keep British forces penned up until George Washington forced their evacuation by sea the following March. A Tuscan-style pillar was erected in 1794 in honor of Dr. Joseph Warren, a Boston revolutionary leader who died in the battle, but Charlestown citizens felt something grander was in order. They began raising funds for the Bunker Hill Monument in 1823, laid the cornerstone in 1825, and dedicated the 221-ft (67-m) granite obelisk in 1843. The building has no elevator, but 294 steps lead to the top, giving spectacular views of Boston harbor. Exhibitions recount the significance and drama of the bloody battle.

🏛 John Harvard Mall

Ten families founded Charlestown in 1629, a year before the rest of Boston was settled. They built their homes and a palisaded fort on Town Hill, a spot now marked by John Harvard Mall. A small monument within the enclosed park pays homage to John Harvard (see p112), the young cleric who ministered to the settlers.

When John Winthrop arrived with three shiploads of Puritan refugees in 1630 (see p20), they settled nearby in the marshes at the base of Town Hill, now City Square.

🏛 Charlestown Navy Yard

Tel (617) 242-5601. **Open** 9am–5pm daily (Nov–mid-Mar: Thu–Sun). 🆓 🆗

Municipal art in City Square

Established in 1800 as one of the country's first military shipyards, for 174 years Charlestown Navy Yard played a key role in supporting the U.S. Atlantic fleet, as the Navy moved from wooden sailing ships to steel giants. The men and women working at the yard built more than 200 warships and carried out maintenance repairs on thousands of others. The yard was designed by Alexander Parris, architect of Quincy Market (see p66), and was one of the first examples of industrial architecture in Boston.

On decommissioning, 30 acres of the Navy Yard were transferred to the National Park Service, and rangers now give tours of the facility on a daily basis, including the Chain Forge (where die-lock anchor chain was first made), the Rope Walk, and Dry Dock 1 (one of the first dry docks in the U.S.). A Visitor Center is located at Building 5.

VISITORS' CHECKLIST

Practical Information
Ⓣ Community College.
🚇 Wed.

Transport
🚌 93. ⛴ from Long Wharf.

🏛 U.S.S. *Constitution*

Charlestown Navy Yard. **Tel** (617) 242-5671. **Open** mid-Apr–Oct: 2:30–6pm Tue–Sun (from 10am Sat & Sun); Nov–mid-Apr: 2:30–4pm Thu–Sun (from 10am Sat & Sun). 🆓 🆗
🆆 **navy.mil/local/constitution**

The oldest commissioned warship afloat, the U.S.S. *Constitution* saw action in the Mediterranean protecting American shipping from the Barbary pirates. In the War of 1812, she won fame and her nickname of "Old Ironsides" when cannonballs bounced off her in a battle with the British ship *Guerriere*. In the course of her active service, she won 42 battles, lost none, captured 20 vessels, and was never boarded by an enemy. She underwent an overhaul in time for her 1997 bicentennial and is now in drydock for further restoration, but open for visits, until 2018. On July 4 each year, she is taken out into the harbor for a turnaround that reverses her position at the pier to ensure equal weathering on both sides. A small museum documents her history.

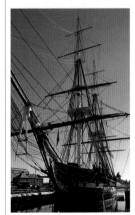

U.S.S. *Constitution*, built in 1797, moored in Charlestown Navy Yard

❾ Concord

First settled in 1635, Concord is linked with neighboring Lexington in the battles of April 19, 1775. Colonials favoring separation from Great Britain hid munitions here and British troops, seeking these supplies, marched on the town, passing first through Lexington *(see p121)*. The resulting battles in Concord, along with the Lexington skirmish, are considered the first of the American Revolution. Half a century later, with the gathering of American writers including essayist Ralph Waldo Emerson, Concord blossomed as the literary heart of the U.S. The homes of many writers of the era are now preserved as museums.

North Bridge in Minute Man National Historical Park

🏛 Monument Square

At Concord's center is Monument Square. The square was the focus of a battle between British troops and Colonists on what has become known as Patriots Day. Having seized the gun cache of rebel forces, British soldiers began burning them. Nearby Colonial forces saw the smoke and, believing the British were torching the town, rushed to Concord's defense.

🏛 Minute Man National Historical Park – North Bridge Visitor Center

174 Liberty St. **Tel** (978) 318-7810. **Open** Apr–Oct: 9:30am–5:30pm daily. **Closed** Nov–Mar. 🚻
Ⓦ nps.gov/mima

Although British troops met little resistance on Lexington Battle Green and managed to prevail in Concord center, they fared less well in the countryside. Colonial militia and citizen-soldiers (Minute Men) successfully hid their cannon and powder stashes from a contingent of British soldiers by burying the munitions in newly plowed fields. They then confronted British troops who were patrolling North Bridge. The so-called "shot heard round the world," memorialized in Emerson's "Concord Hymn" (1837), is widely considered to have set off the war, as the Colonials

Minute Man statue
in Concord

drove three British companies from the bridge and chased them back to their occupation barracks in Boston.

Across the bridge is the famous Minute Man statue, crafted by Concord native Daniel Chester French (1850–1931). A short trail leads from the bridge to the North Bridge Visitor Center. A re-enactment of the battle takes place every year in April.

🏛 Emerson House

28 Cambridge Tpk. **Tel** (978) 369-2236. **Open** mid-Apr–late Oct: 10am–4:30pm Thu–Sat, 1–4:30pm Sun. 🈲 🈳

Following his graduation from Harvard, Ralph Waldo Emerson (1803–82) spent his early adulthood as a schoolteacher and then as a Unitarian minister. But as he grew away from religious orthodoxy and began to promulgate his Transcendental philosophy, Emerson withdrew from the ministry and moved to Concord, living first in The Old Manse where he wrote his manifesto *Nature*. On marrying Lydia Jackson in 1835, he settled into Emerson house, writing essays, organizing lecture tours, and entertaining friends and admirers as the honored "Sage of Concord". Emerson lived in this house until his death in 1882. Much of his furniture, writings, books, and family memorabilia are on display here.

Along the Battle Road, by John Rush is located in the Minute Man Visitor Center

Concord's Old Manse: home to 19th-century literary giants

⊞ The Old Manse

269 Monument St. **Tel** (978) 369-3909.
Open mid-Apr–Oct: noon–5pm Tue–
Sun; call for winter hours. 🐾 🧺

The parsonage by the North Bridge was built in 1770 by the grandfather of writer Ralph Waldo Emerson. Author Nathaniel Hawthorne (1804–64) lived here as a newlywed in 1842–45 and wrote *Mosses from an Old Manse* (1846), giving the house its name. On view are Emerson family possessions and period furniture. The garden was planted by essayist Henry David Thoreau (1817–62) as a wedding gift to Hawthorne.

🏛 Concord Museum

200 Lexington Rd. **Tel** (978) 369-9763.
Open Jan–Mar: 11am–4pm Mon–Sat,
1–4pm Sun; Apr–Dec: 9am–5pm
Mon–Sat, noon–5pm Sun (Jun–Aug:
9am–5pm Sun). 🐾 ♿
w concordmuseum.org

Begun in 1850, the Concord museum contains one of the oldest and best-documented collections of Americana. Holdings include decorative arts from the 17th, 18th, and 19th centuries that can be traced to original Concord owners; the lantern that Paul Revere ordered hung to warn of the British advance; and American Revolution artifacts that include powder horns, muskets, cannonballs, and

fifes. The museum is also the repository of the contents of Emerson's study, and the largest collection of personal items that belonged to essayist Henry David Thoreau. The "Why Concord?" exhibit traces the community from initial settlement some 10,000 years ago through the 20th century.

A View of the Town of Concord April 19, 1775, Concord Museum

Concord Town Center

① Monument Square
② Minute Man National Historical Park
③ North Bridge Visitor Center
④ North Bridge
⑤ Minute Man Statue
⑥ The Old Manse
⑦ Concord Museum
⑧ Emerson House
⑨ Sleepy Hollow Cemetery

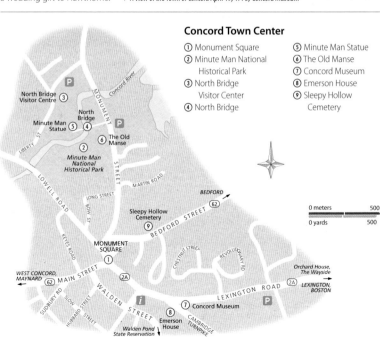

0 meters 500
0 yards 500

For keys to symbols *see back flap*

Author's Ridge, Sleepy Hollow Cemetery

🏛 Sleepy Hollow Cemetery

Bedford St, east of Monument Sq.
Open dawn–dusk daily.

This rolling green cemetery is the final resting place of many Concord literary giants. Pilgrims seek the graves of Henry David Thoreau (1817–62), Nathaniel Hawthorne (1804–64), Louisa May Alcott (1832–88), and Ralph Waldo Emerson (1803–82), among other notables, on "Author's Ridge." They often leave pebbles on Emerson's head-stone, acorns on Thoreau's, and pennies on the grave of sculptor Daniel Chester French. Although his most famous work is the Lincoln Memorial in Washington, DC, French also sculpted the Civil War Memorial in Sleepy Hollow.

🏛 Orchard House

399 Lexington Rd. **Tel** (978) 369-4118.
Open Apr–Oct: 10am–4:30pm Mon–Sat, 1–4:30pm Sun; Nov–Mar: 11am–3pm Mon–Fri, 10am–4:30pm Sat, 1–4:30pm Sun. 🅿 🚫 **Closed** Jan, Easter, Thanksgiving, Dec 25.
W louisamayalcott.org

Louisa May Alcott was the most successful member of the Alcott family, but in his day, her father Bronson was well-regarded as a Transcendental philosopher and founder of the now-defunct Concord School of Philosophy. Orchard House was the Alcott family home from 1858–77, and Louisa May set *Little Women* (1868) here. Since the house has been little altered since

the Alcotts lived in it, visitors often comment that a tour is like walking through the book.

Room at Orchard House, the Alcott family residence from 1858–77

🏛 The Wayside

455 Lexington Rd. **Tel** (978) 318-7863.
Open Jun–Oct, call for hours.

This National Historic Site has a long literary history. It was home to the Alcott family while Louisa May was growing up, and became the only home ever owned by author Nathaniel Hawthorne. Children's author Margaret Sidney (1844–1924) of *Five Little Peppers* fame bought it from Hawthorne's daughter. Guided tours are offered at limited hours by Minute Man National Park rangers.

🏛 Walden Pond State Reservation

915 Walden St. **Tel** (978) 369-3254.
Open call for hours. 🅿 🚫 ♿
W mass.gov/dcr

Essayist Henry David Thoreau (1817–62) lived at Walden Pond from 1845 to 1847. It was here that he compiled the material for his seminal work *Walden; or, Life in the Woods* (1854), which called for a return to simplicity and a respect for nature, which he cast as the source of all morality. Although he depicted himself living in isolation, Thoreau would visit the Concord Center to have Sunday dinners with the Emerson family, and the pond and its woodlands are no more wilderness than they were in Thoreau's day. His significance in American thought and letters, however, led to the designation of the pond as a National Historic Landmark. The area is popular for walking, fishing, and swimming, though the reservation limits visitors to 1,000 people at any one time. A bronze statue of Thoreau stands outside a re-creation of his cabin.

Directly across busy Route 2 from Walden Pond is the Walden Woods Project which demonstrates the enduring appeal of Thoreau's ideas. A one-mile (1.6-km) walking trail is punctuated by aphoristic inscriptions in granite from Thoreau's writings, and bronze-tipped columns devoted to such issues as pacifism and environmentalism. Within Walden Woods is a "reflection circle." The granite columns surrounding it bear yet more quotations from thinkers who were influenced by Thoreau, including civil rights leader Martin Luther King, Jr. (1929–68) and Sioux chief Luther Standing Bear (1868–1939).

Fisherman on the tranquil waters of Walden Pond

⑩ Lexington

The peaceful prosperity of the modern-day suburb of Lexington belies its role in the birth of American independence. On the village common at dawn on April 19, 1775, British regulars and Colonial militia exchanged shots. The skirmish proved to be the opening salvo of the American Revolution, and Lexington Battle Green has been hallowed ground for Americans ever since. Many visitors like to bicycle the 5.5 miles (9 km) from Alewife "T" station in Cambridge along the Minuteman Bikeway, which roughly parallels the British route on their march to Lexington.

VISITORS' CHECKLIST

Practical Information
🛈 1875 Massachusetts Ave.
(781) 862-1450. 📅 Patriots Day
(Apr). 🌐 **lexingtonchamber. org**

Transport
✈ Boston.

Minute Man Bikeway, part of the Minute Man National Historical Park

🐾 Minute Man National Historical Park – Minute Man Visitor Center
Rte 2A. **Tel** (781) 674-1920. **Open** Apr–Oct: 9am–5pm daily; Nov–Mar: 11am–3pm Tue–Sat. 🌐 **nps.gov/mima**

This 990-acre (400-ha) park, with access from both Concord *(see pp118–120)* and Lexington, preserves the site and interprets the story of the first battles of the American Revolution. It explains that British forces were seeking to uncover colonial munitions hidden in the countryside, and how both Massachusetts militia and citizen-soldiers, known as Minute Men, managed to rout the British regulars. The Visitor Center features a massive battle mural and a 22-minute multimedia show, *Road to Revolution*. A significant portion of the national park runs along the five-mile (8-km) Battle Road Trail. This is the path that was followed by British forces as they advanced from Lexington and marched on to Concord – the same route the forces took in retreat.

🏛 Lexington Battle Green
Tranquil churches surround the leafy green where, each year in April, historic re-enactors re-create the Battle of Lexington. The rest of the year, a statue of a Massachusetts militia man erected in 1900 recalls the event, as do the graves of seven of the eight colonial casualties.

🏛 Historical Society Houses
Hancock-Clarke House: 36 Hancock St; Buckman Tavern: 1 Bedford St; Munroe Tavern: 1332 Massachusetts Ave; **Tel** (781) 862-1703. **Open** call for seasonal opening hours. 📷 📷 🌐 **lexingtonhistory.org**

These three structures all played a role in the events of April 19, 1775 (now known as Patriots Day). **Buckman Tavern** served as the meeting place for the Massachusetts militia before the confrontation and as a makeshift hospital for their wounded. Bostonian Paul

Historic re-enactor

Revere undertook his "midnight ride" to **Hancock-Clarke House** to warn patriots Samuel Adams and John Hancock, two of the signatories to the Declaration of Independence, of the approaching British *(see p23)*. **Munroe Tavern** was a headquarters for British forces. All display artifacts from the Revolutionary era.

🏛 Scottish Rite Masonic Museum & Library
33 Marrett Rd. (at intersection of Rte 2A and Massachusetts Ave.) **Tel** (781) 861-6559. **Open** 10am–4:30pm Wed–Sat. **Closed** Jan 1, Thanksgiving, Dec 24–25. 🌐 **srmml.org**

This museum tells the story of the Freemasons in the context of American history, serving as the "historical society" of American Freemasonry. Among its prized artifacts is a copy of the Lexington Alarm, a broadside detailing the events at Lexington and calling on American colonists to revolt against the British Crown.

Buckman Tavern, where militia met to plan their revolt against British forces

THREE GUIDED WALKS

Given the difficulties of driving in Boston, it is fortunate that its compact layout and ubiquitous sidewalks make it an ideal walking city. These three walks show the city's extremes – the dense riches of a university campus, the unexpected pleasures of an intensely residential neighborhood, and Boston's most famous walking tour along the historic Freedom Trail. While Harvard (see pp112–6) gets the lion's share of attention among the Boston-area universities, its younger neighbor in Cambridge, the Massachusetts Institute of Technology (MIT), is known for its modern art. South Boston is a secret often jealously guarded by its inhabitants. Although Dorchester Heights was a critical site in the American Revolution, few Freedom Trail walkers ever make the detour to appreciate the high vantage on Boston's outer harbor. In addition to these three walks, each of the five areas of Boston described in the Area by Area section of this book indicates a walk on its Street-by-Street map.

CHOOSING A WALK

The Three Walks
This map shows the location of the three guided walks in relation to the main sightseeing areas of Boston.

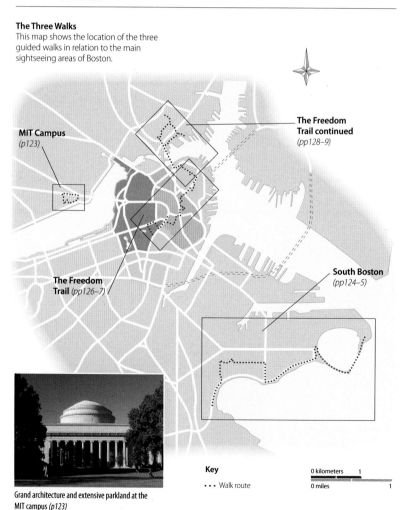

MIT Campus
(p123)

The Freedom Trail continued
(pp128–9)

The Freedom Trail *(pp126–7)*

South Boston
(pp124–5)

Grand architecture and extensive parkland at the MIT campus *(p123)*

Key

• • • Walk route

0 kilometers   1

0 miles   1

A 45-Minute Walk on the MIT Campus

Perhaps best known for its advances in science and engineering, the Massachusetts Institute of Technology has embraced cutting-edge art and architecture as surely as it has pioneered artificial intelligence and robotics. This walking tour samples some of the best of Modern and Post-Modern sculpture and buildings located around the campus. These highlights represent the institute's innovative use of unconventional materials and techniques.

⑨ The Stata Center designed by Frank Gehry

From the Kendall/MIT "T" station, walk to Main Street and turn right. Take the second right down Wadsworth Street to the corner of Amherst Street, then head to the back courtyard of the Arthur D. Little Building, where Pablo Picasso's

right onto Ames Street at the Media Lab Extension building. Next door, the sleekly banded white box with dark windows is the List Visual Arts Center ③, where galleries display changing exhibitions of innovative, contemporary art. Note Alexander

to the walkway that leads into the heart of the campus. Set at the edge of the sidewalk on the left is a complex sculpture of curves, angles, and twisted planes commissioned in 1975 from sculptor Louise Nevelson. Although painted, *Transparent Horizon* ⑥

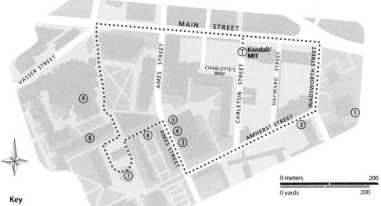

Key

• • • Walk route

Figure Découpée ① from 1963 stands in a small garden. Cross the intersection to the Tang Building, where Frank Stella's 1988 abstract wall relief of acrylic and enamel on aluminum, *Heads or Tails* ②, fills the wall at the base of the staircase atrium. Continue down Amherst Street and turn

Calder's intermediate model for his sculpture, *The Big Sail*, in the lobby ④. In the central atrium, Kenneth Noland's 1985 *Here-There* ⑤ carries the minimalist abstraction of the List building to its logical artistic extreme in a four-story interior wall mural.

Join the students rushing to classes as you cross Ames Street

was constructed of non-rusting corten steel. Continue past the Nevelson and look to the left for a view of Alexander Calder's fully realized, 40-ft-(12-m)-high sculpture, *The Big Sail* ⑦. Turn right to enter the Whitaker Building, where a projection screen in the ground-level corridor shows experimental film and video. The Media Test Wall ⑧, as the installation is called, is emblematic of the school's commitment to technology in the arts. Cross through the Whitaker building for a view of the south side of the Stata Center ⑨. Frank Gehry's metal-sheathed complex constitutes a research and teaching village devoted to computer, information, and intelligence sciences. Walk past the center to return to Main Street and the "T" station.

Tips for Walkers

Starting point: Kendall/MIT "T"
Length: 0.8 miles (1.3 km).
Stopping-off points: Amelia's Trattoria (111 Harvard St.) serves gourmet pizzas and pasta dishes.
Visitor information: See page 111 for museum opening hours.

⑤ *Here-There* mural (1985) by minimalist artist Kenneth Noland

For keys to symbols *see back flap*

A Two-Hour Walk in South Boston

The harbor is the main attraction in quickly gentrifying South Boston. Initially populated by refugees from the mid-19th century Irish famine, the area evolved into the third-largest Irish-American community in the U.S. Recent gentrification has diversified the population and turned Victorian tenements into trendy condominiums. But the defining characteristic of South Boston has always been its relation to the harbor – a bevy of soft sand beaches and headlands that guard the entry to the Port of Boston. The steep hill to Dorchester Heights can be skipped in favor of a continued seaside promenade.

① Stone column at the entrance to Joe Moakley Park

The last stop of the No. 5 bus is at the playing fields and green walkways of Joe Moakley Park ①, named after the late South Boston-born Congressman. Some of Moakley's sayings celebrate the neighborhood's identity and are etched on granite columns that can be found around the park. One such saying reads "Everyone I knew growing up in South Boston was baptized, issued a union card, and enrolled in the Democratic Party." Cross the park to the broad swath of fine brown sand known as Carson Beach ②, a public swimming beach with a bath house and bocce courts.

The steep walk up Old Harbor Street leads to the grand hilltop oval of Thomas

② Time out on Carson Beach

Park, where the Dorchester Heights Monument ③ stands like a lighthouse to mark the spot where George Washington erected cannons in 1776 to force the British withdrawal from Boston.

The massive building at one end of the park is South Boston High School ④. Walk along East 7th Avenue past renovated homes to L Street and turn right toward the harbor. Woody's L Street Tavern ⑤, Southie's most old-fashioned pub and the set for scenes in the film *Good Will Hunting*, is at the corner of East 8th Street.

At the foot of the street is the L Street Bath House ⑥,

the toddler-friendly L Street Beach ⑦, and M Street Beach ⑧. The bath house, which actually stretches between K and M streets, was a municipal gift from notoriously corrupt mayor James Curley (last elected to office from jail) to his friends and cronies of South Boston. The bath house now serves a broad public. Walk east along William J. Day Boulevard as it winds past the yacht club and private moorings and concludes at Pleasure Bay.

Standing sentinel over the harbor on the traffic circle connecting the boulevard to Farragut Road is a bronze of Admiral David Farragut ⑨, commander in chief of the U.S. Navy during the Civil War.

Across the street is the section of South Boston beach

Tips for Walkers

Starting point: Joe Moakley Park
Getting there: No. 5 bus from Andrew Sq. to Moakley Park (McCormack Housing).
Length: 3 miles (5km).
Stops: Sullivan's (next to Fort Independence) and Seapoint Restaurant (at Carson Beach) serve fried seafood and American favorites. Supreme House of Pizza, across from Moakley Park, offers an Italian alternative.

⑭ Cannons at Fort Independence, Castle Island

officers, and soldiers. The walkway brings you to a pointed obelisk monument ⑬. This granite-block shaft is a memorial to Donald McKay whose shipyard, directly across the channel, launched some of the fastest clipper ships of the mid-19th century and helped cement Boston as an international trading port. Bas-reliefs of some of McKay's most famous vessels are mounted near the base. The shipyard site is now Logan International Airport. Most planes coming to Boston make their final approach and touchdown on the runway directly opposite Castle Island.

Because Castle Island controls the throat of Boston harbor, it has been fortified since 1634. The current structure, Fort Independence ⑭, was erected in 1779 on George Washington's orders so that no enemy could ever again occupy Boston as the British had done. It never saw action, though it did serve as a prisoner of war camp during the Civil War. Author Edgar Allen Poe served here briefly in the 1820s and is said to have based one of his macabre tales, *A Cask of Amontillado*, on a fort legend of a man deliberately confined in a dungeon. (Just such a skeleton was uncovered during a renovation in 1905.) The No. 11 bus, which runs along Day Boulevard, will take you back to downtown Boston.

Key

• • • Walk route

gas storage tank in Dorchester. The tank was first painted in rainbow colors by abstract artist Corita Kent in 1971.

The causeway concludes at Castle Island, which has not been a real island since the channel to the mainland was filled in 1891. Follow the seaside walkway which passes by a number of memorials to fallen South Boston firefighters, police

known as the "Sugar Bowl" ⑩. This beach lines Pleasure Bay, a circular body of water protected from the harbor by an extensive breakwater, the Pleasure Bay Causeway ⑪. The causeway walk of nearly 1 mile (1.5 km) is a favorite spot for local mothers to show off their infants, as well as a good exercise route for joggers and speed walkers. Halfway along the causeway is the Head Island light pavilion ⑫, with picnic tables, benches, and sweeping views of the harbor, looking all the way down to the landmark

⑭ U.S.S. *Constitution* gliding past Fort Independence

A 90-Minute Walk Along the Freedom Trail

Boston has more sites directly related to the American Revolution than any other city. The most important of these sites, as well as some relating to other freedoms gained by Bostonians, have been linked together as "The Freedom Trail." This 2.5-mile (4-km) walking route, marked in red on the sidewalks, goes from Boston Common to Bunker Hill in Charlestown (see pp128–9). This first section weaves through the central city and Old Boston. See www.thefreedomtrail.org for more information.

③ Elegant Georgian steeple of Park Street Church

② Nurses Hall in Massachusetts State House

Central City

The Freedom Trail starts at the Visitor Information Center on Boston Common ① (see pp48–9). This is where angry colonials rallied against their British masters and where the British forces were encamped during the 1775–76 military occupation. Political speakers still expound from their soapboxes here, and Boston Common remains a center of much activity.

Walking around to the north corner of the Common gives a great view of the Massachusetts State House ② (see p52) on Beacon Street, designed by Charles Bulfinch as the new center of state

governance shortly after the Revolution. Along Park Street, at the end of the Common, you will come to Park Street Church ③ (see p50), built in 1810 and a bulwark of the antislavery movement. The church took the place of an old grain storage facility, which in turn gave its name to the adjacent Granary Burying Ground ④ on Tremont Street, one of Boston's earliest cemeteries and the final resting place of patriots John Hancock and Paul Revere (see p23). Continuing along Tremont Street you will come to King's Chapel and Burying Ground ⑤ (see p60).

The atmospheric cemetery is Boston's oldest, containing, among others, the grave of colonial city founder John Winthrop. As the name suggests, King's Chapel was the principal Anglican church in Puritan Boston, and more than half of its congregation fled to Nova Scotia at the outbreak of the Revolution. The box pew on the right just inside the front entrance was reserved for condemned prisoners to hear their last sermon before going to the gallows on Boston Common.

Heart of Old Boston

Head back along Tremont Street and turn left down School Street, where a hopscotch-like mosaic embedded in the sidewalk commemorates the site of the First Public School ⑥, established in 1635. At the end of the street is the Old Corner Bookstore ⑦ *(see p61)*, a landmark more associated with Boston's literary emergence of 1845–65 than with the Revolution.

The Old South Meeting House ⑧, a short way to the south on Washington Street, is a graceful, white-spired brick church, modeled on Sir Christopher Wren's English country churches. As one of the largest meeting halls in Revolutionary Boston, "Old South's" rafters rang with many a fiery speech urging revolt against the British. It was a crucible for free-speech debates and taxation protests. A few blocks north, the Old State House ⑨ presides over the head of State Street. The colonial government building, it also served as the first state legislature, and the merchants' exchange in the basement was where Boston's colonial shipping fortunes were made. The square in front of the Old State House is the Boston Massacre Site ⑩, where British soldiers opened fire on a taunting mob in 1770, killing five and providing propaganda for revolutionary agitators.

Follow State Street down to Congress Street and turn left to reach Faneuil Hall ⑪, known as the "Cradle of Liberty" for the history of patriotic speeches made in its public meeting hall. Donated to the city by Huguenot merchant Peter Faneuil, the building was built primarily as Boston's first central marketplace.

Tips for Walkers

Starting point: Boston Common. Maps available at Boston Common Visitors' Center.
Length: 2.5 miles (4 km).
Getting there: Exit at Park Street "T" station to start. Other "T" stations also located on route: State, Haymarket, and Government Center. Follow red stripe on sidewalk for the full route.

⑪ Faneuil Hall, popularly known as "the Cradle of Liberty"

⑨ Old State House, once the seat of colonial government

Use the red stripe to negotiate your way down to North End and the Paul Revere House ⑫ on North Square. Boston's oldest private residence, it was home to the man famously known for his "midnight ride" *(see p23)*. From here, walk to Hanover Street and turn right, following the red stripe towards the next point on the Freedom Trail, Old North Church *(see p128)*.

Key

• • • Walk route

For keys to symbols *see back flap*

The Freedom Trail continued

Distances begin to stretch out on the second half of the Freedom Trail as it meanders through the narrow streets of the North End, then continues over the Charles River to Charlestown, where Boston's settlers first landed. The key Revolutionary and colonial-era sites here embrace two wars – the War of Independence and the War of 1812.

⑭ View from Copp's Hill terrace, Copp's Hill Burying Ground

The North End

Following the Freedom Trail through the North End from Paul Revere House (see p127), allow time to try some of the Italian cafés and bakeries along the neighborhood's main thoroughfare, Hanover Street. Cross through the Paul Revere Mall to reach Old North Church ⑬ (see p73), whose spire is instantly visible over the shoulder of the statue of Paul Revere on horseback. Sexton Robert Newman famously hung two lanterns in the belfry here, signaling the advance of British troops on Lexington and Concord in 1775. The church retains its 18th-century interior, including the unusual box pews.

The crest of Copp's Hill lies close by on Hull Street. Some of Boston's earliest gallows stood here, and Bostonians would gather in boats below to watch the hangings of heretics and pirates. Much of the hilltop is covered by Copp's Hill

Gravestone at Copp's Hill Burying Ground

Burying Ground ⑭.This was established in 1660, and the cemetery holds the remains of several generations of the Mather family – Boston's influential 17th- and 18th-century theocrats – as well as the tombstones of many soldiers of the Revolution slain in the fight for freedom. Boston's first free African American community, "New Guinea," covered the west side of Copp's Hill. A broken column marks the grave of Prince Hall, head of the Black Masons, distinguished veteran of the Revolution, and prominent political leader in the early years of the Republic. The musketball-chipped tombstone of patriot Daniel Malcolm records that he asked to be buried "in a stone grave 10 feet deep" to rest beyond the reach of British gunfire.

Map showing: CHARLESTOWN BRIDGE, Boston Inner Harbor, KEANY SQUARE, COMMERCIAL STREET, PRINCE STREET, HULL STREET, SNOWHILL STREET, SHEAFE STREET, PRINCE STREET, SALEM STREET, NORTH BENNETT STREET, TILESTON STREET, HANOVER STREET, COPP'S HILL BURYING GROUND ⑭, CHARTER STREET, FOSTER ST, ATLANTIC AVENUE, NORTH E PLAYGRO, ⑬

0 meters		200
0 yards		2 00

⑬ Unusual box pews inside Old North Church

⑯ The Bunker Hill Monument viewed from Charlestown harborfront

Key

••• Walk route

Charlestown

The iron bridge over the Charles River that links the North End in Boston with City Square in Charlestown dates from 1899. Across the bridge, turn right along Constitution Road, following the signs to Charlestown Navy Yard ⑮. The National Park Service operates the Visitor Center at Building 5, which has exhibits explaining the historic role of the Navy Yard and the history of the warships – one from the late 18th century, another from the mid-20th century – that are berthed at its piers. The colonial navy had been no match for the might of Britain's naval forces during the Revolution, and building a more formidable naval force became a priority. This was one of several shipyards that were set up around 1800. Lying at her berth alongside Pier 1, the 200-year-old wooden-hulled

⑮ Lion carving, **U.S.S. Constitution**

U.S.S. *Constitution* is probably the most famous ship in U.S. history and still remains the flagship of the U.S. Navy. Built at Hartt's shipyard in the North End, she was completed in 1797. In the War of 1812, she earned the nickname "Old Ironsides" for the resilience of her live oak hull against cannon fire. Fully restored for her bicentennial, the *Constitution* occasionally sails under her own power.

The granite obelisk that towers above the Charlestown waterfront is Bunker Hill Monument ⑯, commemorating the battle of June 17, 1775 that ended with a costly victory for British forces against an irregular colonial army that finally ran out of ammunition. British losses were so heavy, however, that the battle would presage future success for the colonial forces. As a monument to the first large-scale battle of the Revolution, the obelisk, based on those of ancient Egypt, was a prototype for others across the U.S. Catch a bus from Chelsea Street back to the North End and city center.

⑮ Defensive guns at Charlestown Navy Yard with view of the North End

For keys to symbols *see back flap*

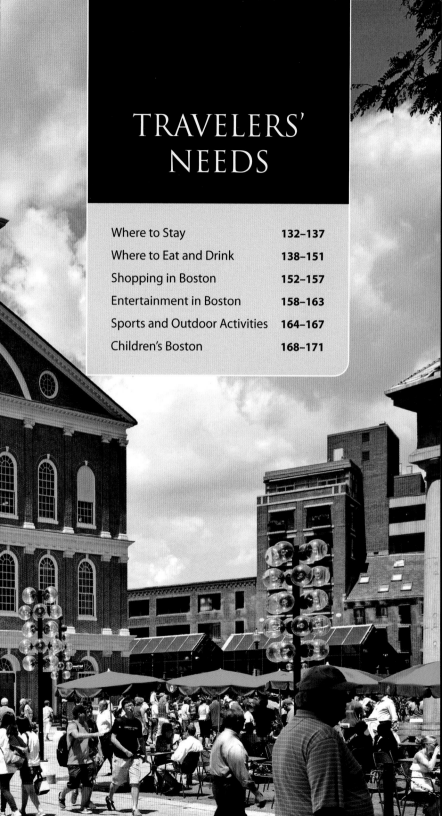

TRAVELERS'
NEEDS

WHERE TO STAY

Boston offers the visitor almost every type of accommodation: modest guesthouses, luxury hotels, chain motels, Victorian brownstone bed and breakfasts (B&Bs), and designer "boutique" hotels. Many older hotels have been renovated to provide traditional charm with modern conveniences, while new hotels keep opening in the city. Nevertheless,

Boston has a perennial hotel shortage, which keeps prices high and makes it difficult to book rooms during peak times. Even in winter, it's rare to find rooms under $100 per night; in summer, "budget" rates can approach $200 or more. It is advisable to contact the city's tourist information offices for room availability and prices.

The elegant Omni Parker House, set along the Freedom Trail (see p135)

Where to Stay

The centrally located Back Bay has the greatest concentration of hotels and is convenient for tourists as well as business travelers. In the gentrified South End, an increasing number of restored Victorian brownstones have been converted to B&Bs. Accommodation in the Financial District, close to the waterfront, caters to business people during the week, but often offers good value to vacationers on the weekends. Across the Charles River, Cambridge has a large number of hotels, particularly around Harvard Square and Kendall Square. In the more suburban Brookline, situated a little way west of Back Bay, there are several guesthouses, as well as a selection of more upscale B&Bs.

Hotel Grading and Facilities

Boston does not have an official hotel grading system. While higher prices generally indicate more amenities, some lodgings in prime locations, or with unique historic features, may command prices that exceed what the facilities might otherwise warrant.

B&Bs generally do not offer fitness facilities, business services,

or restaurants, and may be less expensive. However, some at the higher end of the price scale now have amenities, and prices, that rival the best hotels. Most large hotels have at least a basic fitness room, while some have arrangements with nearby clubs for guest use. Swimming pools are less common, except at the big hotels, and outdoor pools generally open only between June and early September.

One recent development that travelers may find beneficial is that Boston's hotels now house many of the city's top restaurants. High-speed Internet access, wired and wireless, is standard but may incur a fee.

How to Book

Most hotels have toll-free reservation numbers, and some offer discounts for online booking. Room rates are often quoted for two people sharing a room, not including tax or breakfast, although some places provide a breakfast. Prepay only the first night in case the place does not meet expectations. There is some last-minute room availability

during the winter months, but Boston hotels are busy in May and June for college graduations; July and August for summer vacations; and September and October for the fall season.

Hidden Extras

If you have a car in Boston, you'll pay dearly for parking. Ask your hotel if parking is included; if not, budget at least $20–50 extra per day. Taxes in Boston will also add 14.75 per cent to the hotel bill. If breakfast is not included, expect to spend at least $3 for coffee and a pastry in a nearby café, or $15 and up for a full hotel breakfast.

Discounts

Hotel prices vary significantly with the seasons, with the lowest rates found in January and February. Through the year, many hotels catering to business travelers, such as in the Financial District, in Cambridge's Kendall Square, and around Hynes Convention Center offer discount weekend rates. B&Bs may offer better prices mid-week.

Stylishly furnished room at the Revere Hotel, Theater District (see p134)

◀ The bustling Faneuil Hall Marketplace, also known as Quincy Market

The elegant interior of the Presidential suite at Taj Boston, Back Bay *(see p136)*

Bed and Breakfasts

Boston has a good selection of small hotels and B&Bs, offering personal service and charm. If you are looking for a classic B&B, contact one of Boston's B&B booking agencies. A recent trend is the "boutique" hotel, a small, elegant place, with prices reflecting the level of service and luxury. Contact the **Bed & Breakfast Agency of Boston**, **Bed and Breakfast Associates Bay Colony**, or **Boston Homestay, Inc.** for more information.

Business Travelers

Business travelers will find that all major hotels provide fax and Wi-Fi access. Some new or newly refurbished hotels offer in-room fax machines, multi-line phones, and private voice mail. It is wise to check whether older hotels have the facilities you require.

Disabled Travelers

Disabled travelers may be most comfortable in the city's newer hotels that have been built to conform to access requirements. Some of the older hotels have been refitted, but many small B&Bs have steps, narrow hallways, or other architectural features that may make access difficult. For information, contact the **Massachusetts Network of Information Providers for People with Disabilities**.

Children

Children are welcome in most of the larger hotels and often stay free in their parents' rooms. Some deluxe hotels provide child-friendly amenities such as bedtime milk and cookies, and complimentary kids' DVD rentals. Suites are available in many big hotels, giving families space to spread out. For families on more moderate budgets, some guesthouses offer apartment-style accommodations. Be aware that many B&Bs cannot accommodate young children.

Budget Options

It can be hard to find budget options in Boston. The centrally located **Boston Hostel (HI-Boston)** has 468 beds in modern, eco-friendly private and dorm rooms. Many travelers find rentals through **airbnb** to be the most flexible and cost-effective option. The North Shore towns of Salem and Rockport, an hour north of Boston, have mid-priced B&Bs and are accessible by the MBTA commuter rail – contact the **North of Boston Convention and Visitors Bureau** for details.

Recommended Hotels

The accommodations featured in this guide have been selected for their excellent facilities, outstanding location, and good value. These hotels run the gamut across all environments, from small, family-owned B&Bs and hotels catering to Business executives to Historic hotels. While there are enough Value options to choose from, Luxury choices also abound, offering the best in service and amenities. For the best of the best, look out for hotels highlighted as "DK Choice". These establishments stand out for an exceptional feature, be it a stunning location, notable history, or an inviting atmosphere.

DIRECTORY

Bed and Breakfast Agencies

Bed & Breakfast Agency of Boston
Tel (617) 720-3540.
or (800) 248-9262.
w boston-bnbagency.com

Bed and Breakfast Associates Bay Colony, Ltd.
Tel (617) 720-0522.
or (888) 486-6018.
w bnbboston.com

Boston Homestay, Inc.
w bostonhomestay.com

Disabled Travelers

Massachusetts Network of Information Providers for People with Disabilities
Tel (800) 642-0249.
TTY (for people who cannot hear).
Tel (800) 764-0200.
w disabilityinfo.org

Budget Options

airbnb
w airbnb.com

Hostelling International's Boston Hostel (HI-Boston)
19 Stuart St.
Map 1 C5
Tel (617) 536-9455.
w bostonhostel.org

North of Boston Convention and Visitors Bureau
17 Peabody Sq, Peabody, MA 01960.
Tel (978) 977-7760.
w northofboston.org

Where to Stay

Business

Back Bay and South End

Copley Square Hotel $$$
47 Huntington Ave, 02116
Tel *(617) 536-9000* **Map** 3 C5
Ⓦ copleysquarehotel.com
Modern, comfortable rooms and premier service. Centrally located. Trendy on-site restaurant.

Loews Boston Hotel $$$
350 Stuart St, 02116
Tel *(617) 266-7200* **Map** 4 D2
Ⓦ loewshotels.com
Chic, well-appointed rooms with contemporary atmosphere. Ideal for tourists and shoppers.

Sheraton Boston Hotel $$$
39 Dalton St, 02199
Tel *(617) 236-2000* **Map** 3 B3
Ⓦ sheratonbostonhotel.com
Conveniently located modern hotel provides comforts of home while catering to business needs.

Westin Copley Place $$$
10 Huntington Ave, 02116
Tel *(617) 262-9600* **Map** 3 C3
Ⓦ westincopleyplaceboston.com
Comfortable, well-furnished rooms. Linked to the Hynes Convention Center via a skybridge.

Beacon Hill and West End

The Boxer Boston $$$
107 Merrimac St, 02109
Tel *(617) 624-0202* **Map** 1 C2
Ⓦ theboxerboston.com
Contemporary rooms with large beds, big Beaux-Arts windows and modern technology.

Well-stocked bar in the Ruby Room at the Revere Hotel in Theater District

Onyx Hotel $$$
155 Portland St, 02114
Tel *(617) 557-9955* **Map** 1 C2
Ⓦ onyxhotel.com
Stylish place with modest-sized rooms and warm decor. Morning car service to the Financial District.

Wyndham Boston Beacon Hill $$$
5 Blossom St, 02114
Tel *(617) 742-7630* **Map** 1 B3
Ⓦ wyndham.com
Pleasant rooms featuring modern amenities. Well-equipped fitness center. Close to area attractions.

Chinatown and the Theater District

DoubleTree by Hilton $$$
821 Washington St, 02111
Tel *(617) 956-7900* **Map** 4 E2
Ⓦ doubletree3.hilton.com
Spacious rooms with meticulous decor and modern comforts. Warm, attentive service.

Revere Hotel $$$
200 Stuart St, 02116
Tel *(617) 482-1800* **Map** 4 D2
Ⓦ reverehotel.com
Luxurious property in a prime location. Lounge and restaurant are both popular. Well-furnished rooms with many additional perks.

W Boston $$$
100 Stuart St, 02116
Tel *(617) 261-8700* **Map** 4 E2
Ⓦ starwoodhotels.com
Trendy place with well-appointed rooms. Restaurant and lobby bar are popular hangouts.

Farther Afield

Hotel Marlowe $$$
25 Edwin H. Land Blvd, Cambridge, 02141
Tel *(617) 868-8000* **Map** 1 A2
Ⓦ hotelmarlowe.com
Modern and lavish rooms. Complimentary evening wine reception by the lobby fireplace. Steps away from Charles River.

North End and the Waterfront

Renaissance Boston Waterfront $$$
606 Congress St, 02210
Tel *(617) 338-4111*
Ⓦ marriott.com
Waterfront place offering well-appointed rooms with stunning views. Exceptional service.

Seaport Boston Hotel $$$
1 Seaport Lane, 02210
Tel *(617) 385-4000*
Ⓦ seaportboston.com
Modern place connected to the World Trade Center. Regular shuttles offer access to other areas.

Westin Boston Waterfront $$$
425 Summer St, 02210
Tel *(617) 532-4600*
Ⓦ starwoodhotels.com
Rooms featuring all modern conveniences. Several restaurant options on site.

Old Boston and the Financial District

Club Quarters $$
161 Devonshire St, 02110
Tel *(617) 357-6400* **Map** 2 D4
Ⓦ clubquarters.com
Conveniently located near Faneuil Hall. Full-service accommodations offered in a club-like atmosphere. Complimentary services.

DK Choice

Hilton Boston Downtown/ Faneuil Hall $$$
89 Broad St, 02110
Tel *(617) 556-0006* **Map** 2 E4
Ⓦ hiltonbostondowntown.com
Located in the financial district, this Art Deco hotel is popular with business executives. It also caters to families as Faneuil Hall, Quincy Market, and the North End are all a short stroll away. Rooms are spacious and have all modern amenities. The welcoming restaurant/lounge and library are ideal spots for closing deals as well as social meetings.

Historic

Back Bay and South End

Commonwealth Court Guest House $
284 Commonwealth Ave, 02116
Tel *(617) 424-1230* **Map** 3 B2
Ⓦ commonwealthcourt.com
This former private residence often rents rooms, each with a kitchenette, by the week or month.

Newbury Guest House $$
261 Newbury St, 02116
Tel *(617) 670-6000* **Map** 3 B2
W newburyguesthouse.com
Formerly a row of several houses, this place offers cozy rooms with eclectic furnishings. Good value.

The Eliot Hotel $$$
370 Commonwealth Ave, 02215
Tel *(617) 267-1607* **Map** 3 A3
W eliothotel.com
Late 19th-century landmark with spacious suites and deluxe amenities. Exceptional service.

Fairmont Copley Plaza Hotel $$$
138 St James Ave, 02116
Tel *(617) 267-5300* **Map** 3 C2
W fairmont.com
This 1912 landmark has opulent public areas, tastefully appointed rooms, and grand suites.

hotel140 $$$
140 Clarendon St, 02116
Tel *(617) 585-5600* **Map** 3 C3
W hotel140.com
The country's first YWCA stylishly refurbished as a buget option with trendy, minimalist decor.

Lenox Hotel $$$
61 Exeter St, 02116
Tel *(617) 536-5300* **Map** 3 B2
W lenoxhotel.com
Family-run place with intimate, European-style rooms, some with fireplaces. Multiple dining options.

Chinatown and the Theater District

Boston Park Plaza $
64 Arlington St, 02116
Tel *(617) 426-2000* **Map** 4 D2
W bostonparkplaza.com
Boston's largest historic lodging option with an elegant lobby and comfortable rooms.

Farther Afield

Mary Prentiss Inn $$
6 Prentiss St, Cambridge, 02140
Tel *(617) 661-2929*
W maryprentissinn.com
Greek Revival mansion boasting rooms with period furniture and antiques. Wood-burning fireplaces are featured in some rooms. Beautiful terrace.

Sheraton Commander $$$
16 Garden St, Cambridge, 02138
Tel *(617) 547-4800*
W sheratoncommander.com
A Cambridge Common landmark built in 1927. Rooms are small but comfortable and have luxurious amenities. Complimentary breakfast and evening *hors d'oeuvres*.

Plush interiors of a suite at The Eliot Hotel in Back Bay

North End and the Waterfront

Boston Harbor Hotel $$$
70 Rowes Wharf, 02110
Tel *(617) 439-7000* **Map** 2 E4
W bhh.com
Elegant hotel with deluxe rooms boasting harbor or skyline views. Known for the winter wine festival.

Old Boston and the Financial District

DK Choice

Omni Parker House $$$
60 School St, 02108
Tel *(617) 227-8600* **Map** 1 C4
W omniparkerhouse.com
America's oldest continuously-operating luxury hotel (c. 1855), Omni Parker House serves as an ideal base for guests looking to soak in Boston's historical sites. The hotel sits along the Freedom Trail, across the street from Beacon Hill. Guests can sample Parker House rolls and Boston creme pie, both invented here at the hotel's restaurant.

Inn/B&B
Back Bay and South End

463 Beacon Street Guest House $$
463 Beacon St, 02116
Tel *(617) 536-1302* **Map** 3 A2
W 463beacon.com
This handsome brownstone house offers affordable studio rooms with cooking facilities.

Chandler Inn Hotel $$
26 Chandler St, 02116
Tel *(617) 482-3450* **Map** 4 D3
W chandlerinn.com
This affordable hotel has simple, tastefully decorated and comfortable rooms. Friendly, homey feel.

Beacon Hill and West End

DK Choice

John Jeffries House $
14 David G Mugar Way, 02114
Tel *(617) 367-1866* **Map** 1 B3
W johnjeffrieshouse.com
Former nurses' quarters dating back to 1909. The hardwood floors, original moldings, and traditional furnishings give it a cozy town house feel. The handy location provides an ideal base for those looking to explore the gorgeous neighborhood and key historical sites that are within walking distance.

Farther Afield

A Friendly Inn $
1673 Cambridge St, Cambridge, 02138
Tel *(617) 547-7851*
W afinow.com
Just steps from Harvard Square, this Queen Anne-style house has large rooms. Friendly service.

Beech Tree Inn $
83 Longwood Ave, Brookline, 02446
Tel *(617) 277-1620*
W thebeechtreeinn.com
Victorian-style home boasting rooms with private baths. Has a parlor where guests can mingle.

Yun's Place $
66 Hopedale St, Allston, 02134
Tel *(617) 987-2085*
W yunsplace.com
Comfortable rooms in a quaint Victorian home. Friendly innkeepers. Near Cambridge attractions.

Irving House $$
24 Irving St, Cambridge, 02138
Tel *(617) 547-4600*
W irvinghouse.com
A favorite of visiting scholars, this B&B is tucked away in a quiet, leafy area, next to Harvard University.

For more information on types of hotels *see page 133*

Isaac Harding House $$
288 Harvard St, Cambridge, 02138
Tel *(617) 876-2888*
W harding-house.com
This 1860s Victorian home in a quiet neighborhood. Has spacious, comfortable rooms.

Oasis Guest House & Adams Bed & Breakfast $$
22 Edgerly Road, 02115
Tel *(617) 267-2262* **Map** 3 A3
W oasisguesthouse.com
Three adjacent townhouses near the Berklee College of Music. Great location and bargain rates.

Green Turtle Floating Bed and Breakfast $$$
1 Pier 8, Charlestown, 02129
Tel *(617) 337-0202*
W greenturtlebb.com
Unique option offering rooms on three yachts. Boasts expansive views of the Boston Harbor skyline.

North End and the Waterfront

Bricco Suites $$
241 Hanover St, 02113
Tel *(617) 523-9020* **Map** 2 E2
W briccosuites.com
Studios and one- to two-bedroom apartments in Little Italy offer contemporary style and comfort.

Luxury

Back Bay and South End

The Inn at St Botolph $$
99 Saint Botolph St, 02116
Tel *(617) 236-8099* **Map** 3 B3
W innatstbotolph.com
Cozy rooms with contemporary decor and traditional touches.

Mandarin Oriental, Boston $$$
776 Boylston St, 02199
Tel *(617) 535-8888* **Map** 3 B2
W mandarinoriental.com
Enjoy true luxury in large rooms with state-of-the-art electronics. Full spa and dining options on site.

DK Choice

Taj Boston Hotel $$$
15 Arlington St, 02116
Tel *(617) 536-5700* **Map** 1 A5
W tajhotels.com
Opened in 1927 as the original Ritz-Carlton, this is one of New England's most inviting hotels. The scenic location ensures that most attractions are within walking distance. This grand dame epitomizes opulence and "old Boston" style.

Sweeping city views from the rooftop restaurant at Taj Boston, Back Bay

The Colonnade Hotel $$$
120 Huntington Ave, 02116
Tel *(617) 424-7000* **Map** 3 B3
W colonnadehotel.com
Large rooms with modern comforts. Outdoor rooftop pool.

Beacon Hill and West End

Beacon Hill Hotel & Bistro $$
25 Charles St, 02114
Tel *(617) 723-7575* **Map** 1 B4
W beaconhillhotel.com
Renovated town house with small, Euro-chic rooms. Private roofdeck.

Liberty Hotel $$$
215 Charles St, 02114
Tel *(617) 224-4000* **Map** 1 B3
W libertyhotel.com
Deluxe hotel in a former jailhouse with beautiful architecture. Offers bicycle rentals and yoga classes.

Chinatown and the Theater District

Four Seasons Hotel Boston $$$
200 Boylston St, 02116
Tel *(617) 338-4400* **Map** 1 B5
W fourseasons.com
Afternoon tea, children's activities, and other amenities make for a great stay at this luxurious hotel.

Ritz-Carlton Boston Common $$$
10 Avery St, 02111
Tel *(617) 574-7100* **Map** 1 C5
W ritzcarlton.com
Located on the upper levels of the tallest Downtown building. Classy rooms with post-modern decor.

Farther Afield

The Charles Hotel $$$
1 Bennett St, 02138
Tel *(617) 864-1200*
W charleshotel.com
Modern decor. Outstanding jazz club and top-notch restaurant.

Hotel Commonwealth $$$
500 Commonwealth Ave, 02215
Tel *(617) 933-5000*
W hotelcommonwealth.com
Modern property offers gracious hospitality close to historical sites.

The Hotel Veritas $$$
1 Remington St, Cambridge, 02138
Tel *(617) 520-5000*
W thehotelveritas.com
Intimate, modern rooms. Cozy lounge serves cocktails. Ideal for visitors focusing on Cambridge.

Hyatt Regency Boston Harbor $$$
101 Harborside Dr, 02128
Tel *(617) 568-1234*
W bostonharbor.hyatt.com
Giant glass wall facing the harbor maximizes water views. Rooms are spacious and comfortable. Water shuttle to the nearby docks.

Le Méridien Cambridge-MIT $$$
20 Sidney St, Cambridge, 02139
Tel *(617) 577-0200*
W starwoodhotels.com
A favorite of investors, scientists, and academics visiting MIT. Ideal for exploring Central Square's famous restaurants.

North End and the Waterfront

Battery Wharf $$$
3 Battery Wharf, 02109
Tel *(617) 994-9000* **Map** 2 E2
W batterywharfhotelboston.com
Swanky hotel on a quiet waterfront. Many of the elegant rooms have stunning harbor views. Sophisticated service.

InterContinental Boston $$$
510 Atlantic Ave, 02210
Tel *(617) 747-1000* **Map** 2 D5
W intercontinentalboston.com
Posh rooms with superb harbor views. Luxurious service. Also offers extensive business amenities.

Key to Price Guide *see page 134*

Old Boston and the Financial District

Ames Hotel $$$
1 Court St, 02108
Tel *(617) 979-8100* **Map** 2 D3
w ameshotel.com
Old world architecture meets modern style at this luxury option in a prime location.

Langham Boston Hotel $$$
250 Franklin St, 02110
Tel *(617) 451-1900* **Map** 2 D4
w langhamboston.com
Art Nouveau building with 19th-century French decor. Spacious rooms with deluxe amenities.

Millennium Bostonian $$$
26 North St, 02109
Tel *(617) 523-3600* **Map** 2 D3
w millenniumhotels.com
Upscale accommodations near Faneuil Hall Marketplace. Elegant rooms range in size. There is a gas-burning fireplace in the lobby.

XV Beacon $$$
15 Beacon St, 02108
Tel *(617) 670-1500* **Map** 1 C4
w xvbeacon.com
Designer decor and attentive service. Chic but cozy rooms feature high-tech extras. Popular with business execs.

Value

Back Bay and South End

Midtown Hotel $
220 Huntington Ave, 02115
Tel *(617) 262-1000* **Map** 3 B4
w midtownhotel.com
This 1960s-style motor inn boasts simple style, great value, and secure parking. The connecting rooms are perfect for big families.

Charlesmark Hotel $$
655 Boylston St, 02116
Tel *(617) 247-1212* **Map** 3 C2
w charlesmarkhotel.com
Contemporary, European-style hotel set in an 1892 town house. Rooms feature custom-made furniture and Italian tiles.

Beacon Hill and West End

Friend Street Hostel $
234 Friend St, 02114
Tel *(617) 248-8971* **Map** 1 C2
w friendstreethostel.com
Clean and inexpensive dormitory-style accommodations close to all area attractions. Rooms have many amenities. Friendly atmosphere.

Holiday Inn Express Hotel & Suites Boston Garden $$$
280 Friend St, 02114
Tel *(617) 720-5544* **Map** 1 C2
w hiexboston.com
Modern accommodations located across the TD Banknorth Garden and just a few minutes walk away from area attractions. Complimentary hot breakfasts.

Chinatown and the Theater District

Courtyard Boston Downtown $$
275 Tremont St, 02116
Tel *(617) 426-1400* **Map** 4 E2
w marriott.com
Designed in a dramatic style, this Marriott property has crystal chandeliers and marble columns. Rooms feature modern amenities with a 1920s allure.

Farther Afield

DK Choice

Constitution Inn $
150 Third Ave, Charlestown, 02129
Tel *(617) 241-8400*
w constitutioninn.org
Conveniently located in the historic Charlestown Navy Yard, the Constitution Inn offers clean, comfortable rooms, some of which have attached kitchenettes. Guests enjoy standard amenities such as Wi-Fi, cable TV, along with use of a pool and a fitness center. The property sits on the Freedom Trail, just a short stroll to key sites such as the U.S.S. *Constitution* and the Bunker Hill Monument.

Days Hotel Boston $
1234 Soldiers Field Rd, 02135
Tel *(617) 254-1234*
w daysinn.com
Clean and basic accommodations on the Charles River. Rooms boast attractive water views. Just a short ride away from Harvard Square.

enVision Hotel Boston $$
81 South Huntington Ave, Jamaica Plain, 02130
Tel *(617) 383-5229*
w envision-hotel-boston.com
Upscale decor, local historic architecture, modern style, comfortable rooms and personal service make this a great option to stay. Evening receptions feature regional appetizers and desserts.

Harvard Square Hotel $$
110 Mt. Auburn St, Cambridge, 02138
Tel *(617) 864-5200*
w harvardsquarehotel.com
Former motor inn offers modern, sophisticated rooms. Friendly service. Excellent location in the midst of Harvard Square.

Holiday Inn Express Hotel & Suites Boston - Cambridge $$
250 Monsignor O'Brien Hwy, Cambridge, 02141
Tel *(617) 577-7600*
w hiecambridge.com
Dependable roadside option, just a short walk to the nearest transportation.

Hotel Indigo Boston-Newton Riverside $$
339 Grove St, Newton, 02462
Tel *(617) 454-3399*
w newtonboutiquehotel.com
Eco-friendly, state-of-the-art rooms. Decor changes seasonally. Outdoor pool has private cabanas. Popular on-site restaurant.

Kendall Hotel $$$
350 Main St, Cambridge, 02142
Tel *(617) 577-1300*
w kendallhotel.com
A century-old firehouse converted by an artist-architect duo. Offers spacious rooms. Decor includes firehouse memorabilia and antiques.

Old Boston and the Financial District

Harborside Inn $$
185 State St, 02109
Tel *(617) 723-7500* **Map** 2 E3
w harborsideinnboston.com
Modest property in an old spice warehouse. Rooms have wooden floors, exposed brick walls, oriental rugs, and traditional furnishings.

Luxurious studio appointed with all modern comforts at XV Beacon Hotel

For more information on types of hotels *see page 133*

WHERE TO EAT AND DRINK

For a number of years, Boston had a reputation of serving stodgy, old New England fare. Today, however, this is no longer the case, as the city now has a wide variety of exciting places to eat. Along with more traditional cuisine, Boston restaurants show many diverse influences, with dynamic immigrant restaurateurs and innovative chefs transforming the local restaurant culture. Celebrated chefs also bring classic Boston cuisine to life for modern palates, and eateries all over the city delight in using fresh New England produce to create their innovative dishes. The top restaurants serve a medley of styles, such as French and Italian, often using other Mediterranean and Asian accents. For other flavors of the world, Boston has many Indian, Southeast Asian, Latin American, Caribbean, Chinese, and Japanese restaurants, which are located in small neighborhoods and fashionable streets alike. Boston has an excellent selection of cafés and bars as well.

The old-world elegance of the dining room at Grill 23 *(see p147)*

Eating the Bostonian Way

If your lodgings do not include breakfast, you can join locals on their way to work and have a bagel and a cup of steaming coffee in one of the city's many delis and coffee bars. Most places also offer pastries, muffins, coffee cake, tea, and fruit juices. Diners offer richer, more substantial breakfasts of bacon, eggs, potatoes, and toast, with a "bottomless" cup of coffee – one with free refills.

Lunches in Boston may also be a simple sandwich or a larger meal in a restaurant, depending on how much time travelers have, and how hungry they are. Business districts abound with lunch options – join office workers at a lunch counter in Downtown for a "sub" or a grinder (long rolls stuffed with meat).

Dinner is the biggest meal of the day for Bostonians. Many of the most exclusive and elegant restaurants are in the Financial District and Downtown. Those in Back Bay, North End and South End tend to be trendy and youthful, while eateries in Cambridge are generally more relaxed. The websites **bostonchefs.com** and **boston.menupages.com** are useful for menus and prices.

Opening Hours

The types of meals served at many restaurants vary according to the establishment and its location. Many downtown restaurants are open only for breakfast and lunch, while some finer restaurants are open only for dinner. Some restaurants close for a few hours between lunch and dinner, while smaller family-run places may stay open throughout the afternoon, making them a good bet for eating at more unusual times. Generally, lunch is served from 11:30am to 2:30pm, and dinner from 5:30 to 10:30pm. Massachusetts state law prohibits the sale of alcohol, including beer and wine, after 2am, so bars and most restaurants will close by then. There are some very late night restaurants in Chinatown and Kenmore Square, supported mostly by the ravenous crowds leaving dance clubs and bars. On Sundays, restaurants begin serving alcohol at noon. Cocktails at brunch are very popular, especially in the South End.

Paying and Tipping

Most restaurants with table service will bring diners their bill at the end of the meal. The bill will have a 7 per cent state and local meals tax added to the total. All restaurants with table service expect diners to tip their waiter, who is paid a very low rate with the expectation that tips will fill out their salary. The standard tip is 15–20 per cent of the pre-tax bill. If service is especially good or bad, adjust the tip accordingly. If paying by credit card, guests may include the tip in the charged amount. Fast food restaurants may have optional tip jars next to the cashier.

The Barking Crab restaurant, near downtown Boston *(see p144)*

The well-stocked bar at The Oceanaire Seafood Room, a restaurant in Boston *(see p144)*

Booking

Finer restaurants often require a reservation, although in most cases (especially on weeknights) this can be made at short notice. There are a few very popular places that do not accept reservations, and guests must put their names on the waiting list. The host will tell guests how long they can expect to wait.

Alcohol and Smoking

The tide has turned in favor of non-smokers throughout Greater Boston, with complete bans on indoor smoking in public places including restaurants and bars. Outdoor smoking is also prohibited at playgrounds and other posted areas.

Twenty-one is the legal drinking age, so under-age travelers should be aware that they will be denied access to most bars. They will not be able to order wine with dinner in restaurants, either. If there is any doubt that a person is old enough, proof will be required, so use I.D. or passport if asked.

Etiquette

Bostonians tend to dress casually when dining out. Restaurants that enforce dress codes usually require a reservation, so ask when booking. For the top dining rooms, a jacket and tie for men is expected. Ladies may wear slacks, although skirts or dresses are more traditional. Formal evening wear is uncommon, but not out of place in the finer restaurants.

Children

Children are welcome in most mid-range restaurants, although in the business areas, restaurants are often less accustomed to them. Avoid restaurants that have a large bar and young crowds, as they are less likely to permit under-21s on the premises.

Disabilities

A number of restaurants in Boston and Cambridge are accessible by wheelchair, and many are accessible to people with other disabilities. Doors may be fitted with an automatic opener, and restrooms usually include the appropriate stalls and sinks.

Fast Food

Being a college city, Boston is teeming with fast food options. Sandwiches come in infinite varieties – the classic sandwich being found along with "wraps" (fillings wrapped up in a flatbread), "grinders", and gourmet sandwiches on baguette or focaccia. Pizza is another ubiquitous meal, and bagels, spread with cream cheese, are a popular snack eaten on the go. Burritos are hearty portable meals of meat, beans, and cheese rolled into a flour tortilla. Downtown and Harvard Square are good places for fast food, with their many lunch counters catering to business people. These are reliable and easy on the wallet.

Recommended Restaurants

The restaurants featured in this guide have been selected across a wide price range for their value, good food, atmosphere, and location. These restaurants range from no-frills seafood shacks to pricey temples of gastronomy. Many venues often host private events or close unexpectedly due to any number of issues, so it's always wise to consult a restaurant's website or call before visiting.

For the best of the best, look out for restaurants featured as "DK Choice". These establishments have been highlighted in recognition of an exceptional feature – a celebrity chef, exquisite food, or an inviting atmosphere. Since most of these are very popular among local residents and visitors alike, it is advisable to inquire about reservations to avoid facing a lengthy wait for a table.

Enjoying a beer outside at one of Quincy Market's bars

The Flavors of Boston

Geography and history have given New England some fine and highly distinctive culinary traditions. Its long coastline accounts for the region's abundance of superb seafood. Early settlers brought dishes from England, such as boiled dinners and puddings, that remain popular to this day, as do a range of staples introduced to them by Native Americans, such as corn, maple syrup, and cranberries. The ethnic make-up of Boston has also led to some surprising culinary highlights. Thanks to a large Italian community, Boston boasts some of the best and most authentic pizza in America, and the large Irish population ensures there are plenty of hearty Irish dishes to enjoy.

New England apples

Lobster meal at one of Boston's seafood restaurants

Gifts from the Sea

Seafood is king in New England. The cold waters along the coast yield a bounty of delicious fish such as scrod (young cod), haddock, and swordfish. Lobster is a particularly coveted delicacy. Tanks of live lobsters are shipped to restaurants all around America, but nowhere are they as succulent and sweet as they are in their home region. Several of Boston's best restaurants serve mouth-watering lobster dishes, where diners can pick their own freshly-caught lobster from a tank, then sit back and relax while it is steamed or boiled, according to their wishes. Lobster dishes are usually served up with an accompaniment of melted butter for dipping the meat into and cups of clear, steaming seafood broth.

The Mighty Clam

No food is more ubiquitous in New England than clams. They are served in so many different ways: steamed, stuffed, baked, minced in fish cakes or in the famous New England clam chowder. Large hard-shelled quahog clams are often stuffed and baked for a dish known in nearby Rhode Island as a "stuffie." Clam chowder styles show

Corn on the cob   Baked potato   Steamed clams   Melted butter   Boiled lobster

A typical New England clambake dinner

Local Dishes and Specialties

Like most Americans, New Englanders tend to have a light lunch and their main meal in the evening. Perhaps because of the cold winters, breakfasts are hearty. Some New England dining experiences are too good to miss. At least one breakfast should include wild blueberry pancakes or muffins, and another an omelette made with tangy Vermont cheddar. Other musts are a lunch of lobster roll (chunks of sweet lobster meat in a mayonnaise-based dressing, stuffed into a toasted bun), New England clam chowder, and one of the region's famous clambake dinners. A visit to Boston is hardly complete without sampling the superb local scrod and its rich, classic Boston cream pie, both found on menus all over the city, along with Vermont's favorite ice cream, Ben and Jerry's.

Maple Syrup

Blueberry pancakes Small wild blueberries are stirred into batter to make a stack of these thick pancakes.

Colorful display of pumpkins at a local farmers' market

New American Cuisine

Boston's best chefs are masters of "New American" cuisine, emphasizing the use of the freshest ingredients, in-season fruits and vegetables, and light, healthy sauces. Often dishes have touches of Mediterranean and Asian spices. Seasonal menus include game in winter and fall, and fresh seafood year round. In the growing season, many dishes also feature fresh fruit and berries. To ensure freshness, produce comes from nearby growers. Presentation is important, with dishes planned to please the eye as well as the palate.

considerable regional variation. Boston has a distinctive interpretation of this broth, made with a cream sauce, potatoes, and onions, which makes it much richer than the clear tomato-based version served in Manhattan.

Sweet Offerings

Sugar maples, which bring a dazzling display of color to the hillsides in autumn, yield yet another bonus in late winter. They can then be tapped and their sap boiled down to produce maple syrup. This is served on pancakes and made into candy (sweets) and sauces. New England's vast acres of wild blueberries, along with its many apple orchards and pumpkin fields, also lend themselves to a variety of delectable desserts.

In the 19th century, molasses from the Caribbean was used as a sweetener, and it is still added to many traditional sweet treats, such as Indian pudding, a delicious slow-baked confection of spiced cornmeal, molasses, and milk.

Freshly picked wild blueberries, from the bumper summer harvest

WHAT TO DRINK

Poland Spring water This bottled water from Maine is popular with Bostonians.

Frappé A New England-style milkshake made with ice cream and chocolate syrup.

Westport Rivers wines These are always a favorite at the annual Boston wine festivals.

Samuel Adams and Harpoon beers New England's best known brands have roots in Boston.

Micro-brewery beers Sample Boston Beer Works' "Boston Red," named after the city's Red Sox baseball team, or any one of the English-style pale ales made by Tremont Brewery.

Baked scrod Fillets of young cod (scrod) are rolled in breadcrumbs, baked, and then served with tartare sauce.

New England clam chowder Fresh clams, either left whole or chopped, and chunks of potato fill this creamy soup.

Boston cream pie Layers of sponge cake, sandwiched with egg custard, are topped with chocolate icing.

Where to Eat and Drink

Beacon Hill and West End

Anna's Taqueria $
Mexican   **Map** 1 B3
242 Cambridge St, 02114
Tel *(617) 227-8822*
Cafeteria-style chain serving
Mexican-American burritos.
Popular among students and the
surrounding medical community.
Al pastor (spit-grilled meat) and
carnitas (shredded fried or roasted
pork) are favorites. No alcohol.

Panificio $
Italian   **Map** 1 B3
144 Charles St, 02114
Tel *(617) 227-4340*
Much sought after bakery
specializing in rustic Italian
breads, pastries, and coffee
drinks. Light meals, soups, and
sandwiches are served all day
long in the friendly dining room.
Brunch is a huge draw. No alcohol.

75 Chestnut $$
American   **Map** 1 B4
75 Chestnut St, 02108
Tel *(617) 227-2175*
Converted town house in a quiet
area offering a welcoming dining
experience. Delicious, upscale
bistro fare includes Nantucket
seafood stew and black truffle
ravioli. The casual bar area is
great for watching sports.

Artú $$
Italian   **Map** 1 B4
89 Charles St, 02114
Tel *(617) 227-9023*
Visit this casual spot for Tuscan
specialties from an exposed
sizzling grill. Juicy roast pork,
seasoned chicken, and grilled

Elegantly laid-out tables at No. 9 Park, an
upscale restaurant in Beacon Hill

veggies are crowd-pullers. Be
prepared for long waits at lunch.
Dinner is quiet and romantic.

Beacon Hill Bistro $$
New American   **Map** 1 B4
25 Charles St, 02114
Tel *(617) 723-1133*
Staples such as pancakes and
homefries are served for breakfast
and lunch in an authentic bistro
setting. Dinner features a New
American spin on French bistro
cuisine, with dishes such as steak-
frites and pan-seared hake. Sample
from the wine list at the bar.

Cheers $$
American   **Map** 1 B4
84 Beacon St, 02108
Tel *(617) 227-9605*
This celebrated bar was the
inspiration for the legendary
1980s TV show of the same name.
Standard bar food such as buffalo
wings, fish-and-chips, and paninis
are on offer. A variety of memorabilia is available for purchase.

Figs $$
Pizza   **Map** 1 B4
42 Charles St, 02114
Tel *(617) 742-3447*
Well-known pizza place in
the heart of Beacon Hill. The
signature pie is topped with
caramelized figs, prosciutto,
and gorgonzola cheese. Baked
pastas are also a crowd puller.
Lively environs.

Grotto $$
Italian   **Map** 1 C3
37 Bowdoin St, 02114
Tel *(617) 227-3434*
Welcoming eatery with a varied
menu of dishes such as home-
made pasta, grilled calamari with
white beans, grilled beef tender-
loin, and crab ravioli. Friendly staff.

Harvard Gardens $$
American   **Map** 1 B3
316 Cambridge St, 02114
Tel *(617) 523-2727*
Attracts a diverse crowd of
diners with an extensive menu
of comfort food served till late.
The handsome bar hosts
a renowned singles scene.

King and I $$
Thai   **Map** 1 B3
145 Charles St, 02114
Tel *(617) 227-3320*
Savory, authentic Thai staples are
served in this small casual eatery.
Vegetarians are well-catered to.
The food can be very spicy.
Takeout is popular.

Lala Rokh $$
Middle Eastern   **Map** 1 B4
97 Mt Vernon St, 02114
Tel *(617) 720-5511*
Authentic Persian cuisine served
in romantic surroundings. Citrus-
based glazes and relishes give
meats a piquant flavor. Decadent
desserts feature dates and nuts.

The Paramount $$
American   **Map** 1 B4
44 Charles St, 02114
Tel *(617) 720-1152*
A comfort-food destination open
since 1937. Pancakes and french
toast are favorites. Dinner features
table service and hearty dishes
such as pasta and noodles. Busiest
during breakfast and lunch, which
are served cafeteria-style.

Tip Tap Room $$
American   **Map** 1 C3
138 Cambridge St, 02114
Tel *(857) 350-3344*
This bar and grill draws
government workers with its
menu of burgers, plus fried
avocado and some gnocchi,
risotto, and steak plates. Good
selection of local craft beers.

Bin 26 Enoteca $$$
Italian   **Map** 1 B4
26 Charles St, 02114
Tel *(617) 723-5939*
Stylish contemporary restaurant
that puts emphasis on its extensive wine list. The menu features
an adventurous take on traditional
Italian food. The *stuzzichini* (small
bites) are impressive. Cocoa pasta
with wild mushrooms is a must-try.

DK Choice

No. 9 Park $$$
French-Italian   **Map** 1 C4
9 Park St, 02108
Tel *(617) 742-9991*
Perhaps the most popular of
celebrity chef Barbara Lynch's
local culinary empire, this chic
restaurant is frequented by
Beacon Hill high flyers. The
inventive fare includes prune-
stuffed gnocchi with *vin santo*
glaze. The hip bar serves
cocktails and a slightly less
expensive, more casual menu.

Lively crowds enjoying beer and pub grub at The Black Rose, Financial District

Scampo $$$
Italian Map 1 B3
215 Charles St, 02114
Tel *(617) 536-2100*
Located within the stylish
Liberty Hotel, this trendy
spot offers a modern Italian-
accented menu. Highlights
include suckling pig, baby
lamb, home-made pastas,
and a range of dishes made
with fresh mozzarella.

Toscano Restaurant $$$
Italian Map 1 B4
47 Charles St, 02114
Tel *(617) 723-4090*
Prestigious Italian restaurant
with interesting upscale versions
of popular pasta dishes. The
beautiful setting and excellent
service add to the romantic
atmosphere. Extensive wine
list boasts many bold labels.

Old Boston and the Financial District

Boloco $
Café Map 2 D4
284 Congress St, 02210
Tel *(617) 284-7488*
Casual area chain known for
an eclectic menu of burritos
and wraps. Fresh, healthy
ingredients attract mostly
locals looking for a quick,
nutritious lunch. No alcohol.

Chacarero $
Deli Map 2 D4
101 Arch St, 02108
Tel *(617) 542-0392*
This no-frills Downtown Crossing
lunch spot is famous for its
authentic Chilean sandwiches
of smoky grilled meat and
flavorful toppings piled onto
spongy fresh bread. Watch
out for the fiery hot sauces.
No alcohol.

Sam LaGrassa's $
Deli/Latin American Map 2 D4
44 Province St, 02108
Tel *(617) 357-6861*
Busy downtown eatery that
creates some of the city's best
sandwiches stuffed with freshly
carved meats. Share a table with
local workers or enjoy your
sandwich on the Boston Common.

Anthem $$
American Map 2 D3
101 South Market St, 02109
Tel *(617) 720-5570*
A greenhouse-like place with wall-
to-wall windows facing Faneuil
Hall. The menu features steak
house grub and wood-grilled
flatbread pizzas. The congenial
setting includes two bar areas.

The Black Rose $$
Irish Map 2 E3
160 State St, 02109
Tel *(617) 742-2286*
Irish bar filled with interesting
bric-a-brac. The extensive
beer list is accompanied by
standard Irish pub grub. Very
crowded on St Patrick's Day
and other Irish festivals.

Durgin Park $$
American Map 2 D3
340 Faneuil Hall Marketplace, 02109
Tel *(617) 227-2038*
Historic spot dating back to 1826.
Family-style seating makes for a
bustling atmosphere. Traditional
dishes include baked beans,
Indian pudding, and grilled
prime rib. Generous portions.

The Kinsale $$
Irish Map 1 C3
2 Center Plaza, 02108
Tel *(617) 742-5577*
Handsome Irish bar and restaurant
with a huge sidewalk patio.
The lengthy menu incorporates
both Irish and American dishes.
Popular hangout for watching

sports, playing trivia, and
enjoying live Irish music.

Sakura-Bana $$
Japanese Map 2 E4
57 Broad St, 02109
Tel *(617) 542-4311*
This sushi house in the Financial
District appeals to those looking
for fresh, affordable maki rolls,
sashimi, and other Japanese
fare. Friendly servers patrol the
simply decorated environs.

DK Choice

Silvertone $$
American Map 1 C4
69 Bromfield St, 02108
Tel *(617) 338-7887*
A subterranean hangout near
Downtown Crossing and the
Boston Common, Silvertone
is a favorite among industry
crowds and foodies looking for
well-prepared American fare.
The rich mac 'n' cheese and
juicy burgers are legendary.
The lively bar area is an ideal
spot for couples or groups,
thanks to an impressive drink
menu, featuring hand-crafted
cocktails and an assortment
of shareable snacks.

Society on High $$
New American Map 1 D4
99 High St, 02110
Tel *(857) 350-4555*
Smart and contemporary, this
bistro in the Financial District
has New England specialties
like fish and chips and clam
chowder, alongside a huge
choice of tapas. The lobster
poached in butter is heavenly.

Union Oyster House $$
Seafood Map 2 D3
41 Union St, 02110
Tel *(617) 227-2750*
One of the oldest restaurants in
America, this place was a favorite
of President Kennedy. The menu
features a bounty of seafood.
Boston scrod and the raw bar are
recommended. Feast on oysters
from around the world.

**Bond Restaurant
and Lounge** $$$
New American Map 2 D4
250 Franklin St, 02110
Tel *(617) 451-1900*
The locavore menu at this
cosmopolitan spot boasts an
array of dishes featuring local
seafood and farm-fresh veggies.
House charcuterie leads into such
entrées as steaks, braised lamb
shank, and diver scallops. The
decor exudes an air of privilege.

For more information on types of restaurants *see page 139*

Mooo...
Steak House　　　$$$
Map 1 C4
15 Beacon St, 02108
Tel *(617) 670-2515*
Unusually named steak house in the chic XV Beacon Hotel. The extensive menu has plenty of options beyond fine steaks and chops. Efficient service.

The Oceanaire Seafood Room　　$$$
Seafood　　　Map 2 D3
40 Court St, 02108
Tel *(617) 742-2277*
Part of a small national chain of upscale fish restaurants, that offers a versatile menu of outstanding seafood, both local and flown in fresh. The setting retains the marble charm of the bank that once occupied the space.

Ruth's Chris Steakhouse　　$$$
Steak House　　　Map 2 D4
45 School St, 02108
Tel *(617) 742-8401*
Prime cuts of beef and rich, sinful sides such as sauteed mushrooms and potatoes au gratin, are served at this restaurant in the old City Hall building. Part of an international chain, Ruth's has an extensive list of high-end wines and a sommelier to guide you through it.

North End and the Waterfront

Ernesto's Pizzeria　　$
Pizza　　　Map 2 D2
69 Salem St, 02113
Tel *(617) 523-1373*
Simple place with plastic seating offering 24 different pizza topping combinations. The signature *mala femina* pie is topped with artichoke hearts, fresh tomatoes, and blue cheese. Delivery available to most Boston hotel rooms.

Pizzeria Regina　　$
Pizza　　　Map 2 D2
11 1/2 Thatcher St, 02113
Tel *(617) 227-0765*
Open since 1926, this is one of the city's best-known pizza spots. Feast on amazing brick-oven pies accompanied by inexpensive wine.

Antico Forno　　$$
Italian　　　Map 2 D2
93 Salem St, 02108
Tel *(617) 723-6733*
Tasty wood-fired pizzas draw in locals and tourists alike to two casual dining rooms with colorful murals and brickwork. Menu also includes home-made pastas. Reserve in advance.

Classy interiors of The Oceanaire Seafood Room, Financial District

Barking Crab　　$$
Seafood　　　Map 2 E5
88 Sleeper St, 02110
Tel *(617) 426-2722*
This vibrant fish shack is at its peak in summer. Choose from exceptionally fresh local seafood such as lobster, clams, haddock, and cod. Lovely skyline views. Outdoor seating.

Dino's Café　　$$
Italian/Deli　　　Map 2 D2
141 Salem St, 02113
Tel *(617) 227-1991*
Tiny, no-frills eatery offering a variety of hearty meals. The huge Italian sandwiches are a favorite with locals. Pasta dishes are also delicious and can serve two. Impeccable service.

Giacomo's Ristorante　　$$
Italian　　　Map 2 E2
355 Hanover St, 02113
Tel *(617) 523-9026*
One of North End's most enduring restaurants, Giacomo's serves classic Italian dishes, including hearty portions of pasta. Casual atmosphere. Cash only.

James Hook & Co.　　$$
Seafood　　　Map 2 E4
440 Atlantic Ave, 02111
Tel *(617) 423-5501*
Located on Fort Point Channel, this seafood market is popular with locals who pop in for freshly cooked lobster, clams, crab, and fish to-go. Superb lobster rolls. No alcohol.

La Famiglia Giorgio　　$$
Italian　　　Map 2 D2
112 Salem St, 02113
Tel *(617) 367-6711*
Known for its generous portions and upbeat ambience, this is a great place for families and couples. Serves pastas, pizzas, and other Italian staples. Coffee and dessert are served – a North End rarity.

Maurizio's Ristorante Italiano　　$$
Italian　　　Map 2 E2
364 Hanover St, 02113
Tel *(617) 367-1123*
Lovely spot with a menu featuring Sardinian dishes and focusing on excellent seafood preparations. Sardinian and Ligurian white wines complement the bold flavors. The hand-made stuffed pastas are a must-try.

Neptune Oyster　　$$
Seafood　　　Map 2 D2
63 Salem St, 02113
Tel *(617) 742-3474*
Expect a wait for a table at this small seafood eatery. Exceptionally fresh raw bar items jockey for attention with expertly prepared dishes. Friendly staff.

Sportello　　$$
Italian　　　Map 2 E5
348 Congress St, 02116
Tel *(617) 737-1234*
Home-made pastas, gourmet soups, grilled paninis, veal sweetbreads, day boat scallops, and elegant decor. The takeout counter has freshly baked breads and imported Italian treats.

State Street Provisions　　$$
New American　　　Map 1 E3
265 State St, 02210
Tel *(617) 863-8363*
This classy bar and bistro at the foot of Long Wharf serves modern comfort fare, from a great house charcuterie and cheese board to inventive pizzas, daily pasta specials, and lobster rolls. The bar can get loud in evenings.

Terramia　　$$
Italian　　　Map 2 D2
98 Salem St, 02113
Tel *(617) 523-3112*
This snug *trattoria* eschews the red-sauce neighborhood heritage in favor of Piedmontese roasted

meats, savory dishes with dark mushrooms and caramelized onions, and Ligurian-style seafood dressed with capers and lemon.

Trade $$
New American   Map 2 E4
540 Atlantic Ave, 02210
Tel (617) 451-1234
Breezy after-work hot spot serving Mediterranean-inspired bites, flatbreads, craft beers, and designer cocktails. Huge windows look out onto the Kennedy Greenway. The bar is popular.

Yankee Lobster Company $$
Seafood
300 Northern Ave, 02210
Tel (617) 345-9799
Simple seafood eatery close to the waterfront. Popular patio area provides a breezy setting to enjoy steamed lobster, fish and chips, and clam chowder.

Bricco $$$
Italian   Map 2 D2
241 Hanover St, 02113
Tel (617) 248-6800
Stylish *trattoria* that is a great spot for socializing over Abruzzo-style pastas or inventive dishes such as steamed mussels with smoked red pepper and braised broccoli rabe. Window tables afford colorful North End views.

Carmen $$$
Italian   Map 2 E2
33 North Sq, 02113
Tel (617) 742-6421
Cozy eatery specializing in small plates – such as mussels and cheeses – with great wine pairings. Fine pastas with classic sauces are also available. Close quarters and seating below street level make for a romantic atmosphere.

Legal Harborside $$$
Seafood
270 Northern Ave, 02210
Tel (617) 477-2900
Legendary local chain serving fresh fish in a waterfront, fine-dining setting. Their clam chowder is unrivaled and the raw clams and oysters are impeccable.

Menton $$$
French/Italian   Map 2 E5
354 Congress St, 02210
Tel (617) 737-0099
The crown jewel of celebrity chef Barbara Lynch's fleet of Boston eateries. Pricey set menus are executed by an expert culinary team. Knowledgeable servers explain the menu's many intricacies and guide patrons through the impressive wine list.

Meritage $$$
New American   Map 2 E4
70 Rowes Wharf, 02110
Tel (617) 439-3995
A superb destination for wine lovers. The varied menu features suggested wine pairings for each dish. Rich desserts and fine cheeses matched to ports and Sauternes provide a great finish.

DK Choice

Prezza $$$
Italian   Map 2 E2
24 Fleet St, 02113
Tel (617) 227-1577
The menu here is based on the cuisine of Abruzzo, in Italy, with handmade pastas and meat and fish dishes cooked on a wood-burning grill. The extensive wine list has the perfect pairings for the hearty Tuscan fare and the desserts are deliciously decadent.

Scopa $$$
Italian   Map 2 E2
319 Hanover St, 02113
Tel (857) 317-2871
Maybe the best handmade pasta in the North End, along with classic starters, boldly roasted meats, and four gourmet pizza options.

Chinatown and the Theater District

Dong Khanh $
Vietnamese   Map 1 C5
81 Harrison Ave, 02111
Tel (617) 426-9410
A favorite among Boston's Vietnamese residents, this homey market bistro offers light noodle soups and classic dishes such as chopped salads, lemongrass chicken, and mixed seafood plates. Good vegetarian choices. No alcohol.

Gourmet Dumpling House $
Chinese   Map 1 C5
52 Beach St, 02111
Tel (617) 338-6223
Simple Chinatown eatery that tempts with authentic hand-made dumplings and other Chinese comfort food such as spicy fish Szechuan, eel noodles, and herbal squid and oxtail soup.

My Thai Vegan Cafe $
Vegan   Map 1 C5
3 Beach St, 02111
Tel (617) 451-2395
Casual Asian eatery specializing in vegetarian and vegan dishes such as curry rice noodles with bean sprouts, ginger tofu, and mango fried rice. Many of the meatless options on the lengthy menu feature imitation proteins. Friendly staff. No alcohol.

Pho Pasteur $
Vietnamese   Map 1 C5
682 Washington St, 02111
Tel (617) 482-7467
Popular restaurant serving steaming bowls of *pho* (Vietnamese noodle soup) and other pan-Asian treats such as wontons, fried rice, and seafood dishes. No alcohol.

Chau Chow City $$
Chinese   Map 4 F2
83 Essex St, 02111
Tel (617) 338-8158
Modern Hong Kong seafood dishes, such as scallops with green beans and macadamia nuts, top the menu on the lower two floors. A third level serves dim sum. The shrimp dumplings are renowned.

East Ocean City $$
Chinese   Map 4 E2
27 Beach St, 02111
Tel (617) 542-2504
Legendary spot where seafood is taken from tanks in front of diners and cooked immediately. Friendly servers help in choosing from the wide-ranging menu.

Casual dining area with an open kitchen at Sportello *(see opposite)*, in Fort Point

For more information on types of restaurants *see page 139*

DK Choice

Jacob Wirth Restaurant $$
German   Map 4 E2
31 Stuart St, 02116
Tel *(617) 338-8586*
Open since 1868, this landmark old-fashioned spot has a welcoming atmosphere and is best known for its bratwurst with *sauerkraut* and potato salad. Walls are lined with historical memorabilia. Friday night piano sing-alongs are enjoyed by lively collegiate groups.

Peach Farm $$
Chinese   Map 4 F2
4 Tyler St, 02111
Tel *(617) 482-1116*
Dine in one of the several rooms that make up this local favorite. Sesame jellyfish, and salt and pepper eel are house specialties. Open till late.

Penang $$
Malaysian   Map 1 C5
685 Washington St, 02111
Tel *(617) 451-6373*
A chiefly Malaysian menu ranging from noodle staples and spicy curry dishes to more contemporary concoctions. Popular with homesick expats.

Shabu-Zen $$
Chinese   Map 4 F2
16 Tyler St, 02111
Tel *(617) 292-8828*
Swirl raw vegetables and slivers of meat and fish in hot broth with accompanying seasonings and choice of noodles at this eatery. Popular for its delectable hot pot.

Taiwan Café $$
Taiwanese   Map 4 F2
34 Oxford St, 02111
Tel *(617) 426-8181*
Locals flock here to dine on Taiwanese comfort food such

as duck tongue, steamed taro, or clay pot meatballs. Lunch specials are a steal. Cash only.

Teatro $$
Italian   Map 1 C5
177 Tremont St, 02111
Tel *(617) 778-6841*
This converted synagogue features a high, arched open kitchen, and a theatrical ambience. Offers a light grill menu and a broad selection of northern Italian seafood and veal dishes. Reserve ahead for pre-theater dining.

Winsor Dim Sum Cafe $$
Chinese   Map 1 C5
10 Tyler St, 02111
Tel *(617) 338-1688*
A much sought-after spot for authentic dim sum. Patrons order from the menu rather than selecting from carts. Be prepared for long queues on weekends.

Bristol Lounge $$$
New American   Map 1 B5
200 Boylston St, 02116
Tel *(617) 351-2037*
Located in the Four Seasons hotel, this all-purpose restaurant is one of the city's best spots for afternoon tea, upscale dining with kids, or a romantic rendezvous. On the menu are seafood dishes, risotto, ravioli, pasta, and chowder.

Doretta Taverna & Raw Bar $$$
Greek   Map 1 B5
79 Park Plaza, 02116
Tel *(617) 422-0008*
This hip spot pays homage to the family recipes of the chef's Greek wife. Small plates *(mezze)* offer savory tastes, while the catch of the day forms the backbone of the entrée menu. Do not miss the lamb shoulder.

Erbaluce $$$
Italian   Map 4 D2
69 Church St, 02116
Tel *(617) 426-6969*

A dish of spicy dry-fried salted squid at Peach Farm, Chinatown

Gourmet regional Italian fare served in style in an attractive, clandestine Bay Village space. A romantic find for a quiet pre-theater dinner. The well-curated wine list features many rare varietals.

Legal Sea Foods $$$
Seafood   Map 1 B5
26 Park Plaza, 02116
Tel *(617) 426-4444*
This local chain is a national leader in setting quality standards for fish. Extensive wine cellar. Popular for Back Bay business lunches and after-dinner drinks.

Troquet $$$
French   Map 1 B5
140 Boylston St, 02116
Tel *(617) 695-9463*
Wine lovers fill the diminutive dining room of this old building facing the Boston Common. The kitchen prepares modern French-inspired dishes, which are perfectly paired with selections from the owner's vast wine collection.

Back Bay and South End

Mike's City Diner $
American   Map 3 C5
1714 Washington St, 02118
Tel *(617) 267-9393*
Eager customers line up early at Mike's for filling, greasy breakfast classics such as corned beef hash and home fries. The menu also features hearty home-made soups and stews, meaty sandwiches and triple-layer burgers. No alcohol.

Trident Booksellers & Café $
Café   Map 3 A3
338 Newbury St, 02115
Tel *(617) 267-8688*
This bookstore café has a huge breakfast menu of home-made

Outside tables shaded by umbrellas at Jacob Wirth Restaurant, Theater District

corned beef hash, burritos, and omelets. A long bar faces the open kitchen. Window tables overlook Newbury Street.

Coppa $$
Italian   **Map** 4 D4
253 Shawmut Ave, 02118
Tel *(617) 391-0902*
Award-winning restauarnt and *enoteca* (wine store) serving small plates of flavorful Italian fare such as *stuzzichini, salumi* (cured meat), *antipasti* (Italian appetizers), pastas, and wood fired pizzas. Well-chosen wine list.

Orinoco $$
Latin American   **Map** 3 C5
477 Shawmut Ave, 02118
Tel *(617) 369-7075*
Enjoy specialties such as *arepas* and plantain-stuffed empanadas while being serenaded with Latin music under the tin ceiling of this 1890s building.

Parish Café $$
Café   **Map** 1 A5
361 Boylston St, 02116
Tel *(617) 247-4777*
Casual bar-restaurant featuring menu items crafted by some of the most famous chefs in Boston. Inventive sandwiches include the delicious lobster salad on pepper brioche. Popular outdoor seating.

Post 390 $$
New American   **Map** 3 C3
406 Stuart St, 02118
Tel *(617) 399-0015*
Handsome urban tavern with two bars and an open kitchen spread over two floors. The extensive menu has upscale dishes such as turkey pot pie and house-smoked barbecue ribs.

Scoozi $$
Italian
580 Commonwealth Ave, 02215
Tel *(617) 536-7777*
Small, casual eatery with a huge sidewalk patio. Students and young international visitors throng the place for delicious sandwiches and other light fare such as tater tots, salads, and crab cakes.

Stephanie's on Newbury $$
American   **Map** 3 B2
190 Newbury St, 02116
Tel *(617) 236-0990*
A local institution known for filling dinner salads and pasta dishes. Signature plates include smoked salmon potato pancakes and meatloaf layered with cheese and caramelized onions. Offers Back Bay's best outdoor seating.

Tapeo $$
Spanish   **Map** 3 B2
266 Newbury St, 02116
Tel *(617) 267-4799*
Authentic tapas bar specializing in small plates. Serves true *jamón serrano* (dry-cured Spanish ham slices), a rarity in the area, plus exquisite dishes such as boneless pheasant breast and garlicky squid.

Tico $$
Latin American   **Map** 1 A5
222 Berkeley St, 02116
Tel *(617) 351-0400*
The menu here features a range of regional dishes such as *ceviches, tostadas,* and tacos. Try the roasted cauliflower with chipotle and crunchy favas. The stylish bar has an impressive list of fine tequilas.

B&G Oysters $$$
Seafood   **Map** 4 D4
550 Tremont St, 02116
Tel *(617) 423-0550*
Subterranean spot for mollusk fans. Features a marble bar and an open kitchen. At least a dozen varieties of oysters are available at any given time. Broad selection of mineral-rich white wines.

Brasserie Jo $$$
French   **Map** 3 B3
120 Huntington Ave, 02116
Tel *(617) 425-3240*
Alsatian eatery serving great meals till late. French beers are available on tap. Menu is replete with classics, from steak-frites to *tarte tatin* (upside down tart). Popular in evening for sharing glasses of the cocktail *kir* and plates of pâté.

Deuxave $$$
New American   **Map** 3 A3
371 Commonwealth Ave, 02115
Tel *(617) 517-5915*
Elegant spot frequented by a chic clientele to relax over cocktails. The chef blends local, seasonal ingredients to create dishes such as pan-seared halibut and lobster gnocchi.

L'Espalier $$$
French   **Map** 3 B3
774 Boylston St, 2138
Tel *(617) 262-3023*
This premier restaurant serves award-winning, modern French cuisine that emphasizes local, artisanal ingredients. Try the butter-poached Maine lobster and cocoa-rubbed venison.

Grill 23 $$$
Steak House   **Map** 4 D2
161 Berkeley St, 02116
Tel *(617) 542-2255*
Serving prime cuts of beef since 1983. The bar offers exquisite martinis and the menu is based on seasonal ingredients. The 900-plus label wine list is considered among the city's best.

Oishii $$$
Japanese   **Map** 4 E4
1166 Washington St, 2116
Tel *(617) 482-8868*
Top-rated spot for gourmet Japanese fare. Fresh ingredients are diced, rolled, and torched into artfully presented platters of sushi and sashimi. Minimalist interior and courteous servers.

Sonsie $$$
Italian/International   **Map** 3 A3
327 Newbury St, 02116
Tel *(617) 351-2500*
This Newbury Street stalwart has open glass doors and outdoor tables in summer. Serves delicious dishes from the French and Italian rivieras, with the occasional Indo-Chinese delight.

Sorellina $$$
Italian   **Map** 3 C3
1 Huntington Ave, 02116
Tel *(617) 412-4600*
The northern Italian menu defines the experience here. The food ranges from the traditional, such as herb-roasted chicken and plain grilled steaks, to the adventurous venison carpaccio with cherries. Impressive designer decor.

Sophisticated Crystal dining room at L'Espalier, a French restaurant on Boylston Street

Top of the Hub $$$
New American **Map** 3 B3
800 Boylston St, 02199
Tel *(617) 536-1775*
Perched atop the regal Prudential Tower, this restaurant boasts the best skyline views in Boston. The menu features New England seafood and savory aged meats. A classy bar and superb service are also a draw.

DK Choice

Toro $$$
Spanish **Map** 3 C5
1704 Washington St, 02118
Tel *(617) 536-4300*
The restaurant is named for the chef-owner's love of Spanish tapas and Japanese sushi and sashimi bars. An assortment of modern tapas includes house-cured meat dishes and imported items such as cripsy pork belly with snails. A preferred date spot among the stylish, well-dressed Bostonians.

Tremont 647 $$$
International **Map** 3 C4
647 Tremont St, 02118
Tel *(617) 266-4600*
Trendy eatery in the heart of the South End. Menu includes international touches as well as smoky meats with bold flavors. *Momos* (Tibetan dumplings) are a signature dish. Weekend pajama brunches bring diners in their sleepwear.

UNI Clio $$$
Japanese **Map** 3 A3
370-A Commonwealth Ave, 02215
Tel *(617) 536-7200*
Celebrity chef Ken Oringer creates a contemporary izakaya at the Eliot Hotel, with innovative sashimi and spectacular seafood. Small plates inspired by global street food are offered late at night on weekends.

Farther Afield

Clover Food Lab $
Vegetarian
1326 Massachusetts Ave, Cambridge, 02138
Fast-food reinvention emphasizes seasonal ingredients, with many vegan options and kid-friendly choices. French fries with fried rosemary and BBQ seitan platters are cult favorites.

Crema Café $
Café
27 Brattle St, Cambridge, 02138
Tel *(617) 876-2700*

This sunny café whips up gourmet coffee drinks, healthy sandwiches, and tasty snacks. Small, split-level space. Most patrons buy food to go, while others eat outside in Harvard Square.

L.A. Burdick Chocolates $
Café
52 Brattle St, Cambridge, 02138
Tel *(617) 491-4340*
Welcoming café run by a gourmet chocolatier in a small space. Indulge in exquisitely crafted chocolates, designer pastries, and the famously thick hot chocolate.

Sofra $
Café
1 Belmont St, Cambridge, 02138
Tel *(617) 661-3161*
Inviting café-bakery on a busy corner churning out modern interpretations of hummus, *tzatziki* (Greek yogurt), *kibbeh* (Greek croquette), and stuffed flatbreads. A small seating area is available, but many opt to take treats to go.

Border Café $$
Mexican
32 Church St, Cambridge, 02138
Tel *(617) 864-6100*
One of Harvard Square's most popular options for inexpensive eats. Tex-Mex favorites such as fajitas and nachos as well as spicy Cajun fare. The margaritas are tasty.

Bronwyn $$
German
255 Washington St, Somerville, 02143
Tel *(617) 776-9900*
Chic upscale eatery offering an exploration of authentic German sausages and beers. Hip, young crowds fill the bustling bar space to hoist steins of imported beers and snack on hearty, soft pretzels.

Cambridge Brewing Company $$
American
1 Kendall Square, Cambridge, 02139
Tel *(617) 494-1994*
Award-winning beers brewed on site and a menu of standard

pub grub attract crowds of local aficionados to this place. The outdoor patio is sought-after in summer. Grab a growler to go.

The Helmand $$
Afghan
143 1st St, Cambridge, 02142
Tel *(617) 492-4646*
One of the country's most famous Afghan restaurants with a stylish dining room. The menu features fiery curries and freshly baked breads. Go for the *aushak* (Afghan stuffed ravioli) and *kaddo* (pumpkin topped with ground meat and yogurt sauce).

Il Casale $$
Italian
50 Leonard St, Belmont, 02462
Tel *(617) 209-4942*
This old fire station houses this delightful eatery that serves homemade pasta dishes as well as wood-grilled meats and fish. Many dishes are from family recipes.

Le's $$
Vietnamese
36 Dunster St, Cambridge, 02138
Tel *(617) 864-4100*
A favored haunt of Harvard students, this congenial restaurant serves steaming bowls of delectable *pho*. A range of other noodle dishes, as well as healthy entrées and rice plates, are also available.

Mr. Bartley's Gourmet Burgers $$
Burgers
1246 Massachusetts Ave, Cambridge, 02138
Tel *(617) 354-6559*
Quintessential burger shop specializing in filling gourmet burgers. Some of the sandwiches are humorosly named after a celebrity or politician. Expect long waits on weekends.

Redbones $$
Barbeque
55 Chester St, Somerville, 02144
Tel *(617) 628-2200*

The eclectic interior of Mr. Bartley's Gourmet Burgers

Popular spot just off the lively Davis Square, known for authentic Southern barbeque. Groups of students and families fill the multiple dining spaces to gorge on platters of expertly prepared meats and down-home sides.

Russell House Tavern $$
New American
14 JFK St, Cambridge, 02138
Tel *(617) 500-3055*
Stylish, all-purpose restaurant and lounge in the heart of Harvard Square. There are two levels for dining and a small alley patio. The varied menu includes designer cocktails, sandwiches, and more substantial bistro fare.

Tanjore $$
Indian
18 Eliot St, Cambridge, 02138
Tel *(617) 868-1900*
Friendly, family-owned spot with a menu featuring dishes ranging from mild *dosas* (crêpe made from fermented rice or black lentil batter) and spicy *vindaloos* (an Indian curry) to *tandoori* dry roasts. Authentic desserts, too.

Temple Bar $$
American/Pub
1688 Massachusetts Ave, Cambridge, 02138
Tel *(617) 547-5055*
Local hangout serving mouth-watering burgers, sandwiches, and gourmet pizzas. The evening menu is more elaborate and features dishes such as seared chicken breast, steak frites, crispy soy roasted lamb and *ceviches*.

Tory Row $$
International
3 Brattle St, Cambridge, 02142
Tel *(617) 876-8769*
This elegant hangout buzzes with students, tourists, and locals. The eclectic menu offers multi-cultural comfort food such as *croque monsieur* (grilled ham and cheese sandwich), baked *raclette* (a Swiss dish of melted cheese), and roasted red pepper hummus.

Tupelo $$
American/Southern
1193 Cambridge St, Cambridge, 02139
Tel *(617) 868-0004*
This Inman Square spot thrills with superb Southern fare with a definite accent of the Gulf Coast and New Orleans. Gumbos include classic chicken and andouille, and an artful vegetarian option playing up the Cajun Trinity. Fried alligator and oysters are choice bar bites.

Veggie Galaxy $$
Vegetarian
450 Massachusetts Ave, Cambridge, 02139
Tel *(617) 497-1513*
Casual, diner-style eatery famous for its healthy vegetarian fare. Savory vegetable burgers and fresh, filling salads are the main draws. Friendly servers patrol the bright environs.

Blue Ginger $$$
Asian Fusion
583 Washington St, Wellesley, 02113
Tel *(781) 283-5790*
Adventurous diners head to this restaurant owned and operated by famous chef Ming Tsai for signature items such as sake-miso marinated Alaskan butterfish and *foie gras-shiitake shumai* (foie gras dumplings with mushrooms).

Café ArtScience $$$
New American
650 Kendall St, Cambridge, 02142
Tel *(857) 999-2193*
Conceived as the intersection of art, food, and design, this high-tech venue in the heart of the robotics/biomed research hub emphasizes intense dishes with French/Italian origins tempered by experimental kitchen techniques.

Catalyst $$$
New American
300 Technology Square, Cambridge, 02139
Tel *(617) 576-3000*
Elegant, high-ceilinged dining area offering several seating options. The modern American fare served here is based on local, sustainable ingredients. A lively bar, eclectic background music, and a busy, open kitchen make this a popular choice with local academics and visitors alike.

DK Choice

Craigie on Main $$$
New American
853 Main St, Cambridge, 02138
Tel *(617) 497-5511*
With its focus on the best local, seasonal, and organic ingredients, this handsome Central Square restaurant remains a favorite with the city's gourmands. The à la carte as well as tasting, and bar menus change daily. Patrons can expect intricate preparations of exotic ingredients like cockscombs, pork belly, and monkfish cheeks.

A beautifully presented dish at Harvest, a high-end restaurant in Cambridge

Harvest $$$
New American
44 Brattle St, Cambridge, 02139
Tel *(617) 868-2255*
Boston's pioneer in the creation of New American cuisine, this dining room has launched three generations of celebrity chefs. The inventive kitchen continues to discover new ways to serve largely local fish, veggies, meat and dairy. The bar and patio are well-known literary haunts.

Josephine Restaurant Parisien $$$
French
468 Commonwealth Ave, 02215
Tel *(617) 375-0699*
Feast on classic bistro fare made by a French master chef. Try the simple takes on classics such as steak-frites, beef Bourguignon, and lemon meringue tart.

Les Zygomates $$$
French
129 South St, 02111
Tel *(617) 542-5108*
A relaxed atmosphere, live jazz, and an extensive selection of wines by the glass complement the French bistro fare at this restaurant. The menu always has a few vegetarian entrées.

Oleana $$$
Mediterranean
134 Hampshire St, Cambridge, 02139
Tel *(617) 661-0506*
The menu here is inspired by cuisines from all sides of the Mediterranean, including Lebanese, Moroccan, and Catalan. Aromatic spices and intense sauces characterize most dishes. There is also a nightly vegetarian tasting menu.

Cafés and Bars

The social fabric of Boston is held together through its abundance of places to meet with friends and while away the hours. With a rich mix of students, working folk, and executives, the city provides a selection of cafés and bars that cater to all tastes, and to people who keep all hours. There are places where you can find a pick-me-up, rest your feet, and meet local people. A further selection of bars is listed on pp162–3.

Cafés

Cafés tend to cluster in a few areas of the city, most notably Harvard Square and its environs, the South End, the North End, and Beacon Hill. **Crema Café**, one of Harvard Square's long line of cafés, serves both hot and iced tea, along with delicious pastries and sandwiches. The oldest of the square's coffee culture joints, the hip **Café Pamplona**, dates back to the Beatnik days. For an especially genteel treat, make your way to **L.A. Burdick Chocolates** and order a sampler plate of their innovative chocolates or one of their superb buttery fruit tarts. They also have some fine teas, including herbals. There are two branches of the **1369 Coffeehouse**, which are spacious, upbeat and frequented by a clientele of all ages, who come mainly for the excellent cookie bars.

The South End's secluded cafés are home to a thriving café society. Many are popular with the vibrant gay community *(see p163)* that has made its home in this neighborhood, but also happily welcome all visitors, regardless of sexual preference. **Berkeley Perk Cafe** is colorful and spacious, with a wide selection of juices, quality sodas, and sweet treats. Pastry chef Joanne Chang's first **Flour Bakery & Café**, in the South End, met with such over-whelming neighborhood support that she opened branches at additional locations in Cambridge. Each location is a surefire venue for artisanal breads, generous sandwiches, and warming soups, as well as fine tarts, cakes, cookies, and breakfast breads.

Cafés cluster around the main thoroughfares of the North End, where many local restaurants do not even bother to serve coffee or dessert because the cafés in this lively Italian neighbor-hood do it so much better – espresso or cappuccino and *tiramisu* or *cannoli* are a must. **Caffè Vittoria**, decorated in marble and chrome, has a wide array of pastries and liqueurs, and its own cigar parlor. **Caffè Pompei** is a more chaotic place, which features murals of its doomed namesake crowding the walls. While many like **Mike's Pastry** for their *cannoli*, it is said that the best are found alongside the nougat at **Maria's Pastry Shop**, which sadly does not have seating. **Lulu's Sweet Shop** is known for its tempting variety of cup-cakes. On Beacon Hill, **Tatte** has a range of exquisite gourmet coffee and inviting pastries.

Tea Rooms

A couple of grand hotels have preserved a genteel tradition of offering afternoon tea: **Bristol Lounge** at the Four Seasons Hotel serves a lovely tea (especially enjoyable if you are seated by the fireplace), while on weekends the **Taj Boston** continues the formal afternoon tea tradition established by its predecessor the Ritz-Carlton, complete with a full Old World service. In the heart of the Boston Public Library, the **Courtyard Restaurant** serves classic tea 11:30am–3:30pm Mon–Sat. More recently, tea has found aficionados among the college-aged crowd, and a number of tea houses designed for the younger and more budget-conscious flourish in the city, especially near college campuses and on Newbury Street. In the heart of Harvard Square, **Tealuxe** lets customers peruse an impressive catalog of hundreds of teas from around the world. Fine Asian teas, with a touch of tranquility and a hint of enlight-enment, are the specialty at **Dado Tea**, which is situated both in and east of Harvard Square in Cambridge.

Ice Cream Parlors

Bostonians eat more ice cream, per person, year round, than just about anyone else in America. They are highly discerning customers, and fiercely loyal to their favorite parlor. Many restaurants make a point of serving one of the locally made ice creams with their dessert menus. When ordering ice cream, you can get it served in a dish with a spoon, or in a cone to lick. You usually get a choice of wafer cone (light, crispy, slightly bland) or a sugar cone (thin, crisp, sweet cookie wafer). Some may decide to order one of the enormous waffle cones, which is really just an over-grown sugar cone custom-made for the truly indulgent. Parlors are open most of the day and late into the evening. In central Boston the best ice creams can be hard to find, but Newbury Street *(see p95)* has some of the most popular options. **Emack & Bolio's** is a long-time favorite for its sinful sundaes featuring homemade fudge. The New England ice cream giant **Ben and Jerry's** has several parlors featuring all their flavors.

If possible, the ice-cream talent in Cambridge is even greater than in Boston. Adult lovers of gourmet ice cream swear by the Burnt Caramel and Earl Grey flavors at **Toscanini's**, in Central Square With the demise of Herrell's, **Lizzy's Ice Cream** has emerged as the new standard bearer of Harvard Square. Try the Charles River Crunch (dark chocolate ice cream with almond toffee nuggets). Competition for most inventive flavors is stiff. For example, **Christina's Homemade Ice Cream** in Inman Square makes the best green tea ice cream in the city, as well as a wide range of other flavors, ranging from the sublime to the simply gooey.

A little farther afield, **Ron's Gourmet Ice Cream and Twentieth Century Bowl** features specialty flavors such as peanut sunrise, as well as a chance to work off some calories on their candlepin bowling lanes.

Bars

The legal drinking age in Boston is 21, and you may be asked to show proof of identification *(see p174)*.

Boston has scores of bars which offer live music and other types of entertainment *(see also pp162–3)*. Those listed here are a good place to relax and simply have a drink, though some of them can still be quite lively.

For good, down-to-earth bars, you cannot go wrong with the youthful **Shay's Pub and Wine Bar**, **The Sevens**, the cheap and cheerful **Beacon Hill Pub**, the well-heeled **21st Amendment**, or the kitschy lounge paradise of **The Good Life**. Parker's Bar at the Omni Parker House Hotel has the atmosphere of a gentleman's club, while around the city are dotted a number of good wine bars, notably **Les Zygomates** and **Troquet**. **Jacob Wirth** *(see p87)*, which is also a restaurant, is situated in the Theater District and has good beer and a lively ambience.

DIRECTORY

Cafés

1369 Coffeehouse
1369 Cambridge St., Cambridge.
Tel (617) 576-1369.
757 Massachusetts Ave.
Tel (617) 576-4600.

Berkeley Perk Cafe
69 Berkeley St.
Map 4 D3.
Tel (617) 426-7375.

Café Pamplona
12 Bow St., Cambridge.
Tel (617) 492-0352.

Caffè Pompei
278 Hanover St.
Map 2 E2.
Tel (617) 227-1562.

Caffè Vittoria
290–296 Hanover St.
Map 2 E2.
Tel (617) 227-7606.

Crema Café
27 Brattle St., Cambridge.
Map 4 D3.
Tel (617) 876-2700.

Flour Bakery & Café
1595 Washington St.
Map 3 C5.
Tel (617) 267-4300.
12 Farnsworth St.
Map 2 E5.
Tel (617) 338-4333.
190 Massachusetts Ave., Cambridge.
Tel (617) 225-2525.
131 Clarendon St.
Map 3 C3.
Tel (617) 437-7700.

L.A. Burdick Chocolates
52 Brattle St., Cambridge.
Tel (617) 491-4340.

Lulu's Sweet Shop
57 Salem St.
Map 2 D2.
Tel (617) 742-0070.

Maria's Pastry Shop
46 Cross St.
Map 2 D3.
Tel (617) 523-1196.

Mike's Pastry
300 Hanover St.
Map 2 E2.
Tel (617) 742-3050.

Tatte
70 Charles St.
Map 1 B2.
Tel (617) 523-9200.

Tea Rooms

Bristol Lounge
200 Boylston St.
Map 4 D2.
Tel (617) 338-4400.

Courtyard Restaurant
Boston Public Library,
700 Boylston St.
Map 3 C2.
Tel (617) 859-2251.

Dado Tea
955 Massachusetts Ave., Cambridge.
Tel (617) 497-9061.
50 Church St., Cambridge.
Tel (617) 547-0950.

Taj Boston
15 Arlington St.
Map 4 D2.
Tel (617) 536-5700.

Tealuxe
Brattle St., Cambridge.
Tel (617) 441-0077.

Ice Cream Parlors

Ben and Jerry's
174 Newbury St.
Map 3 B2.
Tel (617) 536-5456.
20 Park Plaza.
Map 4 D2.
Tel (617) 426-0890.
36 John F. Kennedy St., Cambridge.
Tel (617) 864-2828.

Christina's Homemade Ice Cream
1255 Cambridge St.
Tel (617) 492-7021.

Emack & Bolio's
290 Newbury St.
Map 3 B2.
Tel (617) 536-7127.

Lizzy's Ice Cream
29 Church St., Cambridge.
Tel (617) 354-2911.

Ron's Gourmet Ice Cream and Twentieth Century Bowl
1231 Hyde Park Ave., Hyde Park, MA 02136.
Tel (617) 364-5274.

Toscanini's
899 Main St., Cambridge.
Tel (617) 491-5877.

Bars

21st Amendment
150 Bowdoin St.
Map 1 C3.
Tel (617) 227-7100.

Beacon Hill Pub
149 Charles St.
Map 1 B3.
Tel (617) 625-7100.

The Good Life
28 Kingston St.
Map 2 D5.
Tel (617) 451-2622.

Jacob Wirth
31–37 Stuart St.
Map 4 E2.
Tel (617) 338-8586.

Les Zygomates
129 South St.
Map 4 F2.
Tel (617) 542-5108.

Parker's Bar
60 School St.
Map 2 D4.
Tel (617) 227-8600.

The Sevens
77 Charles St. **Map** 1 B3.
Tel (617) 523-9074.

Shay's Pub and Wine Bar
58 John F. Kennedy St., Cambridge.
Tel (617) 864-9161.

Troquet
140 Boylston St.
Map 4 E2.
Tel (617) 695-9463.

SHOPPING IN BOSTON

Shopping in Boston has evolved dramatically in recent years. Long known as an excellent center for antiques, books, and quality clothing, the city's shopping options now cover a much broader spectrum, influenced both by its booming economy and its large, international student population. From the fashionable boutiques of Newbury Street, to the many stores selling cosmopolitan home furnishings or ethnic treasures, to the varied art and crafts galleries, Boston caters to every shopping need. Whether you are looking for the latest fashion accessory, an unusual antique, or a special souvenir, choices abound to accommodate every sense of style and budget. Boston is no longer simply traditional, and now holds its own in providing a vibrant, eclectic and world-class shopping experience.

Large glass atrium of the busy Prudential Center shopping mall

Sales

There are two major sale seasons in Boston: July, when summer clothes go on sale to make room for fall fashions, and January, when any winter clothing and merchandise is cleared after the holidays. Most stores also have a sale section or clearance rack throughout the year.

Payment and Taxes

Major credit cards and traveler's checks with identification are accepted at most stores. There is a tax of 6.25 per cent on all purchases except groceries and clothing, although any item of clothing over $175 will be taxed.

Opening Hours

Most stores open at 10am and close at 6pm from Monday to Saturday, and from noon to 5 or 6pm on Sunday. Many stores stay open later on Thursday nights, and most department stores stay open until 7:30 or 8pm throughout the week. Weekday mornings are the best times to shop. Saturdays, lunch hours, and evenings can be very busy.

Shopping Malls

Shopping malls – clusters of shops, restaurants, and food courts all within one large and open complex – have become top destinations for shopping, offering variety, dining, and entertainment. With long winters and a fair share of bad weather, New Englanders flock to malls to shop, eat, and, in the case of teenagers, simply hang out.

Farm produce on display on Charles Street

Copley Place, with its elegant restaurants, and more than 75 shops over two levels, is based around a dazzling 60-ft (18-m) atrium and waterfall. Across a pedestrian overpass, **Shops at Prudential Center** encompasses **Saks Fifth Avenue** department store, a food court, and many smaller specialty shops. The **Heritage on the Garden**, a collection of upscale boutiques and luxury retailers, looks out over Boston's Public Garden, and features the boutiques of top European designers, fine jewelers, and stores selling other luxury goods. Outside the center of town, across the Charles River, **CambridgeSide Galleria** has over 100 shops and a pond-side food court. For last-minute purchases, **Boston America**, at Logan Airport (Terminal B), has shops, restaurants, banking, and Internet access.

Department Stores

There are several major department stores in Boston offering a large and varied selection of clothing, accessories, cosmetics, housewares, and gifts. Some also have restaurants and beauty salons, and provide a variety of personal shopping services. At Downtown Crossing (see p84), a bustling shopping district between Boston Common and the Financial District, the primary department store is **Macy's**, a large outpost of the legendary New York emporium, which offers an impressive array of fashions, cosmetics, housewares, and furnishings.

Heading uptown, through Boston Common and Public Garden to Boylston Street, you can spot the Prudential Tower, centerpiece of a once nondescript but now revitalized complex of shops, offices, and restaurants. This includes the venerable and elegant **Saks Fifth Avenue**, which caters to its upscale clientele with renowned service, a luxurious ambiance, and strikingly stylish displays. For a similarly comprehensive and upscale department store, head around the corner to **Lord & Taylor**, which has been filling closets with designer clothes since 1826. For the ultimate high fashion, high profile shopping experience, stop by **Neiman Marcus**, which specializes in haute couture, precious jewelry, furs, and gifts. The store is well known for its Christmas catalog, with presents that have included authentic Egyptian mummies, vintage airplanes, a pair of two-million-dollar diamonds, and robots to help out around the

house – or mansion. Other Copley Place merchants include Jimmy Choo, Christian Dior, Louis Vuitton, and Armani Exchange, as well as Boston's outpost of the popular Manhattan trendsetter, Barney's.

Discount and Outlet Stores

Dedicated bargain hunters may want to consider making a day trip to one of New England's famed outlet centers, where many top designers and major brand manufacturers offer last-season and overstocked clothing and goods at big discounts. Generally sold at 20 to 30 per cent less than their regular retail prices, some items can be found reduced by as much as 75 per cent. Closest to downtown Boston, **Assembly Row** in Somerville has more than 30 outlet shops, including Chico's, Kenneth Cole, and Clarks. This development also has several popular eateries and a cinema. **Wrentham Village Premium Outlets** are about 40 miles (65 km) south of Boston. The stores

Boutiques of genteel Newbury Street

Brattle Book Shop's sign

here sell designer clothing, housewares, and accessories from many of the leading manufacturers.

Kittery, 50 miles (80 km) north of Boston, is an even larger outlet destination, with more than 125 shops selling everything from footwear and designer clothes, to sports equipment, perfume, books, china, glass, and gifts. There are also numerous restaurants.

Freeport, Maine, is one of the largest and most famous outlet centers, being home to the renowned outdoor equipment specialist **L.L. Bean**. Roughly a two hour drive from Boston, it is only worth the journey for the dedicated shopper, or for those already visiting Maine.

DIRECTORY

Shopping Malls

Boston America
Terminal B, Logan International Airport, East Boston.
W massport.com

CambridgeSide Galleria
100 Cambridgeside Pl., Cambridge.
Tel (617) 621-8666.
W cambridgeside galleria.com

Copley Place
100 Huntington Ave.
Map 3 C3.
Tel (617) 262-6600.
W simon.com

Heritage on the Garden
300 Boylston St.
Map 4 D2.
Tel (617) 426-9500.
W theheritageonthe garden.com

Shops at Prudential Center
800 Boylston St.
Map 3 B3.
Tel (800) 746-7778.
W prudentialcenter.com

Department Stores

Lord & Taylor
760 Boylston St. **Map** 3 B2.
Tel (617) 262-6000.

Macy's
450 Washington St.
Map 4 F1.
Tel (617) 357-3000.

Neiman Marcus
5 Copley Place, 100 Huntington Ave. **Map** 3 C3.
Tel (617) 536-3660.

Saks Fifth Avenue
Prudential Center. **Map** 3 B3. **Tel** (617) 262-8500.

Discount and Outlet Stores

Assembly Row
340 Canal St., Somerville.
Tel (617) 440-5565.
W assemblyrow.com

Freeport Outlets
Freeport, Maine.
Tel (207) 865-1212. or (800) 865-1994.
W freeportusa.com

Kittery Outlets
Route 1, Kittery, Maine.
Tel (888) 548-8379.
W thekitteryoutlets.com

L.L. Bean
95 Main St., Freeport, Maine. **Tel** (877) 755-2326.
W llbean.com

Wrentham Village Premium Outlets
1 Premium Outlets Blvd, Wrentham.
Tel (508) 384-0600.
W premiumoutlets.com

Fashion

From chain stores stocked with popular brand labels to specialists selling vintage clothing, Boston offers choices in every area of fashion. Well-heeled shoppers frequent high-fashion boutiques, students flock to vintage emporiums, and businessmen visit both traditional outlets and the many fashionable men's outfitters. In this stylish, international city, many stores feature fine clothes from Italy, France, England, and Japan, along with the more prevalent fashions from top American designers.

Mixed Fashion

Many stores in Boston offer quality clothing for both men and women. In Copley Place, **Barney's New York**, a branch of the world-famous Manhattan fashion icon, offers an extensive range of cutting-edge designer labels.

Nearby on Newbury Street, **Giorgio Armani**, **Riccardi**, and **Burberry** all cater to the well-heeled, who like to browse through their outrageously expensive clothing and accessories. **Alan Bilzerian** attracts celebrities in search of both his own label and the latest avant-garde looks from Europe and Japan. The U.K.-based **AllSaints Spitalfields** combines a trendy, urban look (including motorcycle jackets) with the trappings of luxury, while Canadian company **Kit and Ace** designs clothing that is comfortable, fashionable, loose and easy to wear. Made from easy-care, high-tech fabrics usually reserved for athletic gear, the streetwear is ideal for travelers. In Cambridge, **American Apparel** features casual sports-wear for men and women. **Urban Outfitters** offers an eclectic collection of clothing and accoutrements for the young and trendy, and stocks Kikit, Girbaud, and Esprit. America's favorite chain, **Gap**, has simple styles which remain stylish enough for movie stars, yet affordable for the masses. **Banana Republic** is ideal for those after a sleeker more modern look.

The Swedish retailer **H&M**, which stocks trend-setting fashion for adults and children at affordable prices, has shops both downtown and in Back Bay. The Back Bay store is particularly known for its large selection of accessories. For clothing more suited to the great outdoors, visit **Eastern Mountain Sports**, which sells a range of no-nonsense sporting gear, or **Patagonia**, a mecca for serious climbers, skiers, and sailors, which also carries sophisticated, high-tech sporting equipment.

Visitors don't mind going a little out of the way for huge discounts (up to 70 per cent) on athletic and street shoes and apparel at the **New Balance Factory Outlet** store. The locally based athletic-shoe company stocks virtually every size – short and narrow to long and wide.

Women's Fashion

No woman need leave Boston empty-handed, whether her taste is for the *haute couture* of **Chanel** or the earthy ethnic clothing at **Nomad**. Newbury Street is filled with sumptuous, high-fashion boutiques, including **Kate Spade**, **Betsy Jenney**, and **Max Mara**, Italy's largest and most luxurious ready-to-wear manufacturer for women. Boston was instrumental in introducing the colorful and graphic prints of **Marimekko** to the U.S. in the 1960s, and they are now enjoying a resurgence of popularity. On Boylston Street, **Ann Taylor** is undoubtedly the first choice for refined, modern career clothes, while **Talbots**, a Boston institution, features enduring classics. **Anthropologie** stocks an eclectic mix of exotic and whimsical clothing and accessories from around the world.

In Harvard Square, **Oona's** has been selling vintage clothing for 35 years, while **Mint Julep** offers stylish clothing from U.S. and inter—national designers. **Clothware** features natural-fiber clothes from local designers, and **Settebello** carries elegant European apparel and accessories.

Men's Fashion

Gentlemen seeking a quint-essential New England look need go no farther than **Brooks Brothers** on Newbury Street, longtime purveyors of tradi-tional, high-quality men's and boys' wear.

One of America's foremost fashion house, **Polo/Ralph Lauren** offers top-quality and highly priced sporting and formal attire, while **Jos. A. Bank Clothiers** sells private label merchandise as well as most major brands at discounted prices.

Academics and college students alike head to Cambridge, where the ven-erable **Andover Shop** and **J. Press** provide a selection of Ivy-League essentials of impeccable quality.

Discount and Vintage Clothes

Those who equate Downtown Crossing with bargain hunting and lament the closing of the legendary Boston bargain emporium Filene's Basement should pay a visit to the two discount superstores in the area. Prominent discount chains **Marshalls**, and **T.J. Maxx** sell famous designer brands for less, and also offer superb bargains on clothing, shoes, housewares, and accessories. Both stores are conveniently located in the same building.

Bargain-conscious shoppers and lovers of vintage apparel will enjoy the selection of new and used goods at the **Garment District** in Cambridge. Also in Cambridge, **Keezer's Classic Clothing** has provided generations of Harvard students with everything from used tuxedos to sports jackets and loafers. **Second Time Around**, with consignment shops in both Cambridge and Boston, offers a select array of top-quality, gently worn contemporary clothing for women.

Shoes and Accessories

Many stores in Boston specialize in accessories and footware. **Helen's Leather** on Charles Street is well known for leather jackets, briefcases, purses, shoes, and Birkenstock sandals, as well as its huge selection of Western boots. At Downtown Crossing, **Foot Paths** carries a range of shoes from Timberland, Kenneth Cole, Rockport, and others.

Stylish Spanish shoes and bags are the specialty at **Stuart Weitzman** at Copley Place, while the adventurous will find more fashionable and unusual shoes at **The Tannery** in Cambridge. For sports gear, the large and opulent **Niketown** on Newbury Street shows video re-runs of sports events while shoppers peruse the latest designs in athletic clothing and footwear.

DIRECTORY

Mixed Fashion

Alan Bilzerian
34 Newbury St.
Map 4 D2.
Tel (617) 536-1001.

AllSaints Spitalfields
122 Newbury St.
Map 3 C2.
Tel (617) 517-0894.

American Apparel
47 Brattle St., Cambridge.
Tel (617) 661-2770.

Banana Republic
28 Newbury St.
Map 4 D2.
Tel (617) 267-3933.

Barney's New York
Copley Place. **Map** 3 C3.
Tel (617) 385-3300.

Burberry
2 Newbury St. **Map** 3 C2.
Tel (617) 236-1000.

Eastern Mountain Sports
1 Brattle Sq., Cambridge.
Tel (617) 864-2061.

Gap
Copley Place. **Map** 3 C3.
Tel (617) 247-1754.

Giorgio Armani
22 Newbury St. **Map** 3 C2.
Tel (617) 267-3200.

H&M
350 Washington St.
Map 4 F1.
Tel (617) 482-7081.
100 Newbury St. **Map** 3
C2. **Tel** (617) 859-3192.

Kit and Ace
208 Newbury St.
Map 3 B2.
Tel (844) 548-6223.

New Balance Factory Outlet
173 Market St., Brighton.
Tel (617) 779-7429.

Patagonia
346 Newbury St.
Map 3 A3.
Tel (617) 424-1776.

Riccardi
116 Newbury St. **Map** 3 C2.
Tel (617) 266-3158.

Urban Outfitters
361 Newbury St. **Map** 3 A3.
Tel (617) 236-0088.

Women's Fashion

Ann Taylor
800 Boylston St. **Map** 3 B3.
Tel (617) 421-9097.

Anthropologie
203 Newbury St. **Map** 3 B2.
Tel (617) 262-0545.

Betsy Jenney
114 Newbury St. **Map** 3 C2.
Tel (617) 536-2610.

Chanel
6 Newbury St. **Map** 4 D2.
Tel (617) 859-0055.

Clothware
1773 Massachusetts Ave.,
Cambridge.
Tel (617) 661-6441.

Kate Spade
117 Newbury St. **Map** 3 C2.
Tel (617) 262-2632.

Marimekko
140 Newbury St. **Map** 3 C2.
Tel (617) 247-2500.

Max Mara
69 Newbury St. **Map** 3 C2.
Tel (617) 267-9775.

Mint Julep
6 Church St., Cambridge.
Tel (617) 576-6468.

Nomad
1741 Massachusetts Ave.,
Cambridge.
Tel (617) 497-6677.

Oona's
1210 Massachusetts Ave.,
Cambridge.
Tel (617) 491-2654.

Settebello
52 Brattle St., Cambridge.
Tel (617) 864-2440.

Talbots
500 Boylston St. **Map** 3 C2.
Tel (617) 262-2981.

Men's Fashion

Andover Shop
22 Holyoke St.,
Cambridge.
Tel (617) 876-4900.

Brooks Brothers
46 Newbury St. **Map** 4 D2.
Tel (617) 267-2600.

Jos. A. Bank Clothiers
399 Boylston St. **Map** 4 D2.
Tel (617) 536-5050.

J. Press
82 Mount Auburn St.,
Cambridge.
Tel (617) 547-9886.

Polo/Ralph Lauren
93/95 Newbury St.
Map 3 C2.
Tel (617) 424-1124.

Discount and Vintage Clothes

Garment District
200 Broadway,
Cambridge.
Tel (617) 876-5230.

Keezer's Classic Clothing
140 River St., Cambridge.
Tel (617) 547-2455.

Marshalls
350 Washington St.
Map 4 F1.
Tel (617) 338-6205.

Second Time Around
176 Newbury St.
Map 3 B2.
Tel (617) 247-3504.

T.J. Maxx
350 Washington St.
Map 4 F1.
Tel (617) 695-2424.

Shoes and Accessories

Foot Paths
489 Washington St.
Map 4 F1.
Tel (617) 338-6008.

Helen's Leather
110 Charles St.
Map 1 B3.
Tel (617) 742-2077.

Niketown
200 Newbury St.
Map 3 B2.
Tel (617) 267-3400.

Stuart Weitzman
Copley Place.
Map 3 C3.
Tel (617) 266-8699.

The Tannery
39 Brattle St., Cambridge.
Tel (617) 491-1811.

Antiques, Fine Crafts, and Gifts

Visitors hoping to take home a special memento will find an enormous number of antique, craft, and gift stores in Boston. From the huge antique markets and cooperatives, to specialty shops selling everything from rugs to rare books, there are abundant opportunities to indulge a passion for the past. Those favoring more contemporary *objets d'art* will find crafts guilds, galleries, and gift shops selling unique glassware, ceramics, textiles, jewelry, and much more produced by New England artisans, as well as items from every corner of the world.

Antiques

Charles Street is Boston's antiques Mecca, with more antique stores than any other part of town. The neighborhood is extremely affluent with many exclusive and expensive stores, though the occasional bargain may be found in some of the larger stores. **Upstairs Downstairs** sells "affordable antiques," and has four rooms full of furniture, lamps, prints, and a large selection of smaller items.

A prime source of antique pine and painted furniture, **Danish Country** carries antique *armoires* and other furniture from Scandinavia, as well as Royal Copenhagen china and tall case clocks. The shop also carries Chinese lacquered antique furniture that blends well with the Scandinavian pieces.

Antique jewelry from around the world is a specialty at **Marika's Antiques Shop**, along with paintings, glass, porcelain, and silver. True to its name, **Devonia Antiques for the Table** has fine china, glassware, and even antique linens for creating the period dining atmosphere. **Twentieth Century Ltd.** excels particularly in glittery costume jewelry from top designers. They also offer pieces in sterling silver.

In Cambridge, **Reside** specializes in mid-20th-century modern furniture and accessories, with ethnic pillows and weavings. For an eclectic mix of antiques both fine and funky from the 19th century to the 1950s, head to **Easy Chairs**. In neighboring Brookline, **A Room with a Vieux Antiques** excels at Art Deco furniture, much of it purchased in France.

Antique Markets and Cooperatives

If browsing through mountainous inventories with the broadest range of quality, price, and stock is your idea of heaven, then there are several multi-dealer antiques emporiums worth exploring. On Charles Street, **Boston Arts & Antiques** has everything from quilts, candlesticks, and wicker furniture to chandeliers and furniture. Open Sundays, **SOWA Vintage Market** features nearly three dozen dealers in an old brick warehouse. Set decorators love to scout here for film shoots. The adjoining flea market and farmers' market add to the fun. In Cambridge, **Cambridge Antique Market** encompasses more than 100 dealers, offering estate antiques, collectibles, furniture, jewelry, and a vast selection of many other items.

If you have scoured Charles Street, scrutinized the cooperatives and still not found what you are looking for, try **Skinner Inc.** in Boston, which holds auctions throughout the year featuring furniture and fine arts, as well as ethnic art and books.

Specialty Dealers

Collectors in pursuit of more specific pieces will find shops in Boston that specialize in everything from nautical antiques to rare books, maps, jewelry, and rugs. Fine antiques and jewelry featuring Victorian and Art Nouveau designs are beautifully displayed and described by the knowledgeable staff at **Small Pleasures**. Vintage watches from Rolex, Cartier, Vacheron, Constantia, and others are a specialty at **Paul A. Duggan Co.**; while **The Bromfield Pen Shop** has been a purveyor of thousands of new, antique, and limited-edition pens for over 50 years. For nautical antiques, including model ships and marine paintings, **Lannan Ship Model Gallery** boasts an extensive and high quality inventory. Antique Asian furniture, as well as antique and modern hand-woven rugs and carpets from the Asian steppes to northern India and Nepal, are among the specialties of **Mohr & McPherson**, which maintains a large showroom in Back Bay. Bibliophiles will also find an extraordinary range of stores in Boston. In business since 1825, **Brattle Book Shop** (see p85) is the oldest and best known, with a huge selection of used, out-of-print and rare books, magazines, and vintage photographs. Rare books in the fine arts are the focus of **Ars Libri Ltd.**, while **Eugene Galleries** features antiquarian maps, prints, and etchings, in addition to its comprehensive selection of books. Fans of graphic novels, comic books, Japanese and Korean manga, and all sorts of visual story-telling flock to **Million Year Picnic** to get their fix of current titles. A few toys and T-shirts round out the collection, but comics are the main draw. Also in Cambridge, **Schoenhof's Foreign Books** and **Grolier Poetry Book Shop** cater to those seeking specialty volumes. The **Bryn Mawr Bookstore** stocks used books and some rare volumes covering every conceivable subject.

Fine Crafts

Collectors with a more contemporary bent will find several distinguished galleries and shops featuring a wide variety of American crafts by both local and nationally recognized artists. **Mobilia** in Cambridge has a national reputation for its jewelry, ceramics, and other objects. The **Society of Arts and Crafts**, established in 1897, has a shop and gallery, with exhibits from the 350 artists it represents. Works are largely in wood, fiber, metal, glass, and mixed media. The **Cambridge Artists'** **Cooperative**, owned and run by over 250 artists, offers an eclectic collection of items, ranging from hand-painted silk jackets to ornaments and larger items. The **Mudflat Gallery** showcases work in clay by nearly 50 members and students.

Gifts

In addition to the plethora of souvenir shops that threaten to drown tourists in tasteless, predictable merchandise, Boston has numerous shops specializing in original and distinctive gifts that you will not find anywhere else. On Newbury Street browse the **International Poster Gallery**, for original, vintage posters from the 19th and 20th centuries. In Cambridge, **Joie de Vivre** has a fantastic collection of toys, clocks, jewelry, jack-in-the-boxes, and much more beside. Next door, **Paper Source** carries a selection of fine handmade papers, gift wrap, rubber stamps, and other materials for creative indulgence. For quirky, one-of-a-kind trinkets and functional gifts, check out the Beacon Hill and Harvard Square outlets of **Black Ink**.

DIRECTORY

Antiques

A Room with a Vieux Antiques
361 Boylston St., Brookline.
Tel (617) 277-2700.

Danish Country
138 Charles St. **Map** 1 B3.
Tel (617) 227-1804.

Devonia Antiques for the Table
15 Charles St.
Map 1 B4.
Tel (617) 765-2396.

Easy Chairs
375 Huron Ave.,
Cambridge.
Tel (617) 491-2131.

Marika's Antiques Shop
130 Charles St. **Map** 1 B3.
Tel (617) 523-4520.

Reside
266 Concord Ave.,
Cambridge.
Tel (617) 547-2929.

Twentieth Century Ltd.
73 Charles St. **Map** 1 B4.
Tel (617) 742-1031.

Upstairs Downstairs
93 Charles St.
Map 1 B4.
Tel (617) 367-1950.

Antiques Markets and Cooperatives

Boston Arts & Antiques
119 Charles St.
Map 1 B3.
Tel (617) 227-9810.

Cambridge Antique Market
201 Msgr. O'Brien Hwy.,
Cambridge.
Tel (617) 868-9655.

Skinner Inc.
63 Park Plaza.
Map 1 C4.
Tel (617) 350-5400.

SOWA Vintage Market
460c Harrison Ave.
Map 3 E4.

Specialty Dealers

Ars Libri Ltd.
500 Harrison Ave.
Map 4 E4.
Tel (617) 357-5212.

Brattle Book Shop
9 West St.
Map 1 C4.
Tel (617) 542-0210.

The Bromfield Pen Shop
5 Bromfield St.
Map 1 C4.
Tel (617) 482-9053.

Bryn Mawr Bookstore
373 Huron Ave., Cambridge.
Tel (617) 661-1770.

Eugene Galleries
76 Charles St.
Map 1 B4.
Tel (617) 227-3062.

Grolier Poetry Book Shop
6 Plympton St.,
Cambridge.
Tel (617) 547-4648.

Lannan Ship Model Gallery
99 High St.
Map 2 D5.
Tel (617) 451-2650.

Million Year Picnic
99 Mt. Auburn St.,
Cambridge.
Tel (617) 492-6763.

Mohr & McPherson
460 Harrison Ave.
Map 3 E4.
Tel (617) 210-4900.

Paul A. Duggan Co.
333 Washington St.,
Suite 435.
Map 1 C4.
Tel (617) 742-0221.

Schoenhof's Foreign Books
76A Mt. Auburn St.,
Cambridge.
Tel (617) 547-8855.

Small Pleasures
142 Newbury St. **Map** 3 C2.
Tel (617) 267-7371.

Fine Crafts

Cambridge Artists' Cooperative
59a Church St.,
Cambridge. **Tel** (617) 868-4434.

Mobilia
358 Huron Ave.,
Cambridge.
Tel (617) 876-2109.

Mudflat Gallery
Porter Square Shopping Center, 1–37 White St.,
Cambridge.
Tel (617) 491-7976.

Society of Arts and Crafts
175 Newbury St. **Map** 3 B2.
Tel (617) 266-1810.

Gifts

Black Ink
101 Charles St. **Map** 1 B3.
Tel (866) 497-1221.
5 Brattle St., Cambridge.
Tel (866) 497-1221.

International Poster Gallery
205 Newbury St.
Map 3 B2.
Tel (617) 375-0076.

Joie de Vivre
1792 Massachusetts Ave.,
Cambridge.
Tel (617) 864-8188.

Paper Source
1810 Massachusetts Ave.,
Cambridge.
Tel (617) 497-1077.

ENTERTAINMENT IN BOSTON

From avant-garde performance art to serious drama, popular dance music to live classical performances, Boston offers an outstanding array of entertainment options, with something to appeal to every taste: the Theater District offers many excellent plays and musicals, the Wang Theatre hosts many touring productions, and Symphony Hall is home of the renowned Boston Symphony Orchestra. Boston is also well acquainted with jazz, folk music, and blues as well as being a center for more contemporary music, played in big city nightclubs. In summer, entertainment often heads outdoors, with many open-air plays and concerts, such as the famous Boston Pops at the Hatch Shell.

Practical Information

The best sources for information on current films, concerts, theater, dance, and exhibitions include the Thursday and Friday Arts section of *The Boston Globe*. Even more up-to-date listings can be found online at the following sites: www.bostonusa.com; *The Boston Globe* (www.bostonglobe. com); *Improper Bostonian* (www. improper.com); *Boston Magazine* (www.bostonmagazine.com).

Boston entertainment listings magazines

Booking Tickets

Tickets to popular musicals, theatrical productions, and touring shows often sell out far in advance, although theaters sometimes have a few returns or restricted-view tickets available. You can either get tickets in person at theater box offices, or use one of the ticket agencies in Boston. For advance tickets these are **Ticketmaster** and **Live Nation**. Tickets can be purchased from both of these agencies over the telephone, in person, or online. Half-price tickets to most noncommercial arts events as well as to some commercial productions are available from 11am on the day of the performance at **BosTix** booths. Purchases must be made in person and only cash is accepted. BosTix also sells advance full-price tickets. Special Boston entertainment discount vouchers, available from hotel lobbies and tourist offices, may also give a saving on some shows.

Tchaikovsky's *Nutcracker*, danced by the Boston Ballet *(see p160)*

Districts and Venues

Musicals, plays, comedies, and dance are generally performed at venues in the Theater District, although larger noncommercial theater companies are distributed throughout the region, many being associated with colleges and universities.

The area around the intersection of Massachusetts and Huntington Avenues hosts a concentration of outstanding concert venues, including Symphony Hall, Berklee Performance Center at Berklee College of Music, and Jordan Hall at the New England Conservatory of Music.

Many nightclub and dance venues are on Lansdowne and other streets by Fenway Park and around Boylston Place in the Theater District. The busiest areas for bars and small clubs offering live jazz and rock music are Central and Harvard Squares in Cambridge, Davis Square in Somerville, and Allston. The principal gay scene in Boston is found in the South End, with many of the older bars and clubs in neighboring Bay Village.

Boston's Symphony Orchestra performing at Symphony Hall *(see p160)*

Open-Air and Free Entertainment

Boston's best free outdoor summer entertainment is found at the Hatch Shell *(see p94)* on the Charles River Esplanade. The Boston Pops *(see p160)* performs here frequently during the week around July 4, and all through July and August jazz, pop, rock, and classical music is played. On Friday evenings from late June to the week before Labor Day, the Hatch Shell also shows free big-screen family films.

Music is also performed in the summer months at the **Blue Hills Bank Pavilion** on the waterfront, which holds live jazz, pop, and country music concerts. City Hall Plaza and Copley Plaza have free concerts at lunchtimes and in the evenings, and the **Museum of Fine Arts, Boston** *(see pp106–9)* operates a summer musical concert series in its

Free open-air music concert outside City Hall

courtyard. Most of the annual concerts and recitals of the **New England Conservatory of Music** are free, although some require advance reservations.

Other open-air entertainment includes a series of free plays staged on Boston Common by the **Commonwealth Shakespeare Company** in July and August.

An area that has more unusual open-air entertainment is Harvard Square, famous for its nightly and weekend scene of street performers. Many recording artists paid their dues here, and other hopefuls still flock to the square in the hope of being discovered – or at least of earning the cost of dinner. On the waterfront, the **Institute of Contemporary Art**

Entrance to the Shubert Theatre *(see p160)*

offers a program of free live music during summer months, while the **Boston Harbor Hotel** sponsors free weeknight Summer in the City films and concerts at Rowes Wharf.

Details of all free entertainment happening in the city are listed in the Thursday and Friday editions of *The Boston Globe*.

Disabled Access

Many entertainment venues in Boston are wheelchair accessible. **VSA (Very Special Arts) Massachusetts** offers a full Boston arts access guide. Some places, such as **Jordan Hall**, the **Cutler Majestic Theatre**, and the **Wheelock Family Theatre**, have listening aids for the hearing impaired, while the latter also has signed and described performances.

DIRECTORY

Booking Tickets

BosTix
Faneuil Hall Marketplace.
Map 2 D3.
Copley Square. **Map** 3 C2.
Tel (617) 482-2849.
🆆 bostix.com

Live Nation
Various outlets.
Tel (800) 431-3462.
🆆 livenation.com

Ticketmaster
Various outlets
Tel (800) 745-3000.
🆆 ticketmaster.com

Open-Air/Free Entertainment

Blue Hills Bank Pavilion
290 Northern Ave., South Boston. **Map** 2 F5.

Tel (617) 728-1600.
🆆 bluehillsbank pavilion.ticketoffices. com

Boston Harbor Hotel
Rowes Wharf, Boston.
Map 1 E4.
Tel (617) 439-7000.
🆆 bhh.com

Commonwealth Shakespeare Company
Parkman Bandstand,
Boston Common.
Map 1 C4.
Tel (617) 426-0863.
🆆 commshakes.org

Institute of Contemporary Art
100 Northern Ave.
Map 2 F5.
Tel (617) 478-3100.

Museum of Fine Arts, Boston
465 Huntington Ave.
Tel (617) 369-3306.
🆆 mfa.org

New England Conservatory of Music
290 Huntington Ave.
Tel (617) 585-1260.
🆆 newengland conservatory.edu

Disabled Access

Cutler Majestic Theatre
219 Tremont St.
Map 4 E2.
Tel (617) 824-8000.
🆆 cutlermajestic.org

Jordan Hall
30 Gainsborough St.
Tel (617) 585-1260.
🆆 necmusic.edu

VSA (Very Special Arts) Massachusetts
89 South St.
Map 4 F2.
Tel (617) 350-7713.
TTY (617) 350-6385.
🆆 vsamass.org

Wheelock Family Theatre
200 Riverway,
Brookline.
Tel (617) 879-2300.
TTY (617) 879-2150.
🆆 wheelock.edu/wft

The Arts in Boston

Performing arts are vital to Boston's cultural life. Since the 1880s, the social season has revolved around openings of the Boston Symphony Orchestra and many Brahmins *(see p47)* occupy their grandparents' seats at performances. In the past, theaters in Boston were heavily censored *(see p89)*, but today's Bostonians are avid theatergoers, patronizing commercial venues for plays bound to, or coming from, Broadway and attending ambitious contemporary drama at repertory theaters. Many non-commercial theater and dance companies perform in smaller venues in local neighborhoods and at the colleges. Although some theaters are closed on Mondays, there is rarely a night in Boston without performing arts.

Classical Music and Opera

Two cherished Boston institutions, the **Boston Symphony Orchestra** and its popular-music equivalent, the Boston Pops, have a long history of being led by some of America's finest conductors. The BSO performs a full schedule of concerts at Symphony Hall from October through April. The Boston Pops takes over for May and June, performing at the Charles River Esplanade *(see p94)* for Fourth of July festivities that are the highlight of the summer season.

The students and faculty of the **New England Conservatory of Music** present more than 450 free classical and jazz performances each year, many in Jordan Hall *(see p159)*. **Boston Lyric Opera** has assumed the task of reestablishing opera in Boston, through small-cast and light opera at venues around the city.

Boston's oldest musical organization is the **Handel & Haydn Society**, founded in 1815. As the first American producer of such landmark works as Handel's *Messiah* (performed annually since 1818), Bach's *B-Minor Mass* and *St. Matthew Passion*, and Verdi's *Requiem*, H & H is one of the country's musical treasures. Since 1986, the society has focused on performing and recording Baroque and

Classical works using the period instruments for which the composers wrote. H & H gives regular performances in Boston at Symphony Hall, Jordan Hall, and other venues.

Classical music is ubiquitous in Boston. **Emmanuel Music**, for example, performs sacred music, including Bach, at regular services at Emmanuel Church on Newbury Street. The Isabella Stewart Gardner Museum *(see p105)* hosts a series of chamber music concerts, continuing a 19th-century tradition of professional "music room" chamber concerts in the homes of the social elite.

The **Celebrity Series** brings world-famous orchestras, soloists, and dance companies to Boston, often to perform at Jordan Hall, as well as several other venues. Some 40 to 50 events are organized.

Theater

Though much diminished from its heyday in the 1920s, when more than 40 theaters were in operation throughout Boston, the city's Theater District *(see pp80–89)* today still contains a collection of some of the most architecturally eminent, and still commercially productive, early theaters in the United States. Furthermore, during the 1990s, many of the theaters that are currently in use underwent programs of

restoration to their original grandeur, and visitors today are bound to be impressed as they catch a glimpse of these theaters' past glory. The main commercially run theaters of Boston – the **Colonial**, **Wilbur**, and **Shubert** theaters, the **Boston Opera House** and the **Wang Theatre** *(see pp85–9)* – often program Broadway productions that have already premiered in New York and are touring the United States. They also present Broadway "try outs" and local productions.

In stark contrast to some of the mainstream shows on offer in Boston, the most avant-garde contemporary theater in the city is performed at the **American Repertory Theater (ART)**, an independent, non-commercial company associated with Harvard University *(see pp114–15)*. ART often premieres new plays, particularly on its second stage, but is best known for its often radical interpretations of traditional and modern classics. By further contrast, the independent **Huntington Theatre** is widely praised for its traditional direction and interpretation. For example, the Huntington was the co-developer of Pulitzer-Prize winning plays detailing 20th-century African American life, by the late August Wilson, an important chronicler of American race relations.

Several of the smaller companies, including **Lyric Stage**, devote their energies to showcasing local actors and directors and often premiere the work of Boston-area playwrights. Many of the most adventurous companies perform on one of the four stages at the **Boston Center for the Arts**.

Dance

The city's largest and most popular resident dance company, the **Boston Ballet** performs an ambitious season of classics and new choreography between October and May at the restored Boston Opera House (see p85). The annual performances of the *Nutcracker* during the Christmas season are a Boston tradition. The somewhat more modest **José Mateo Ballet Theatre** has earned a reputation for developing a strong and impressive program of repertory choreography. The company performs in the attractive neo-Gothic Old Cambridge Baptist Church, which is situated near Harvard Square. Modern dance in Boston is represented by many small companies, collectives, and independent choreographers, who often perform in the **Dance Complex** and **Green Street Studios** in Cambridge. Boston also hosts many other visiting dance companies, who often put on performances at the **Cutler Majestic Theatre**.

Cinema

Situated in Harvard Square, close to Harvard Yard (see pp112–13), the **Brattle Theatre**, one of the very last repertory movie houses in the Greater Boston area, primarily shows classic films on a big screen. For example, the Brattle was instrumental in reviving moviegoers' interest in the Humphrey Bogart, black-and-white classic *Casablanca*. Something of a Harvard institution, the Brattle has long served as a popular "first date" destination for couples with a shared passion for the movies.

Serious students of classic and international cinema patronize the screening programs of the **Harvard Film Archive**. The **Kendall Square Cinema** multiplex is the city's chief venue for non-English language films, art films and documentaries. Multiplex theaters showing mainstream, first-run Hollywood movies are found throughout the Boston area. Some of the most popular and centrally-located options are the **AMC Loews Boston Common**, and **Regal Fenway** theaters. Tickets for every kind of movie in Boston are often discounted for first shows of the day on weekends and all weekday shows before 5pm.

DIRECTORY

Classical Music and Opera

Boston Lyric Opera
Various venues.
Tel (617) 542-6772.
W blo.org

Boston Symphony Orchestra
Symphony Hall, 301 Massachusetts Ave.
Map 3 A4. **Tel** (617) 266-1200, (617) 266-1492.
W bso.org

Celebrity Series
Various venues.
Tel (617) 482-6661.
W celebrityseries.org

Emmanuel Music
Emmanuel Church, 15 Newbury St. **Map** 4 D2.
Tel (617) 536-3356.
W emmanuelmusic.org

Handel & Haydn Society
Various venues.
Tel (617) 266-3605.
W handelandhaydn.org

New England Conservatory of Music
Jordan Hall,
30 Gainsborough St.
Map 3 A4.
Tel (617) 585-1260.
W newengland conservatory.edu

Theater

American Repertory Theater
Loeb Drama Center, 64 Brattle St., Cambridge.
Tel (617) 547-8300.
W amrep.org

Boston Center for the Arts
539 Tremont St.
Map 4 D3.
Tel (617) 933-8600.
W bostontheater scene.com

Boston Opera House
539 Washington St.
Map 4 E1.
Tel (617) 931-2787.
W broadway acrossamerica.com

Colonial Theatre
106 Boylston St. **Map** 4 E2.
Tel (617) 426-9366.
W artsemerson.org

Huntington Theatre
264 Huntington Ave.
Map 3 B4.
Tel (617) 266-0800.
W huntington theatre.org

Lyric Stage
140 Clarendon St.
Map 3 C3.
Tel (617) 585-5678.
W lyricstage.com

Shubert Theatre
265 Tremont St.
Map 4 E2.
Tel (617) 482-9393.
W citicenter.org`

Wang Theatre
270 Tremont St. **Map** 4 E2.
Tel (617) 482-9393.
W citicenter.org

Wilbur Theatre
246 Tremont St.
Map 4 E2.
Tel (617) 931-2000.
W thewilbur theatre.com

Dance

Boston Ballet
Various venues.
Tel (617) 695-6955.
W bostonballet.org

Cutler Majestic Theatre
219 Tremont St. **Map** 4 E2.
Tel (617) 824-8000.
W cutlermajestic.org

Dance Complex
536 Massachusetts Ave., Cambridge.
Tel (617) 547-9363.
W dancecomplex.org

Green Street Studios
185 Green St, Cambridge.
Tel (617) 864-3191.
W greenstreet studios.org

José Mateo Ballet Theatre
400 Harvard St, Cambridge.
Tel (617) 354-7467.
W ballettheatre.org

Cinema

AMC Loews Boston Common
175 Tremont St.
Map 4 E2.
Tel (617) 423-5801.
W amctheatres.com

Brattle Theatre
40 Brattle St., Cambridge.
Tel (617) 876-6837.
W brattlefilm.org

Harvard Film Archive
24 Quincy St., Cambridge.
Tel (617) 495-4700.
W hcl.harvard.edu/hfa

Kendall Square Cinema
1 Kendall Square, Cambridge.
Tel (617) 499-1996.
W landmark theatres.com

Regal Fenway
201 Brookline Ave.
Tel (617) 424-6266.
W regmovies.com

Music and Nightlife

Boston's mix of young professionals and tens of thousands of college students produces a lively nightlife scene, focused on live music, clubs, and bars. Ever since the 1920s, Boston has been especially hospitable to jazz, and it still has an interesting jazz scene, with Berklee College of Music playing an important part. Cambridge is an epicenter of folk and acoustic music revivals and alt-rock, while Lansdowne Street near Fenway Park (see p166) is the main district for nightclubs. Virtually every neighborhood has a selection of friendly bars, often with live music.

Rock Music

The **House of Blues** chain of rock clubs was born in Greater Boston, and its return to the city has spawned its largest and most successful club yet, on Lansdowne Street, near Fenway Park. There are standing-room concerts on most nights. With four performance spaces, the **Middle East** in Cambridge's Central Square leads the alternative rock scene, featuring both local bands and touring newcomers. Larger rock concert venues are the **Orpheum Theatre** and the arena seating of **TD Garden**, used at other times for hockey and basketball games.

Jazz and Blues

The city's largest concert venue for jazz is the **Berklee Performance Center** in Back Bay, which draws on faculty and students from Berklee College of Music as well as touring performers. More intimate settings include **Scullers Jazz Club** overlooking the Charles River in Brighton, the small hall for aficionados at the **Multicultural Arts Center** in East Cambridge, and the suave elegance of the **Regattabar** just off Harvard Square. No-frills, neighborhood jazz thrives at **Ryles Jazz Club** in Cambridge's Inman Square. The musical parent of jazz, the blues, is also alive and well. **Wally's** in the South End has an ambience that is pure 1940s juke joint, but there's no denying the veracity of the jazz wailing from its narrow confines. The **Cantab Lounge** in Cambridge's Central Square is a music lover's delight, and features open mic sessions on Mondays and bluegrass on Tuesdays, while the weekends feature live blues, R&B, funk, and soul. The Cantab also runs popular Wednesday night poetry "slams."

Folk and World Music

Harvard Square's **Club Passim** is a folk music legend, the hangout in the late 1950s and early 1960s for the likes of Joan Baez and Van Morrison, and still one of the United States' key clubs in the touring life of singer-songwriters. **The Center for Arts at the Armory**, near Somerville's Union Square, houses studio spaces for artists, a café, galleries, and two performance areas in a historic armory. It attracts a wide variety of musical acts from unknown folk artists to international world music acts. Davis Square is a couple of Red Line stops farther out from Harvard station, but well worth the trip for the bustling music scene in bars and periodic performances by comedians, singer-songwriters, and even acoustic string bands at the venerable **Somerville Theatre**.

International acts ranging from Afro-pop to ska play at many large venues across Boston in a concert series presented by the music promoters **World Music**.

Nightclubs and Discos

Boston has a club for just about every type of dance music. Like club scenes everywhere, little happens until late at night; in Boston nothing gets going until at least 11pm. Housed in a centrally located boutique hotel, the **Emerald Lounge** attracts a mix of youngsters and out-of-towners looking to groove on the dance floor. The **Grand Canal** near North Station features techno and house music for a youthful clientele. Located in the heart of the Theater District, **Whisky Saigon** attracts the city's jet set with pricey bottle service and the latest in dance and techno beats. Sleek **Venu** is the top spot where the young and chic go for post-midnight dancing. From its Back Bay subterranean home, **Storyville** provides one of the city's most in-demand dance spots, filled with intimate nooks and crannies. Also popular is the **Royale** in the Theater District, with classy touches such as doormen instead of bouncers, marble walls, and a vast dance floor.

Bars

The legal drinking age in Boston is 21, and you may be asked to show proof of identification (see p174).

Boston has many bars (see also p151), but many, such as those listed below, are specifically themed, offer live entertainment, or place a strong emphasis on being "party" venues. The bar at **Mistral** is typical of the increasingly upscale places springing up in Boston, where the young and the beautiful like to meet and play. More down to earth are some of Boston's Irish bars offering live music and the obligatory pints of Guinness. Among these are **The Phoenix Landing**, a welcoming Irish pub in Central Square lined with mahogany and featuring English football on cable television as well as lively retro-themed dance nights; **The Burren** that features some of the finest live Irish music in the area, and the smaller **Druid**, a welcoming spot in Cambridge's cosy Inman Square.

Bostonians love sports, and the city has dozens of sports bars. The **Cask 'N' Flagon** is adjacent to Fenway Park, perfect for celebrating victory or softening the pain of defeat. At **Kings** big-screen sports TVs vie with bowling lanes, professional pool tables and skee ball and shuffleboard tables. **The Fours** is just one of the numerous bars that cater to Boston Celtics and Boston Bruins fans near the TD Garden Arena.

Gay Clubs and Bars

Boston's gay scene comes into sharpest focus in the South End and Bay Village, but gay and gay-friendly bars and clubs are found throughout the city. The perpetually packed **Club Cafe**, which straddles the busy border between South End and Back Bay, is a stalwart of the city's LGBT social scene. Boston's longest-running gay club, **Jacques**, features lively drag shows and female impersonator cabaret during the rest of the week. The weekly *Bay Windows* newspaper provides wider information as do other Boston listings.

Comedy Clubs

Many clubs and bars program occasional evenings of standup comedy, and several specialize in this form of entertainment. The **Comedy Connection** at the Wilbur Theatre, brings laughter to the historic hall with an impressive line-up of comedians, who are familiar from their work on national television. **Nick's Comedy Stop** in the Theater District, on the other hand, tends to concentrate more on homegrown talent, grooming performers who often go on to the "big time."

DIRECTORY

Rock Music

House of Blues
15 Lansdowne St.
Tel (888) 693-2583.
w hob.com

Middle East
472/480 Massachusetts Ave., Cambridge.
Tel (617) 864-3278 ext. 221.
w mideastclub.com

Orpheum Theatre
1 Hamilton Pl. **Map** 1 C4.
Tel (617) 679-0810.

TD Garden
1 Causeway St. **Map** 1 C2.
Tel (617) 624-1000.
w tdgarden.com

Jazz and Blues

Berklee Performance Center
Berklee College of Music, 136 Massachusetts Ave.
Tel (617) 266-7455.
w berklee.edu/BPC

Cantab Lounge
738 Massachusetts Ave., Cambridge.
Tel (617) 354-2685.

Multicultural Arts Center
41 Second St., Cambridge.
Tel (617) 577-1400.
w multicultural artscenter.org

Regattabar
Charles Hotel, 1 Bennett St., Cambridge.
Tel (617) 395-7757.
w regattabarjazz.com

Ryles Jazz Club
212 Hampshire St., Cambridge.
Tel (617) 876-9330.
w rylesjazz.com

Scullers Jazz Club
Doubletree Guest Suites, 400 Soldiers Field Rd., Brighton.
Tel (617) 562-4111.
w scullersjazz.com

Wally's Cafe
427 Massachusetts Ave.
Tel (617) 424-1408.

Folk and World Music

The Center for Arts at the Armory
191 Highland Ave., Somerville.
Tel (617) 718-2191.
w artsatthearmory.org

Club Passim
47 Palmer St., Cambridge.
Tel (617) 492-7679.
w clubpassim.org

Somerville Theatre
55 Davis Square, Somerville.
Tel (617) 625-4088.
w somervilletheatre. com

World Music
Box Office:
Tel (617) 876-4275.
w worldmusic.org

Nightclubs and Discos

Emerald Lounge
200 Stuart St. **Map** 1 B5.
Tel (617) 457-2626.
w emeraldnightlife.com

Grand Canal
57 Canal St. **Map** 2 D2.
Tel (617) 523-1112.

Royale
279 Tremont St. **Map** 4 E2.
Tel (617) 338-7699.

Storyville
90 Exeter St. **Map** 3 C3.
Tel (617) 236-1134.
w storyvilleboston.com

Venu
100 Warrenton St. **Map** 4 E2.
Tel (617) 338-8061.

Whisky Saigon
116 Boylston St.
Tel (617) 482-7799.

Bars

The Burren
247 Elm St., Somerville.
Tel (617) 776-6896.

The Cask 'N' Flagon
62 Brookline Ave.
Tel (617) 536-4840.

Druid
1357 Cambridge St., Cambridge.
Tel (617) 497-0965.

The Fours
166 Canal St. **Map** 1 C2.
Tel (617) 720-4455.

Kings

50 Dalton St.
Map 3 A3.
Tel (617) 266-2695.

Mistral
223 Columbus Ave.
Map 4 D3.
Tel (617) 867-9300.

The Phoenix Landing
512 Massachusetts Ave., Cambridge.
Tel (617) 576-6260.

Gay Bars and Clubs

Club Cafe
209 Columbus Ave.
Map 3 C3.
Tel (617) 536-0966.

Jacques
79 Broadway.
Map 4 F4.
Tel (617) 426-8902.

Comedy Clubs

Comedy Connection
Wilbur Theatre, 246 Tremont St.
Map 4 E2.
Tel (617) 931-2000.
w thewilbur theatre.com

Nick's Comedy Stop
100 Warrenton St.
Map 4 E2.
Tel (617) 423-2900.
w nickscomedy stop.com

SPORTS AND OUTDOOR ACTIVITIES

Bostonians have a wealth of recreational opportunities, thanks largely to the city's many spacious parks, its long, well-maintained riverfront, sizeable harbor, and excellent sports facilities. Visitors can enjoy many outdoor activities, whether it is going for an early morning jog on Boston Common, sailing on the Charles River, taking to one of the extensive cycle paths, or playing a round at a public golf course. In the winter there is also outdoor ice-skating, and farther afield, skiing. For those who watch sports rather than participate, major-league baseball, football, soccer, basketball, and ice hockey are played at different times through the year.

Water Sports

During all but the winter months, dozens of small plea-sure craft can be seen navigating the Charles River between Cambridge and Boston. At long-established **Community Boating**, only experienced sailors are able to rent sailboats, while farther upriver at the **Charles River Canoe & Kayak Center**, canoes, rowboats, and adult and children's kayaks can be rented.

For those who enjoy swim-ming or sunbathing, there are several good beaches near Boston, and one supervised beach on the **Boston Harbor Islands**, reached by ferry from Long Wharf. Carson Beach and the beach at Castle Island in South Boston are two of the closest, while Revere Beach to the north is larger and busier and served by the subway. From June to September swimmers can use the **Department of Conservation and Recreation** outdoor swimming pools.

Bicycling, Jogging, and Skating

The gentle Boston topography makes sightseeing by bicycle ideal. A number of good trails and bicycle paths crisscross the city, the most popular of which is the Dr. Paul Dudley White Bike Path. This links central Boston with outlying Watertown via a circular 17-mile (27-km) trail that runs along both sides of the Charles River. The Southwest Corridor cycle route links the Back Bay with Roxbury along a section of the Emerald Necklace (see p105), and the Boston harborfront pathways also attract many cyclists. Farther afield, an old railroad line has been transformed into the Minuteman Bikeway, which runs between Cambridge and Bedford via historic Lexington. **Urban AdvenTours** offers cycle tours along with rental bikes, while other rental stores include **Back Bay Bicycles** and **Community Bicycle Supply**.

In-line skating and jogging are also popular activities in Boston, with riverside esplanades and Boston Common being the favorite areas. If you are looking to buy some gear, try **City Sports**.

Cyclist riding through historic Concord, northwest of Boston

Golf and Tennis

Along with its many excellent private golf clubs, the Boston area also boasts a number of public golf courses, including some municipal links. The **William J. Devine Golf Course** in Franklin Park is the city's public golf course and there is also the nine-hole **Fresh Pond Golf Course** in Cambridge.

The **Department of Conservation and Recreation** maintains a dozen public tennis courts in Boston. Those in North End Park on Commercial Street and Charlesbank Park on the Charles River Esplanade are the most central. Court time can not usually be reserved, so availability is on a first-come-first-served basis.

Sailboats on the Charles River with the Back Bay in the distance

Winter Sports

Freezing winter weather sees large groups of heavily clothed ice skaters heading for the Frog Pond on Boston Common. A modest fee is charged for skating, and skate rental is available in the pavilion by Frog Pond, or else a few blocks away at the **Beacon Hill Skate Shop**. Each winter, the Department of Conservation and Recreation also opens its many indoor rinks in Boston and Cambridge to the public, including Steriti Rink in the North End, which also has an indoor bocce court.

Most of the best skiing in New England is found a long way from Boston, in Vermont, Maine, and New Hampshire. Closer options include **Blue Hills Ski Area** in Canton for downhill skiing, and **Middlesex Fells Reservation** in Stoneham for cross-country. These areas depend a lot on the weather, however, and have only a few slopes.

Enthusiastic ice-skaters take to the frozen Boston Common pond

Fitness Facilities

Amenities at most of Boston's large hotels include fitness facilities. Those hotels that don't have facilities on-site usually have an arrangement whereby guests can use a private club in the immediate area. Otherwise, choose from the many other public gyms and health clubs found throughout the city.

Fitcorp has excellent, modern exercise facilities at numerous city locations, while **Boston Athletic Club** in Downtown has both a well-equipped gym, and also a swimming pool, tennis, and squash courts. Across the river, **Cambridge Athletic Club** offers various racquet sports and a good gym.

DIRECTORY

Water Sports

Boston Harbor Islands National Park Area
Tel (617) 223-8666.
W bostonharbor
islands.org

Charles River Canoe & Kayak Center
Soldiers Field Rd., Allston.
Tel (617) 965-5110.
W ski-paddle.com

Community Boating
21 David G. Mugar Way.
Map 1 A3.
Tel (617) 523-1038.
W community-boating.
org

Bicycling and Skating

Back Bay Bicycles
362 Commonwealth Ave.
Map 3 A2.
Tel (617) 247-2336.
W papa-wheelies.com

City Sports
44 Brattle St., Cambridge.
Tel (617) 492-6000.
W citysports.com

Community Bicycle Supply
496 Tremont St.
Map 4 D3.
Tel (617) 542-8623.
W community
bicycle.com

Urban AdvenTours
Boston Common.
Map 1 C4.
Tel (617) 670-0637.
W urbanadventours.com

Golf Courses

Fresh Pond Golf Course
691 Huron Ave.,
Cambridge.
Tel (617) 349-6282.
W freshpondgolf.com

William J. Devine Golf Course at Franklin Park
1 Circuit Drive,
Dorchester.
Tel (617) 265-4084.
W cityofbostongolf.com

Winter Sports

Beacon Hill Skate Shop
135 South Charles St.
Map 4 E2.
Tel (617) 482-7400.
W beaconhill
skateshop.com

Blue Hills Ski Area
Canton, MA 02021.
Tel (781) 828-5070.
W ski-bluehills.com

Middlesex Fells Reservation
MDC, 4 Woodland Rd.,
Stoneham, MA 02180.
Tel (781) 662-2340.
W mass.gov/dcr/parks

Fitness Facilities

Boston Athletic Club
653 Summer St.
Tel (617) 269-4300.
W bostonathletic
club.com

Cambridge Athletic Club
215 First St., Cambridge.
Tel (617) 491-8989.
W cambridgefitness.com

Fitcorp
1 Beacon St. Map 1 C4.
Tel (617) 248-9797.

Prudential Center.
Map 3 B3.
Tel (617) 262-2050.

125 Summer St.
Map 2 D4.
Tel (617) 261-4855.

197 Clarendon St.
Map 3 C2.
Tel (617) 933-5090.
W fitcorp.com

Useful Addresses

Boston Parks and Recreation Department
1010 Massachusetts Ave.
Tel (617) 635-4505.
W cityofboston.gov/
parks

Department of Conservation and Recreation
251 Causeway St.
Tel (617) 626-1250.
W mass.gov/dcr/parks

Spectator Sports

Bostonians watch sporting events with a passion that is unmatched in most other U.S. cities. Boston has had a team in every major professional league for many years, and some of popular sports' greatest athletes have played for home teams. Moreover, such widely known annual competitions as the Boston Marathon and the Head of the Charles Regatta draw amazingly large and enthusiastic crowds, as do the metropolitan area's many college teams, which have long traditions and avid fans.

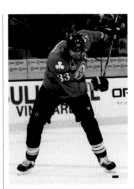

Zdeno Chára of the Boston Bruins on the ice at TD Garden

Baseball

No matter whether they win or lose, the **Boston Red Sox** have an emotional following, especially when the New York Yankees come to town. The Red Sox's beloved Fenway Park stadium is the oldest in the country, and is famous for its enormous 37-ft (11-m) left-field . wall known as the "Green Monster." The small seating capacity, however, means that tickets can be difficult to obtain for the bigger games. Tickets are sold at the gate on the day of the game and are also available from the Fenway Park hotline. The "Bosox" are in the Eastern Division of the American League, one of the country's two major professional leagues. The baseball season runs from early April to the end of September, with championship games in October. In 2004, Boston ended a long drought to win the World Series in dramatic, come-from-behind fashion, and they won again in 2007 and 2013.

Red Sox hitter David Ortiz

Basketball

One of the sport's marquee teams, the **Boston Celtics** have been the most successful of all of Boston's major-league sports teams. They were the dominant team during the 1960s and 80s, winning 16 National Basketball Association (NBA) championships before accomplishing a 17th

trophy in 2008. Banners hang above their home court, the modern 19,000-seat TD Garden arena, paying testament to this record. Even when not playing to their full potential, the Celtics draw big crowds, hoping to see the team rekindle past glories. Tickets are usually available for most games, although they can be pricey – good seats cost at least $50. The season runs from October to April.

American Football

The home football team, the **New England Patriots**, once dominated the sport, and won the game's biggest prize in 2002, 2004, 2005, and 2014. They play against their National Football League (NFL) opponents in Gillette Stadium, about an hour's drive southwest of downtown Boston. Most NFL games are played during the fall on Sundays, or sometimes on Monday evenings to attract a national television audience. Tickets sell out a long way in advance, so the chances of picking one up are remote.

Ice Hockey

Six Stanley Cup wins make the **Boston Bruins** one of the most successful teams in National Hockey League (NHL) history, although their form has been changeable. The hockey season runs from September to April, with the hard-charging "B's" playing in the NHL's Eastern Conference. End-of-season playoff games are often sold out well in advance, but for other games, tickets are usually available for between $10 and $175. Games are played at TD Garden.

Other Sports

Boston's major-league professional soccer team, the **New England Revolution**, plays all of its home games at Gillette Stadium after the New England Patriots have finished their season. The soccer season runs from March through to October, and the game is slowly gaining more widespread support, due

Horses leaving the gates at Suffolk Downs racetrack

partly to its increasing popularity as a college sport.

Suffolk Downs is the Boston area's only thoroughbred racetrack, where bets are taken on both live and simulcast races. Fans of the fast-paced men's lacrosse can watch the **Boston Cannons** (Major League Lacrosse) play their home games at the Harvard Stadium in Allston.

Tennis fans can catch a glimpse of world class tennis players by cheering on the **Boston Lobsters** of the World Team Tennis League. The team's roster and home venue changes almost every year, and most matches are held in July (check the team's website for details).

Each year on Patriots Day (a city holiday on the third Monday of April), the largest event on the sports calendar takes place. The **Boston Marathon** has burgeoned since its inception in 1897, and now approximately 15,000 participants, including many top runners from all over the world, take on the challenge of the 26.2-mile (42.2-km) course. The marathon starts in the town of Hopkinton, west of Boston, and finishes Downtown at the Boston Public Library on Boylston Street. More than half a million people line

Boats taking part in the Head of the Charles Regatta in October

the entire length of the course to cheer on the runners.

The other major event of the sporting year is the **Head of the Charles Regatta**. The world's largest two-day rowing competition is held annually during the third weekend of October on the Charles River. It involves more than 6,000 crew members, who represent clubs, universities, and colleges from around the world. The 3-mile (5-km) course runs upstream from Boston University boathouse to Eliot Bridge. With up to 80 boats in each race, crews set off at short intervals and are timed along the course.

This is a major social event, as well as a sports

Detail from plaque celebrating the Boston Marathon

one, with multitudes of spectators crowding both banks of the river, spread out on blankets and enjoying picnics and beer as they cheer on the rowers.

College Sports

Boston's major colleges actively compete in a number of sports, with the major events occurring during the winter and fall. The annual Harvard–Yale football game takes place on the Saturday before Thanksgiving and is usually a fun and spirited event, both on and off the field. The sport that Boston colleges are best at, however, is ice hockey, and the biggest event on the calendar is the fiercely contested Beanpot hockey tournament. This is held at TD Garden over two weekends in early February and involves the area's major colleges.

DIRECTORY

Baseball

Boston Red Sox
Fenway Park,
4 Yawkey Way.
Tel (617) 267-1700.
W redsox.com

Basketball

Boston Celtics
TD Garden,
1 Causeway St.
Map 1 C2.
Tel (617) 931-2222
(Ticketmaster).
W celtics.com

American Football

New England Patriots
Gillette Stadium,
Route 1, Foxboro.
Tel (617) 931-2222
(Ticketmaster).
W ticketmaster.com
W patriots.com

Ice Hockey

Boston Bruins
TD Garden
(see Boston Celtics).
W bostonbruins.com

Other Sports

Boston Cannons
Harvard Stadium,
65 N Harvard St., Allston.
Tel (617) 746-9933.

Boston Lobsters
Tel (877) 617-5627.
W bostonlobsters.net

Boston Marathon
Boston Athletic
Association.
Tel (617) 236-1652.
W bostonmarathon.org

Head of the Charles Regatta
W hocr.org

New England Revolution
Gillette Stadium
(see New England Patriots).
W revolutionsoccer.net

Suffolk Downs
Route 1a, East Boston.
Tel (617) 567-3900.
W suffolkdowns.com

CHILDREN'S BOSTON

First-time visitors to Boston may wonder what this city, famous for its history and learning, has to offer families with children. The answer is more than can possibly be explored in one visit, with an enormous variety of children's attractions and entertainment, as well as many helpful services and facilities. Whether you begin your adventure at Boston's acclaimed Children's Museum, head out to sea on a whale-watching expedition, take a specially designed children's walking tour of The

Freedom Trail, or visit Franklin Park Zoo, families will soon discover that Boston's unique heritage has as much to interest children as it does adults. A good starting point is the Prudential Center Skywalk (see p100), a 360-degree observatory from where children can locate the city's major landmarks, parks, and attractions. For parents hoping to find some time on their own, a few attractions have supervised children's activities and entertainment, and there are also various baby-sitting agencies.

Boston's Duck Tours – from dry land to the Charles River

Practical Advice

A useful monthly publication, found free at many local children's attractions, is *The Boston Parent's Paper*. This has detailed listings of events, attractions, and activities for kids throughout the Boston region. Children's events are also listed in Thursday's edition of *The Boston Globe*. Short-term baby-sitting can be arranged through **Parents in a Pinch**. **CVS Pharmacy** *(see p177)* is open 24 hours a day for supplies. Boston is easy to explore on foot, but be cautious before crossing streets with children, as Boston's drivers and cyclists can be very assertive. Boston's subway system *(see pp182–3)*, is free for children under 12 with an adult.

Tours and Historical Sights

There are many tours and historical sights in Boston which children will find both fun and interesting. They can board an amphibious World War II vehicle

for a land and water tour of historic Boston with **Boston Duck Tours** *(see p183)*. These drive past the city's historic neighborhoods and landmarks and then splash into the Charles River for a spectacular view of the Boston skyline. Boston's inner harbor and islands can be explored with **Boston Harbor Cruises**. Some cruises also stop at the U.S.S. *Constitution*, commonly known as "Old Ironsides" *(see p117)*. Even more breathtaking are the whale-watching trips, run all through the summer by the New England Aquarium *(see pp78–9)*.

Even if tickets to see the Red Sox games are sold out, baseball fans can still take the 60-minute tour of **Fenway Park** for a behind-the-scenes glimpse of the press box, private suites, and dugouts of this

historic ballpark. The experienced guides of **Boston by Foot** conduct special 60-minute family walking tours of the heart of The Freedom Trail *(see pp126–9)*. History comes alive for children as they walk along the old cobblestone streets, and visit many sites of architectural and historical significance. Tours begin and end in front of the statue of Samuel Adams at Faneuil Hall. This is the gateway to **Quincy Market** *(see p66)*, a lively emporium that sees flocks of tourists and locals alike, attracted by the enormous array of restaurants, shops, and entertainment. Children in particular will enjoy the jugglers, mime artists, musicians, and magicians who perform all around the attractive and traffic-free cobblestone marketplace.

Street entertainer, Quincy Market

Museums

Known as a pioneer of hands-on interactive learning, **Boston Children's Museum** *(see p77)* calls itself "Boston's Best Place for Kids," offering four floors of fun-filled education for toddlers to pre-teens in one building and three stories of exhibits in a new adjoining structure. Children can explore a 170-year-old house transplanted from Tokyo, create giant bubbles or conduct experiments in the Science Playground, and learn about healthy, active lifestyles in the KidPower exhibition. Children aged under three have their own Playspace, a stimulating second-floor area designed especially for them. The **Museum of Science** *(see p55)* could be another full-day stop, housing over 700 permanent exhibits exploring astronomy, energy, industry, anthropology, and nature. Younger children will enjoy the Human Body Connection Animal Care Center, while older kids can explore basic scientific principles in Investigate. All will be impressed by the life-sized Tyrannosaurus Rex and the To The Moon exhibit, with full-size models of the Apollo and Mercury space capsules. Attached to the museum there is also a Planetarium and an Omni IMAX film theater.

Playspace activity, Children's Museum

Few art museums have made their collections so accessible to families as the **Museum of Fine Arts, Boston** *(see pp106–9)*. Multi-session art classes and workshops are offered for kids and adults in several media, including drawing, painting, sculpture, and weaving. For more casual visitors, the MFA schedules children's art activities in the galleries and provides tote bags with suggested activities for families. During February and April school vacations, performances and art-making activities are organized throughout the galleries.

The unique history of Boston's African-American community is presented at two sites. The centerpiece of the **Museum of African American History** *(see p51)* is the oldest black church in the U.S., and the **Abiel Smith School** *(see p51)* was the first schoolhouse for black children in America. The schoolhouse has interactive computer stations where children can learn about slavery, the American abolitionist movement, and the Underground Railroad *(see p51)*, as well as more contemporary issues affecting African-Americans in New England. Older children may be interested in the **Black Heritage Trail** *(see p51)*, a 1.5-mile (2.5-km) guided walking tour that visits 14 sites significant to the history of free African-Americans. The **Boston Tea Party Ships & Museum** *(see p76)*, with models of the two brigantine ships involved in the infamous rebellion, features several interactive attractions after an extensive renovation.

Sports enthusiasts will want to take a trip to the **Sports Museum of New England**, where interactive exhibits,

Having fun, Boston Museum of Science

mini-presentations, and a vast collection of sports memorabilia chronicle the region's sporting history. Children will be fascinated by the life-size wooden statues of Larry Bird, Carl Yastrzemski, and Bobby Orr, and enthusiastically take the chance to try out a variety of sports equipment.

DIRECTORY

Practical Advice

Parents in a Pinch
Tel (855) 781-1303.
W parentsinapinch.com

Tours and Historical Sights

Boston by Foot
87 Mount Vernon Street.
Map 1 B4.
Tel (617) 367-2345.
W bostonbyfoot.com

Boston Harbor Cruises
Long Wharf.
Map 2 E3.
Tel (617) 227-4321.
W bostonharborcruises.com

Fenway Park
4 Yawkey Way.
Tel (617) 226-6666.
W redsox.com

Museums

Sports Museum of New England
TD Garden.
Map 1 C2.
Tel (617) 624-1234.
W sportsmuseum.org

Hands-on exhibit at Boston's Museum of Science

Capybara, one of the many fascinating animals at Franklin Park Zoo

Aquariums, Zoos, and Parks

Visitors are greeted by a group of harbor seals at the entrance to the **New England Aquarium** (see pp78–9), but once inside, all eyes are transfixed by the huge 200,000 gallon (900,000 liter) saltwater tank, which teems with tropical fish, sharks, sea turtles, and even the occasional scuba diver. The gently inclined wheelchair-friendly ramp winds up and around the three-story cylindrical tank, giving a fascinating view of this simulated marine environment. Young children will also enjoy getting their hands wet in the shark and ray touch tank and watching the penguins and the harbor seals. Families can take a whale-watching cruise or just watch a film on the enormous screen in the IMAX Theatre. Animal lovers will want to head directly to **Franklin Park Zoo** (see p104),

with its collection of native and exotic fauna. Don't miss the colorful Tropical Forest, the Giraffe and Zebra Savannah, Bird's World, and the majestic African lions in the Kalahari Kingdom. No visit to the city is complete without a gentle ride on the famous **Swan Boats** (see p48) in the city's Public Garden. The pedal-propelled boats gently glide across a lovely lagoon as ducks clamor alongside for a snack. Nearby are large bronze sculptures of Mrs. Mallard and family, immortalized

Bronze duck sculpture, Public Garden

in Robert McCloskey's 1941 children's classic *Make Way for Ducklings* (see p48). Crossing Charles Street, visitors will come to **Boston Common** (see pp48–9), which separates Downtown

from Beacon Hill and Back Bay. There is a playground here, as well as Frog Pond, which is a huge wading pool in the summer and a skating rink in the winter. Boston's most attractive park, the highlight of the Emerald Necklace, is **Arnold Arboretum** (see p104), in Jamaica Plain. With plenty of opportunities for exploration, it is a good place for children to let off steam.

Children's Theater

Children's theater thrives in Boston. The **Boston Children's Theatre** celebrated its 50th season in 2000, with its acclaimed "live theater for children by children." Mainstage productions run from December through April, and its Stagemobile takes performances outside to Boston's parks in the summer. The **Wheelock Family Theatre**, another highly acclaimed company, uses multi-ethnic and inter-generational casting, with performances on most weekends from September to May. Fables and fairy tales come to life at the **Puppet Showplace Theater**, with shows for pre-schoolers on Wednesday, and performances for families on weekends from September to May.

Visitors enjoying Swan Boat cruises in the pond, Public Garden

Marionettes on stage at the Puppet Showplace Theater

Children's Shopping

While keeping children entertained can often be a challenge, in Boston you will find that even shopping can hold their interest, with enticing window displays, and stores overflowing with desirable products. Do not, however, expect to survive such an outing without spending any money. In Cambridge, **Susi's Gallery for Children** has bright and innovative goods with a sense of whimsy, and **Henry Bear's Park** across town is especially well-stocked with toys graded by age. In Harvard Square, **The Curious George Store** carries one of the country's most complete stocks of children's books, while **Stellabella Toys** has a menagerie of cuddly stuffed animals and fun educational items. **Newbury Comics** features the best selection of comic books in Boston. **Games People Play** stocks a huge assortment of toys and games. The latest in cool clothing can be found at **Baby Gap**, and there's a wide selection of outdoor gear at **Patagonia**. It is well worth the trip to Brookline Village for the **Children's Book Shop**, which has an excellent selection of books for infants to young adults, and to Jamaica Plain for the bubbly **Boing! JP's Toy Shop**. Kids will also enjoy the shops, stalls, and street vendors at **Quincy Market** *(see p66)*.

Eating Out with Children

Though children never seem to tire of fast food, adults generally long for something more substantial and memorable. Both needs can be catered for in many of Boston's restaurants. Children will enjoy sampling Chinese delicacies at **China Pearl** in Chinatown. For pizza in an authentic Italian atmosphere, try the North End's **Pizzeria Regina**. In Cambridge, **The Cheesecake Factory** has an incredibly vast menu of casual fare as well as its eponymous sweets and is sure to please every family member. In the Huron Avenue shopping district in Cambridge, the friendly restaurant **Full Moon** has a play area as well as a varied kid's menu.

Popcorn, a favorite snack

DIRECTORY

Children's Theater

Boston Children's Theatre
316 Columbus Ave.
Map 3 C3.
Tel (617) 424-6634.
w bostonchildrens theatre.org

Puppet Showplace Theater
32–33 Station St.,
Brookline.
Tel (617) 731-6400.
w puppetshow place.org

Wheelock Family Theatre
200 The Riverway,
Brookline.
Tel (617) 879-2300.
w wheelock.edu/wft

Children's Shopping

Baby Gap
Copley Place, 100
Huntington Ave.
Map 3 C3.
Tel (617) 247-1754.

Boing! JP's Toy Shop
667 Centre St.,
Jamaica Plain.
Tel (617) 522-7800.

Children's Book Shop
237 Washington St.,
Brookline.
Tel (617) 734-7323.

The Curious George Store
1 JFK St., Cambridge.
Tel (617) 498-0062.

Games People Play
1100 Massachusetts Ave.,
Cambridge.
Tel (617) 492-0711.

Henry Bear's Park
17 White St., Cambridge.
Tel (617) 547-8424.

Newbury Comics
332 Newbury St.
Map 3 A3.
Tel (617) 236-4930.

Patagonia
346 Newbury St.
Map 3 A3.
Tel (617) 424-1776.

Stellabella Toys
1360 Cambridge St.,
Cambridge.
Tel (617) 491-6290.

Susi's Gallery for Children
348 Huron Ave.,
Cambridge.
Tel (617) 876-7874.

Eating Out with Children

The Cheesecake Factory
100 Cambridgeside
Place, Cambridge.
Tel (617) 252-3810.

China Pearl
9 Tyler St.
Map 4 F2.
Tel (617) 426-4338.

Full Moon
344 Huron Ave.,
Cambridge.
Tel (617) 354-6699.

Pizzeria Regina
11½ Thatcher St.
Map 2 D2.
Tel (617) 227-0765.

SURVIVAL GUIDE

PRACTICAL INFORMATION

More than most American cities, Boston is built to human scale. With the main parts of the city all within a relatively small area, Boston is ideal for the visitor, with walking not only possible, but often preferable, despite an efficient transit system. Boston is also one of the safest major cities in the U.S., and one of the most welcoming to international travelers, making it very easy to feel at home here and comfortable exploring. So long as visitors take a few sensible precautions, they should enjoy a trouble-free stay. Boston's visitor information centers help people get the most from their stay, and the city also deals better than most with the needs of children and the disabled.

Visas and Passports

Citizens of the U.K., most western European countries, Australia, New Zealand, Japan, Canada, Mexico, and Caribbean nations (except Cuba) need a valid, machine-readable passport and must register (and pay a small charge) before traveling with the Electronic System for Travel Authorization (ESTA) at esta.cbp.dhs.gov. The ESTA authorization is for a maximum stay of 90 days in the U.S. and remains valid for two years. Foreign visitors should check with their American consulate for details about passport and visa procedures.

Citizens of all other countries need a valid passport and a tourist visa, which can be obtained from a U.S. consulate or embassy.

Travel Safety

Visitors can get up-to-date travel safety information from the **Foreign and Commonwealth Office** in the U.K., the **State Department** in the U.S. and the **Department of Foreign Affairs and Trade** in Australia.

Tourist Information and Opening Hours

Visitor information desks at the airport can provide guides and maps and answer questions. The **Greater Boston Convention and Visitors Bureau** offers a comprehensive online guide for lodging, with links to make reservations. Major hotels also have helpful guest service desks. All of these places also hold a range of discount tickets for many of Boston's major museums and attractions, nightlife spots, theaters, and restaurants.

Opening hours vary greatly, so check in advance. In general, most shops and attractions are open 10am–6pm daily, with reduced hours on Sundays. Many shops stay open later on Thursdays, while key attractions, like the Museum of Fine Arts (see p106–7), offer extended hours one night a week.

Tax and Tipping

In Boston and the surrounding area, taxes will be added to hotel and restaurant charges and most retail purchases, except groceries and clothing items priced under $175. State sales tax is 6.25 per cent, and hotel tax in the Boston metropolitan area is 14.45 per cent.

Tipping is expected for most services: in restaurants tip 15–20 per cent of the bill, and give $1 per bag to porters and $2 to valet parking attendants. Bartenders expect $1–2 per drink.

Alcohol and Smoking

The legal minimum age for drinking alcohol in Boston is 21; most young people will be required to show photo identification (I.D.) as proof of age in order to get into bars and to purchase alcohol. It is illegal to drink in public spaces, and penalties for driving under the influence of alcohol are severe. The legal age for buying cigarettes is 21, and I.D. may also be required. It is illegal to smoke in public buildings and in all bars and restaurants (see p139).

Travelers with Special Needs

Massachusetts and U.S. law mandate accessibility for persons with handicaps, but wheelchair accessibility is sometimes limited in Boston's historic buildings. Most hotels and restaurants, however, are wheelchair accessible. **VSA (Very Special Arts) Massachusetts** provides useful information on disabled-accessible entertainment. For other information, contact the **Society for Accessible Travel and Hospitality**.

Visitor Information Center on Boston Common

◄ Exterior view of the busy South Station complex in Boston

Traveling with Children

Boston is in general a child-friendly city, boasting its own Children's Museum (*see p77*), as well as numerous other museums and a variety of attractions that offer interesting hands-on exhibits and activities for children (*see pp168–71*).

Families with children will find that the casual and fast-food restaurants cater best to their needs, with menus often tailored to children's tastes and appetites. Children are welcome at most of Boston's restaurants, however.

Traveling on a Budget

Boston hosts a large number of free attractions, exhibitions, and performances. For details, consult the websites of *The Boston Globe* and the **Boston Magazine** (*see p158*).

Students from abroad should purchase an **International Student Identity Card (I.S.I.C.)** before traveling, since there are many discounts available to students in Boston. The I.S.I.C. handbook lists places and services offering discounts to card-holders, including hotels, hostels, museums, tours, attractions, restaurants, and theaters. The **Student Advantage Card** is a similar card available to all American undergraduates.

International Student Identity Card, recognized student I.D. in America

Senior Travelers

Anyone over the age of 65 is eligible for various discounts with proof of age. Contact the **American Association of Retired Persons** for further information. Also the international senior travel organization **Road Scholar**, offers group vacations, courses and events in Boston.

Electricity

Electricity flows at 110–120 volts, and a two-prong plug is used. Non-U.S. appliances will need an adaptor and a voltage converter. Most hotel rooms have hairdriers, as well as sockets for electric shavers.

Cycling along the Charles River

Responsible Tourism

Long considered one of the U.S.'s most environmentally conscious cities, Boston continues to gain national acclaim for its forward-thinking policies, such as requiring all taxicabs to go hybrid by 2015.

It is easy to be green while in Boston. Recycling bins have become quite common, and most new buildings boast Earth-friendly features with respect to energy, lighting, and water supplies. The organization **Boston Green Tourism** aims to guide visitors toward green-certified hotels, restaurants, and shops, and the whole "green movement" has spread throughout the city's economic landscape.

Thousands of college students help boost the area's environmental causes, as do the passionate masses that make a living off of the region's seacoast and farms, while selling their wares at community farmers' markets or family-owned shops.

Seasonal farmers' markets pop up everywhere, from small town parks to Boston's City Hall Plaza (*see p64*). The best way to check when and where the next event will be is to consult www.massfarmers markets.org. For a permanent destination, the family-run Wilson Farm (www.wilson farm.com) has been luring visitors to Lexington (*see p121*) for its fresh apples, corn, and pumpkin since 1884.

Personal Security and Health

Boston is one of the U.S.'s safest cities and its low crime rate reflects its visitor-friendly environment. This has made its police force and community relations programs models for other American cities. Nonetheless, it is still prudent to take a few simple precautions and to keep to the tourist areas. The main sights are all located in safe parts of the city with lots of people and where serious crime is rare. If you are unfortunate enough to be taken ill during your visit, healthcare in Boston is world-class. This does not come cheaply, however, and it is recommended to have adequate insurance coverage before you travel.

Law Enforcement and Police

The most visible uniformed law enforcement personnel in Boston are the National Park Service (or Boston Park Service) rangers, usually dressed in olive green or khaki, and the members of the Boston Police Department (BPD), dressed in blue. You will also see City Parking and Traffic officers, who deal exclusively with traffic violations.

Should you encounter any trouble as a visitor, approach any of the blue-uniformed BPD officers who regularly patrol the city streets. Park rangers can often help with directions and general information.

If you need to report a crime, call the Boston **Police non-emergency line** or call 911 in an emergency.

What to be Aware of

Serious crime is rarely witnessed in the main sightseeing areas of Boston. However, avoid wandering into areas that are off the beaten track, during the day or at night. Police officers regularly patrol the tourist areas, but it is still advisable to use common sense, and to stay alert. Try not to advertise the fact that you are a visitor; prepare the day's itinerary in advance, and study your map

Boston police officer

before you set off. Avoid wearing expensive jewelry, and carry your camera or camcorder securely. Only carry small amounts of cash; credit cards are the most secure option.

Before you leave home, take a photocopy of all important documents, including your passport and visa, and keep them and any other valuables in your hotel safe. Keep an eye on your belongings at all times, whether checking into or out of the hotel, waiting at the airport, or sitting in a bar or restaurant.

Emergencies

If you are involved in a **medical** emergency, go to a hospital emergency room. Should you need an ambulance, call 911 (toll-free) and one will be sent. Also call 911 for **police** or **fire** department assistance.

If you have your medical insurance properly arranged, you need not worry about medical costs. Depending on the limitations of your insurance, it is better to avoid the overcrowded city-owned hospitals listed in the phone book Blue Pages, and opt instead for one of the private hospitals listed in the Yellow Pages. Alternatively, ask at your hotel desk or at the nearest pharmacy for information on your nearest hospital. For **dental referrals** contact the Massachusetts Dental Society. You can also ask your hotel to call a doctor or dentist to visit you.

If you lose your credit cards, most card companies, for example **American Express**, have toll-free numbers for reporting a loss or theft.

Lost Property

Although the chances of retrieving lost property are slim, you should report all stolen items to the police. Use the **Police Non-Emergency Line**. Make sure you keep a copy of the police report, which you will need for your insurance claim. In case of loss, it is useful to have a list of your valuables' serial numbers or a photocopy of any relevant documents or receipts as proof of possession. This should be kept separately. It is also useful to try and remember the taxi companies or bus routes you use, as it might make it easier to retrieve lost items. If your passport is lost or stolen, get in touch with your country's embassy or consulate immediately.

Mounted Boston Park Service ranger, Copley Square

Fire engine

Ambulance

Police car

Hospitals and Pharmacies

Forming one of the country's most renowned medical communities, Boston's hospitals are primarily clustered around the Fenway and near Beacon Hill, with several other facilities dotted around the city. Patients come from all over the world to seek treatment at legendary institutions like **Children's Hospital Boston** and **Massachusetts General**

Hospital (both private). Regardless of one's insurance situation, hospital emergency rooms are required to treat all patients; however, waiting times can reach several hours and costs can be exorbitant. The Massachusetts General Hospital also maintains an **International Patient Center** for those in need of interpreting services, as well as dedicated housing and financial arrangements.

Plan in advance: if you take medication, bring a back-up supply with you. However, if you need a prescription dispensed, there are plenty of pharmacies (drugstores) in and around the city, some staying open 24 hours a day. Ask your hotel for the nearest one. **CVS Pharmacy** is a popular chain of drugstores. The larger pharmacies, such as CVS, can also be a helpful resource for those with basic medical questions and concerns,

from an upset stomach to an allergy.

Those needing dental assistance should check first to see if their travel insurance covers dental aid; like emergency medical fees, unforeseen dentist visits can break the bank. A less expensive option for those without coverage is to visit a clinic such as the **Tufts University School of Dental Medicine** where practicing students work.

Travel Insurance

Travel insurance is not compulsory but strongly recommended when traveling to the U.S. It is important to have insurance for emergency medical and dental care, which can be expensive, even in city-owned hospitals and clinics. Even with coverage you may have to pay for the services, then claim reimbursement from your insurance company.

In addition, it is advisable to make sure your personal property is insured and to obtain coverage for lost or stolen baggage, travel documents, and accidental death or injury.

DIRECTORY

Emergencies

American Express
Tel (212) 758-6510.
W americanexpress.com

Dental Referrals
Tel (800) 342-8747.
W massdental.org

Medical Referrals
Tel (781) 893-4610 or (800) 322-2303.

Police, Fire, Medical (all emergencies)
Tel 911 (toll-free).

Lost Property

Police Non-Emergency Line
Tel Boston
(617) 343-4200.
Tel Cambridge
(617) 349-3300.

Consulates

Australia
150 East 42nd St., 34th floor, New York, NY 10017.
Tel (212) 351-6500.
W australianyc.org

Canada
3 Copley Place. **Map** 3 C3.
Tel (617) 262-3760.
W boston.gc.ca

Ireland
535 Boylston St.
Map 3 C2.
Tel (617) 267-9330.
W dfa.ie/irish-consulate/boston

New Zealand
37 Observatory Circle, NW
Washington, DC 20008.
Tel (202) 328-4800.
W nzembassy.com

United Kingdom
1 Memorial Drive, Cambridge.
Tel (617) 245-4500.
W gov.uk/government/world/organisations/british-consulate-general-boston

Hospitals and Pharmacies

Children's Hospital Boston
300 Longwood Ave.
Tel (617) 355-6000.
W childrenshospital.org

CVS Pharmacy
587 Boylston St. **Map** 3 C2.
Tel (617) 437-8414.
(Store and pharmacy open 24 hours.)

35 White St., Cambridge.
Tel (617) 876-5519.
(Open 24 hours.)

Massachusetts General Hospital
50 Blossom St.
Map 1 B3.
Tel (617) 726-2000.
W massgeneral.org

MGH International Patient Center
55 Fruit St., Blake 180.
Map 1 B3.
Tel (617) 726-2787.
W massgeneral.org/international

Tufts University School of Dental Medicine
1 Kneeland St. **Map** 4 F2.
Tel (617) 636-6828.
W dental.tufts.edu

Banking and Currency

Throughout Boston there are various places to access and exchange your money, from the numerous banks and ATMs to the foreign currency exchanges. The most important things to remember are not to carry all your money and credit cards with you at one time, and to be aware that most banks and currency exchanges are closed on Sundays.

One of Bank of America's many branches in Boston

Banking and Currency Exchange

Boston has branches of numerous national banking chains, including **Bank of America**, **Citizens Bank**, and **TD Bank**. Most banks are open Monday through Friday from 9am to 5pm, although some may open earlier and close later. Most banks also open Saturday mornings from 9am to noon or 1pm. All banks are closed on Sundays and Federal holidays *(see p39)*.

Always ask if there are any special fees or commission charges before you make your transaction. At most banks, traveler's checks in U.S. dollars can be cashed with any form of photo identification, although a passport is usually required if you want to exchange any foreign money. Foreign currency exchange is available at the main branches of large banks, which often have a separate dedicated area or teller window for foreign exchange.

Foreign currency exchanges are generally open weekdays from 9am to 5pm, but some – especially those in busy shopping districts – may have extended opening hours. Among the best-known companies are **American Express Travel Service** and **Travelex Currency Services**, both of which have several branches in and around Boston. Most currency exchanges charge a fee or commission, so it is worth looking around to get the best value rates. Hotels may also exchange money, but their fees will usually be much more expensive.

ATMs

ATMs (cash machines) can be found throughout Boston. They are usually located near the entrance to banks, and sometimes inside convenience stores and supermarkets. The most widely accepted types of bank cards include Cirrus, Plus, NYCE, and some credit cards such as VISA and MasterCard. Note that a fee may be levied on your cash withdrawal depending on the bank. Before you travel, ensure you check with your bank which machines your card can access and the various fees charged.

To minimize the risk of robbery, always be aware of your surroundings and the people around you when using an ATM. Avoid using ATMs in isolated areas. Make sure you shield your PIN and, if available, use a machine located within a bank. Be careful when removing your card from the machine.

American Express charge cards

Credit Cards and Debit Cards

American Express, VISA, MasterCard, Diner's Club, and the Discover Card, as well as most debit cards, are accepted almost everywhere in Boston, from theaters and hotels to restaurants and shops.

Besides being a much safer alternative to carrying a lot of cash, credit and debit cards offer some useful additional benefits, such as insurance on your purchases and access to the daily exchange rate. They are also essential if you want to reserve a hotel or book a rental car. Credit cards can also be useful in emergencies when cash may not be readily available.

Before traveling it would be wise to phone your card provider and inform them that you will be abroad, or you risk finding that your card gets blocked when you start using it in Boston.

DIRECTORY

Banking and Currency Exchange

American Express Travel Service
155 Federal St.
Map 2 D4.
Tel (617) 439-4400.

Bank of America
100 Federal St.
Map 2 D4.
Tel (617) 434-3412.
W **bankofamerica.com**

Citizens Bank
73 Tremont St.
Map 1 C5.
Tel (617) 422-8295.
W **citizensbank.com**

TD Bank
579 Boylston St.
Map 1 A5.
Tel (617) 266-0740.
W **tdbank.com**

Travelex Currency Services
Logan Airport, Terminal E.
Tel (617) 567-1030.
W **travelex.com**

Communications and Media

Boston's communications infrastructure is modern and well developed. Public payphones can still be found on some streets and in hotel lobbies. Visitors will find the city is well supplied with cell phone stores, Internet cafés, and public access to computers and Wi-Fi. News is readily available from Boston's many television and radio stations, newspapers, and magazines, and the postal service is quick and efficient – whether you are sending mail within the U.S. or abroad.

Telephones

Public telephones are found on some street corners and in many hotels. Most accept coins as well as phonecards, which can be purchased at gas stations, convenience stores, and newsstands. Local calls cost 50 cents to $1 from payphones; long-distance call rates vary. All numbers with a 1-800, 866, 877, or 888 prefix, however, are free of charge. Direct calls can also be made from hotel rooms but usually carry hefty surcharges. Unless you are using your own international telephone card, it is cheaper to use the payphone in the lobby.

For directory assistance, dial 411 (local) or 00 (international); for operator assistance, dial 0 (local) or 01 (international.) All operator-assisted calls carry a surcharge. For emergency services (police, fire, or ambulance) call 911.

Cell Phones

In America, there are several cell phone systems (AT&T is one of the largest). Check with your service provider to learn about your options when abroad. Some phones require a chip or need to be unlocked for international usage, while others carry hefty roaming charges. Renting a cell phone while in America (try Cell Hire) is an attractive, and often cheaper, option for many international visitors.

Area Codes

Central Boston's area codes are 617 and 857; include this when dialing local calls. If dialing out of the local area (but within the U.S. or Canada) dial 1, then the area code.

For international calls, dial 011, then the country code, the area code (minus the first 0), and the local number.

Internet and Email

From neighborhood coffee shops and hotel lobbies to parks, there are Wi-Fi hotspots all over the city. Those traveling without their computers or Internet-enabled devices can visit a library – **Boston Public Library**'s main branch has several Internet terminals for public use – or an Internet café.

Postal Service

Post offices are open from 9am to 5pm, Monday through Friday, and most are also open Saturday from 9am to noon. They close on Sundays and for all Federal holidays.

If the correct postage is attached, letters and parcels of less than 13 oz (370 g) can be put in any blue mailbox. Pick-up times are written inside the lid. Always use a zip code to ensure delivery, and send all overseas mail by airmail to avoid long delays.

Boston post office, Charles Street

Newspapers and Magazines

The most widely read newspaper in the Boston area is *The Boston Globe (see p158)*, which is thought of as one of the best newspapers in the U.S. The other widely available local daily is the *Boston Herald* tabloid (www.bostonherald.com). The Thursday and Friday editions of *The Boston Globe*, and *Boston Magazine (see p158)*, published monthly, contain listings of entertainment and cultural events in Boston.

Television and Radio

The Boston media market is highly competitive. Major network television stations include CBS (channel 4), ABC (channel 5), NBC (channel 7), and Fox (channel 25). Public television station PBS is on channel 2. Popular radio stations include NPR (National Public Radio) on WBUR (90.9 FM), KISS-108 (107.9 FM), WCRB (99.5 FM) for classical music, and WMJX (106.7 FM) for easy listening.

DIRECTORY

Cell Phones

AT&T
W att.com

Cell Hire
W cellhire.com

Internet and Email

Boston Public Library
700 Boylston St.
Map 3 C2.
W bpl.org

Post Offices

Financial District
31 Milk St.
Map 2 D4.
Tel (617) 482-1956.

North End
217 Hanover St.
Map 2 E2.
Tel (617) 723-6397.
W usps.gov

TRAVEL INFORMATION

Arriving in Boston is fairly easy. The city is served by Logan International Airport as well as by the smaller satellites in Manchester, NH, and near Providence, RI, which are both located within 50 miles (80 km) of the city center. Amtrak trains come into Boston's South Station, as do bus carriers. From here, the subway, known as the "T," connects to almost every part of the city. Boston also makes an ideal base from which to take day or weekend trips to the numerous places of interest throughout the New England area.

Arriving by Air

Situated in East Boston, **Logan International Airport** is the major airport serving Boston and the surrounding area, although some international charter flights and several domestic carriers use the smaller and less crowded **Manchester New Hampshire Airport** and **T.F. Green Airport** in Warwick, Rhode Island. Both are a bus ride of around an hour from Boston.

Boston is served by almost all North American airlines and by most international airlines, either directly or in partnership with U.S. carriers. Often the least expensive flights, especially between continental Europe and Boston, require making a connection in New York. There are frequent non-stop flights available between Boston and the United Kingdom and Ireland on U.S. carriers, as well as British Airways and Aer Lingus.

Logan International lies within Boston city limits on a peninsula across the inner harbor from the central city. Harbor tunnel crossings tend to act as a bottleneck, which slows taxi services between the airport and downtown. At busy times, a taxi ride ($20–30) can

Control Tower at Boston's Logan International Airport

take 30 minutes or more, with much of the trip spent in bumper-to-bumper traffic. The least expensive means of getting from the airport to downtown Boston is via the M.B.T.A. subway (see pp182–3) on the Silver Line to South Station. This takes 18–25 minutes. There are also bus services that run between the airport and Boston's suburbs. Arguably the most scenic approach into Boston is the **Boston Water Taxi**, with stops at Logan Airport, and Central and Long wharves. The journey takes about 20–25 minutes.

Airfares

For cheap air fares, search online on websites such as www.lastminute.com and www.expedia.com. The more you shop around, the better deal you will get, and it is worth taking the time to do some research. For inexpensive consolidated tickets, contact **Kayak.com** online or give **AirlineConsolidator.com** a try. The easiest way to find the best fare is to use the website **CheapTickets.com**.

High season runs from June to August, as well as around Easter and Christmas, when flights are at their most expensive. Travelers should also be aware of price hikes when scheduling a visit around large events like the Boston Marathon (see p36) and university commencement ceremonies. May, September, and October are generally less expensive, and any other time of the year is considered off-peak. Flights are usually least expensive for travel from Tuesday to Thursday. APEX tickets, usually the best deal, must be booked a few weeks in advance. However, note that these tickets must include a Saturday night.

City Water Taxi, running from Logan Airport to Central and Long wharves

Package Deals

Boston packages are sometimes available in the U.S. as part of a fall foliage bus tour or through the AAA (American Automobile Association; *see p185*). Several airlines arrange packages including travel and lodging. Boston hotels generally post their special event packages on the website of the Greater Boston Convention and Visitors Bureau *(see p175)*.

Arriving by Car

Boston is not called "The Hub" for nothing, as most routes in the northeast converge here. The principal routes from the north are I-95 from the coast and I-93 from northern New England. I-90 comes in from the west as the Massachusetts Turnpike. I-93 approaches from the south as the Southeast Expressway, while I-95, formerly known as Rte 128, circumvents Boston. Exits from the roadway to parts of downtown come up quickly, so check your exit number in advance.

Arriving by Train

A train service between New York and Boston via coastal Connecticut and Rhode Island is provided by **Amtrak**. Conventional train services take 4–5 hours, and arrive at and depart from Boston's South

Amtrak train waiting to depart from Boston's South Station

Station. A high-speed service that takes 3 hours is also available but is more expensive. The Amtrak service extends north to Maine and south to Philadelphia, Washington, D.C., and beyond.

Arriving by Bus

Although taking a bus is easily the slowest and usually cheapest way to get to Boston, it need not be unpleasant. **Greyhound Bus Lines** and **Peter Pan Trailways** both serve the city of Boston as long-distance carriers, sharing quarters at the South Station bus terminal. Both offer routes around the country and provide discounts for children, senior citizens, and U.S. military personnel on active duty. Both also offer bargain excursion tickets for unlimited travel within a certain time period for a single fixed rate.

Discount carriers include the modern **BoltBus** and **MegaBus**, as well as several no-frills companies that depart from Boston's Chinatown.

Greyhound Bus Lines logo

Main concourse of Boston's South Station

Getting Around Boston

Public transportation in Boston and Cambridge is very good. In fact, it is considerably easier to get around by public transportation than by driving, with the added benefit of not having to find a parking space. All major attractions in the city are accessible on the subway, by bus, or by taxi. The central sections of the city are also extremely easy to navigate on foot.

M.B.T.A. commuter bus, with distinctive yellow paintwork

Green Travel

Boston's moniker of "America's Walking City" hints at how easy it is to tour the city in this environmentally friendly way. Those needing to cover some serious ground can lean on one of the U.S.'s oldest public transportation systems. The **M.B.T.A.** has worked with the Environmental Protection Agency on projects like loco-motive engine pollution-control devices, while replacing its diesel-powered bus fleet with natural gas-powered buses. Visitors can reach almost any-where in the metro area – from the historic towns of Lexington and Concord to the Boston Harbor Islands – using public transportation. The Boston "T"'s own website offers public transit and walking directions to just about anywhere in the city. The 17-mile (27-km) Esplanade trail along the **Charles River** (where you can rent canoes and kayaks) and the Minuteman Bikeway (see p164) offer ample opportunities for bikers, joggers, and walkers.

Finding Your Way

The Greater Boston Convention and Visitors Bureau (see p175) provides a helpful contact point. To find out about any upcoming cultural events, check the websites for *Boston Magazine* and *The Boston Globe (see p158).*

Most of Boston is laid out "organically" rather than in the sort of strict grid found in many American cities. When trying to orient yourself, it helps to think of Boston as enclaves of neigh-borhoods around a few central squares. In general, uphill from Boston Common is Beacon Hill, downhill is Downtown. Back Bay begins west of Arlington Street. The North End sticks out from the north side of Boston, while the Waterfront is literally that, where Boston meets the sea.

M.B.T.A. Subway and Trolley Cars

Boston's subway system is the oldest in North America, but it has been vastly expanded and modernized since the first cars rolled between Park Street and Boylston Street in 1897. The street trolley system began in 1846 with trolleys drawn along tracks by horses. In 1889, the system was electrified.

Combined, the subway and trolley lines are known as the "T." The "T" operates 5–12:45am Monday through Saturday, and 6–12:45am Sunday. Week-day service is officially every 3–15 minutes; on weekends it is less frequent.

Charlie Card, valid on Boston's public transit network

There are five lines: the Red Line runs from south of the city to Cambridge, and the Green Line from the Museum of Science westward into the suburbs. The Blue Line begins near Government Center and goes to Logan Airport and on to Revere, while the Orange Line links the northern suburbs to southwest Boston. The Silver Line, a surface bus, runs from Roxbury to Logan Airport via South Station. Maps of the system are available at the Downtown Crossing M.B.T.A. station.

Admission to subway stations is via turnstiles into which you insert a paper Charlie ticket or touch your plastic CharlieCard on the reader. Day or week LinkPasses for unlimited travel can be purchased at stations and Airport "T" stops, and can be loaded on to Charlie tickets or CharlieCards.

M.B.T.A. Buses

The bus system complements the subway system and in effect enlarges the entire transit network to cover more than 1,000 miles (1,600 km). However, buses are often crowded. The Your Bus M.B.T.A. app shows real-time schedules linked to location. Two useful routes for sightseeing are Charlestown–Haymarket, (from Haymarket, near Quincy Market, to Bunker Hill) and Harvard–Dudley (from Harvard Square via Massachusetts Avenue, through Back Bay and the South End, to Dudley Square in Roxbury). Cash, a Charlie ticket, or a plastic CharlieCard is required for the fare.

Walking in Boston

Boston is considered North America's premier walking city – partly because it is so compact, and partly because virtually all streets are flanked by sidewalks. It is nonetheless essential to wear comfortable walking shoes with adequate cushioning and good support.

Because Boston is principally a city of neighborhoods, it is often simplest to use public transportation to get to a particular neighborhood, and then to walk to soak up the atmosphere. Walking also allows you to see parts of the city that are impractical to explore by car because the streets are too narrow – for example, Beacon Hill, parts of the North End, and Harvard Square.

Boston parkland, ideal for walking

Taxis

Taxis can be found at taxi stands in tourist areas or be hailed on the street. They may pick up fares only in the city for which they are licensed – Cambridge taxis in Cambridge, and Boston taxis in Boston. It is possible to call a taxi

company and arrange a pickup time and place.

Rates are calculated by both mileage and time, starting with a standard "pickup" fee (around $3) when the meter starts running. Taxis in Boston and Cambridge are generally more expensive than in other U.S. cities. Taxis to Logan International charge an airport-use fee (around $3), while those coming from Logan charge for the harbor tunnel toll (around $7). Additional surcharges may apply late at night. A full schedule of fares should be posted inside the vehicle, along with the driver's photograph and permit, the taxi's permit number, and directions for reporting complaints. **Uber** coverage is very thorough in Boston and Cambridge.

Cycling

Boston and Cambridge have an extensive network of bike paths, plus a bike rental system

called **HubWay** (www.the hubway.com). Cycling on the highways is illegal, city streets can be hazardous, and cycling on sidewalks is discouraged. Cycling is a fun way to see some of the outlying sights. Cycle shops and some newsstands carry the Boston Bike Map, which details trails and paths across the metropolitan region. For more on cycling, *see p164*.

Guided Tours

Many city tours, including **Old Town Trolley Tours** and theme tours (such as "ghosts" or "chocolate"), depart from the Visitor Information Center on Boston Common. The **Boston Duck Tours** use an open-air amphibious vehicle that tours the streets and navigates the Charles River. Also, **National Park Service** rangers offer free walking tours of Boston's parks, the Freedom Trail (*see pp126–9*), and the Black Heritage Trail (*see p51*).

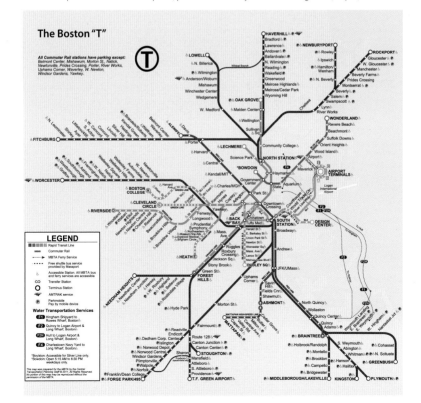

The Boston "T"

Boston traffic by night with the Financial District in the background

Driving

Despite heavy traffic and restricted parking, having your own vehicle in Boston can, at times, be an undeniable convenience. For example, visiting some of the outlying sights of Boston (see *Getting Out of Boston p185*), which may be difficult to reach by public transportation, is much easier with a car. Many U.S. visitors to the city arrive with their own cars, and overseas visitors can rent one quite easily. Even so, driving in and around Boston requires patience, humor, reliable maps, good driving skills, and the ability to read the road swiftly and take decisive actions.

Despite Boston's comparatively small size, its traffic can at times rival that of much larger cities such as Rome or New York. Boston has far too many vehicles for its roads, and the city's many one-way streets can prove confusing to everyone except the locals, who will honk at befuddled visitors. Road construction is ubiquitous, as Boston constantly upgrades underground utilities. Use the Street Finder (see pp188–91) or another good map (the best show the direction of one-way streets) to help you get around. Also avoid the rush hours of 8–9:30am and 4–6pm and plan your route in advance so you can con-centrate on traffic.

Rules of the Road

The highway speed limit in the Boston area is 55 mph (88 km/h) – much lower than in many European countries. In residential areas, the speed limit ranges from 20 to 35 mph (32–48 km/h). Near schools, it can be as low as 15 mph (24 km/h). It is important to obey all signs or you will risk getting a ticket. If you are stopped by the police, be courteous or you may face a larger fine. In addition, all drivers are required to carry a valid driver's license and registration documents for their vehicle.

Parking

Curbside parking is hard to find at the most popular locations, and during morning and afternoon rush hours curbside parking is banned altogether in some areas. If you do manage to find a space on the street, be sure to feed the meter, or you might face a hefty fine. Vehicles parked near fire hydrants, alleyways, in spaces reserved for the handicapped, or at overland "T" and bus stops may be towed away, and you will be able to retrieve them only at considerable cost and inconvenience. Parking at meters is free on Sundays and public holidays,

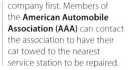

"Tow Zone" sign

and many downtown areas allow parking in loading zones on Sunday as well. Read posted signs carefully. Parking in a public lot or garage can cost more than $10 per hour or $40 per day, but it is sometimes the only choice. Valet parking is available at some restaurants, hotels, and malls for a fee.

In order to avoid traffic congestion in the city center, visitors may consider parking near a "T" or bus stop in the suburbs, and continuing their journey into town by public transportation.

Gas

Compared to much of the rest of the world, gas (petrol) is less expensive in the U.S. However, with the large engines that are often found in older American cars, any savings on fuel may be partially offset. Gas comes in three grades: economy, super, and premium. There are many gas stations in and around Boston, and they often have self-service pumps. The gas at these is often a few cents cheaper per gallon than at pumps with attendants.

Breakdowns

In the unlucky event of a breakdown, the best course of action is to pull off the road completely and put on the hazard lights to alert other drivers that you are stationary. There are emergency phones along some major interstate highways, but in other situations, it is best to contact breakdown services or even the police from land and cell phones. In the event of a breakdown, drivers of rental cars should contact the car rental company first. Members of the **American Automobile Association (AAA)** can contact the association to have their car towed to the nearest service station to be repaired.

Car Rental

You must be at least 21-years old with a valid driving license (plus an international driver's license if from outside the U.S.) to rent a car. Drivers under 25 may be charged additional fees. All rental agencies require a credit card or a cash deposit. Collision and liability insurances are recommended, but they are sometimes offered free with credit cards. Return the car with a full tank of gas to avoid inflated agency fuel prices. Save paying airport fees by picking up and dropping off your car downtown.

Getting Out of Boston

Boston holds enough treasures to satisfy even the most finicky of tourists, but any visitor would be wise to escape the city in order to appreciate the area's historical sites, stunning natural beauty, and world-class dining and entertainment options. Fortunately, most of this can be achieved without the use of a car, as public transportation options abound. Cambridge (see pp110–16) and Charlestown (see p117) are easily accessible using the M.B.T.A.'s subway and bus lines, and the M.B.T.A. commuter rail service links the city with destinations farther out, including historic Salem and Gloucester, as well as the scenic waterfronts and beaches of Newburyport and Cohasset. The commuter boat system also ferries passengers from the city's waterfront to various stops along the South Shore. Consider renting a bike (which you can bring along on the bus, boat, or train) to explore the historic sites and battlefields in Concord (see pp118–20) and Lexington (see p121), or the area's scenic coastline. Several bike shops offer daily rentals, and there are a few companies, such as **Urban AdvenTours**, that offer guided bike tours.

Many visitors to the Boston area also take advantage of seasonal excursions. For the summer, Cape Cod and its islands (Martha's Vineyard and Nantucket), not to mention Rhode Island's stunning coastline, are within a 2-hour journey from the city. It's possible to reach these destinations by plane, bus, or boat, but visitors will have an easier time using a rental car. When fall arrives, the areas north of the city – extending up into Vermont, New Hampshire, and Maine – lure leaf-peepers from all over the world to see breathtaking foliage. Again, to see this region, a car is necessary. Except in the very high season, traffic and parking aren't much of a problem for these getaways.

Amtrak (see p181) provides a scenic, albeit slower and usually more expensive, option when it comes to escaping north – the Downeaster service travels along Maine's rugged coastline up to inviting Brunswick, and south to Rhode Island and Connecticut.

The picturesque, peaceful marina at Newburyport

DIRECTORY

Green Travel

Charles River Canoe & Kayak
Kendall Sq., Cambridge.
Tel (617) 492-0941.
ⓦ paddleboston.com

M.B.T.A.
10 Park Plaza.
Tel (617) 222-3200.
ⓦ mbta.com

Taxis

Boston Cab Dispatch, Inc.
Tel (617) 262-2227.

Checker Cab Co. of Cambridge
Tel (617) 497-9000.

Town Taxi
Tel (617) 536-5000.

Uber
ⓦ uber.com

Yellow Cab
Cambridge.
Tel (617) 547-3000.

Guided Tours

Boston Duck Tours
Prudential Center.
Map 3 B3.
Tel (617) 267-3825.
ⓦ ducktours.com

National Park Service
Tel (617) 242-5642.
ⓦ nps.gov/bost

Old Town Trolley Tours
Boston Common Visitors' Center. **Map** 1 C4.
Tel (617) 269-7010.
ⓦ trolleytours.com

Breakdowns

American Automobile Association (AAA)
125 High St., Boston.
Tel (800) 222-4357 or (617) 443-9300.
ⓦ AAA.com

Car Rental

Alamo
Tel (877) 222-9075.
ⓦ alamo.com

Avis
Tel (800) 331-1212.
ⓦ avis.com

Budget
Tel (800) 527-0700.
ⓦ budget.com

Dollar
Tel (800) 800-4000.
ⓦ dollar.com

Enterprise
Tel (800) 736-8222.
ⓦ enterprise.com

Hertz
Tel (800) 654-3131.
ⓦ hertz.com

Thrifty Car Rental
Tel (800) 847-4389.
ⓦ thrifty.com

Getting Out of Boston

Urban AdvenTours
103 Atlantic Ave.
Map 2 E3.
Tel (617) 670-0637.
ⓦ urbanadventours.com

BOSTON STREET FINDER

The key map below shows the area of Boston covered by the *Street Finder* maps, which can be found on the following pages only. Map references, given throughout this guide, for sights, restaurants, hotels, shops, and entertainment venues refer to the grid on the maps. The first figure in the map reference indicates which *Street Finder* map to turn to (1 to 4), and the letter and number that follow refer to the grid reference on that map.

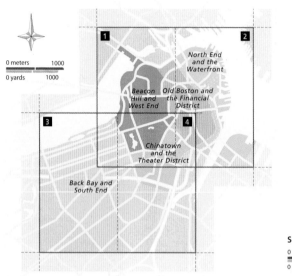

Key

- Major sight
- Place of interest
- Other building
- Ferry boarding point
- Main railroad station
- "T" station
- Bus station
- Tourist information
- Hospital with A&E unit
- Police station
- Church
- Railroad
- Motorway
- Pedestrian street

Scale of Map Pages 1–4

0 meters   250
0 yards   250

A

A Street	4 F4
Acorn Street	1 B4 & 4 D1
Adams Place	1 B3
African Meeting House	1 C3
Albany Street	4 D5
Anderson Street	1 B3
Appleton Street	3 C3
Arch Street	2 D4 & 4 F1
Arlington Street	1 A4 & 4 D1
Ash Street	2 D4 & 4 F1
Ash Street	4 E3
Athens Street	4 F4
Atlantic Avenue	2 D5 & 4 F2
Avenue De Lafayette	1 C5 & 4 F2
Avery Street	1 C5 & 4 E2

B

B Street	4 F5
Back Bay Station	3 C3
Battery Street	2 E2
Battery Wharf	2 E2
Batterymarch Street	2 D4
Beach Street	1 C5 & 4 E2
Beacon Street	1 A4 & 3 A4
Beaver Place	1 A4 & 4 D1
Bedford Street	2 D5 & 4 F2
Bell Atlantic Building	2 D4
Belvidere Street	3 A3
Benton Street	3 A5
Berkeley Street	1 A4 & 3 C1
Blackstone Block	2 D3
Blackstone Square	3 C5

Blackstone Street	2 D3
Blagden Street	3 C3
Blossom Court	1 B2
Blossom Street	1 B2
Bond Street	4 D4
Boston Athenaeum	1 C4
Boston Center for the Arts	4 D3
Boston Globe Store	2 D4 & 4 F1
Boston Opera House	1 C5 & 4 E1
Boston Public Library	3 C2
Boston Tea Party Ship	2 E5
Bosworth Street	1 C4 & 4 F1
Bowdoin Street	1 C4
Bowker Street	1 C3
Boylston Street	1 A5 & 3 B3
Braddock Park	3 B3
Bradford Street	4 D4
Branch Street	1 B4 & 4 D1
Brattle Book Shop	1 C4 & 4 E1
Bridge Court	1 B3
Bristol Street	4 E4
Broad Street	2 E4
Broadway	4 F3
Bromfield Street	1 C4 & 4 F1
Burbank Street	3 A4
Burke Street	3 A5
Byron Street	1 B4 & 4 D1

C

Cambria Street	3 A3
Cambridge Street	1 B3
Camden Street	3 B5
Canal Street	2 D2
Cardinal O'Connell Way	1 B2

Causeway Street	1 C2
Cedar Lane Way	1 B4
Center Plaza	1 C3
Central Wharf	2 E3
Chandler Street	4 D3
Charles Street	1 B2
Charles Street Meeting House	1 B4
Charlesbank Park	1 A2
Charlestown Avenue	1 A1
Charter Street	2 D2
Chatham Street	2 D3
Chauncy Street	1 C5 & 4 F2
Chester Park	3 B5
Chestnut Street	1 A4 & 4 D1
Children's Museum	2 E5
Christian Science Center	3 B3
Christopher Columbus Park	2 E3
Church Street	4 D2
City Square	1 C1
Claremont Park	3 B4
Clarendon Street	1 A5 & 3 C1
Clark Street	2 E2
Clearway Street	3 A3
Clinton Street	2 D3
Clough House	2 E2
Colonial Theatre	1 B5 & 4 E2
Columbia	2 D5 & 4 F2
Columbus Avenue	1 B5 & 3 A5
Commercial Avenue	1 A2
Commercial Street	2 D1
Commercial Street	2 E3
Commercial Wharf	2 E3
Commonwealth Avenue	3 B2
Concord Street	3 C5

Congress Street	2 D3
Cooper Street	2 D2
Copley Place	3 C3
Copley Square	3 C2
Copp's Hill Burying Ground	2 D2
Cortes Street	4 D3
Cotting Street	1 C2
Court Houses	1 C3
Court Street	2 D3
Coventry Street	3 A5
Cross Street	2 D3
Cross Street	2 E3
Cunard Street	3 A5
Custom House	2 E3
Cutler Majestic Theatre	1 C5 & 4 E2

D

Dalton Street	3 A3
Dartmouth Place	3 C3
Dartmouth Street	3 C2
Davenport Street	3 B5
Dedham Street	4 D4
Derne Street	1 C3
Devonshire Street	2 D5 & 4 F1
Dorchester Avenue	4 F5
Dwight Street	4 D4

E

East Street	2 D5 & 4 F2
East Berkeley Street	4 D3
East Brookline Street	4 D5
East Canton Street	4 D5

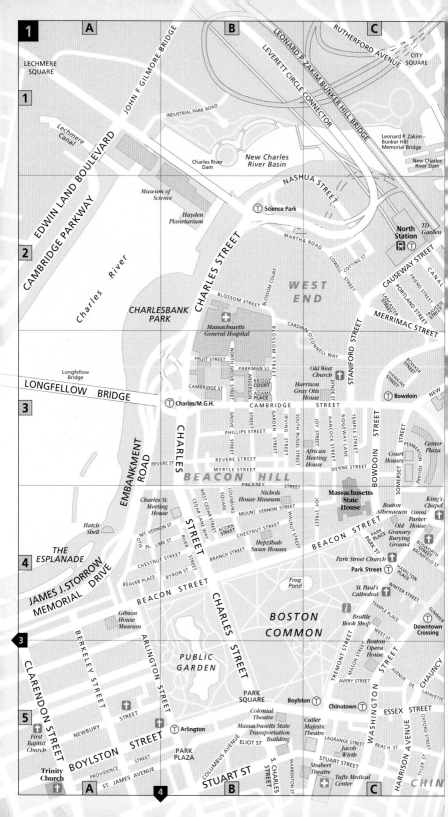

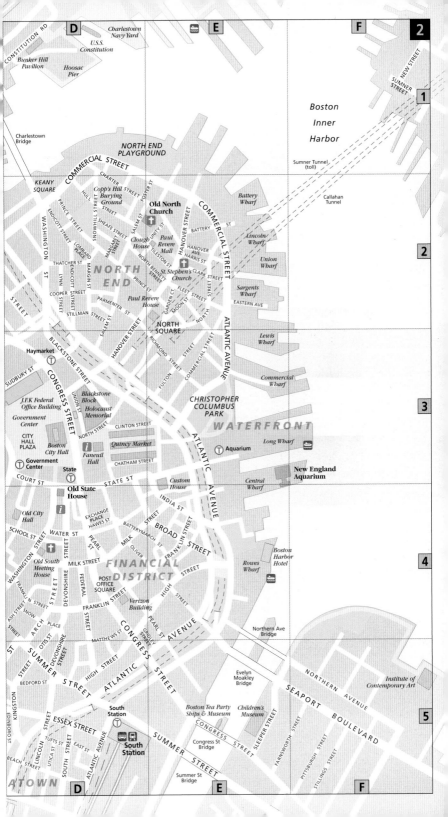

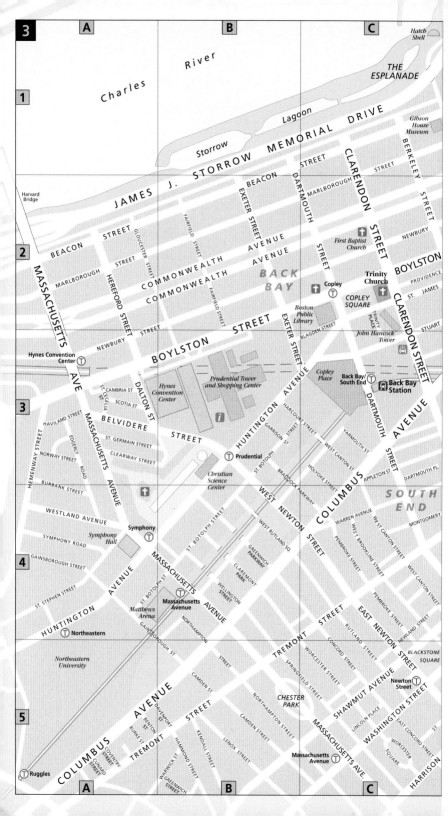

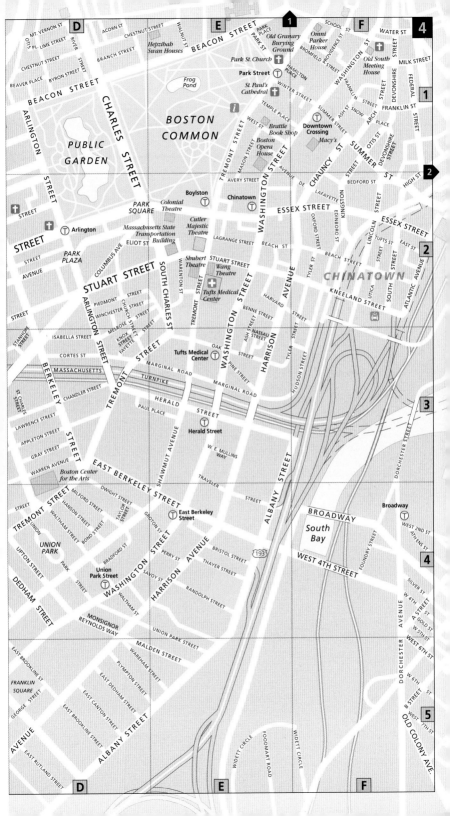

General Index

Page numbers in **bold**
refer to main entries

Acknowledgments

Dorling Kindersley would like to thank the following people whose contributions and assistance have made the preparation of this book possible.

Main Contributors

Patricia Harris and David Lyon are journalists and critics. They review art and restaurants and write extensively about travel, food, and popular culture from their home in Cambridge, Massachusetts. In addition to their books on art and travel, their essays, narratives, and photographs have appeared in a wide variety of online and print publications, including Expedia. com, *The Boston Globe*, the *Los Angeles Times*, *American Craft*, *Arthur Frommer's Budget Travel*, *The Robb Report*, and *Boston Magazine*.

Tom Bross has lived in Massachusetts since 1965 and now lives in Boston's North End, virtually next door to Old North Church. During the past 25 years as a freelance travel journalist Tom has written extensively about U.S., Canadian, and overseas destinations for various guidebooks, national magazines, newspapers, newsletters, and online publications. His domestic specialties are New England and California; overseas, Germany, Belgium, and Austria. He is, in addition, a professional photographer and spent several years in the 1980s as staff photographer of his home city's American League baseball team, the Boston Red Sox.

Kem Sawyer lives in Washington DC and has written children's books, feature articles, and book reviews. She particularly enjoys writing about history and has written the history feature for the *DK Eyewitness Travel Guide to Washington DC* as well as for this guide.

Additional Contributors

Brett Cook, Eric Grossman, Carolyn Heller, Juliette Rogers.

Additional Illustrations

Christopher King.

Additional Photography

Peter Anderson, John Coletti, Patricia Harris, David Lyon, Ian O'Leary, Stephen Oliver, Susannah Sayler, Tony Souter, Clive Streeter.

Design and Editorial

Managing Editor Helen Townsend
Managing Art Editor Kate Poole
Art Director Gillian Allan
Indexer Hilary Bird
Researcher Timothy Kennard

Revisions and Relaunch Team

Ashwin Raju Adimari, Hansa Babra, Shruti Bahl, Mark Bailey, Eleanor Berman, Marta Bescos, Sam Borland, Caroline Elliker, Alice Fewery, Jo Gardner, Eric Grossman, Claire Jones, Priya Kukadia, Sumita Khatwani, Shikha Kulkarni, Esther Labi, Gerrish Lopez, Carly Madden, Nicola Malone, Sam Merrell, Katherine Mesquita, Casper Morris, Scarlett O'Hara, Mary Ormandy, Catherine Palmi, Marianne Petrou, Pete Quinlan, Rada Radojicic, Mani Ramaswamy, Lynne Robinson, Lokamata Sahu, Sands Publishing Solutions, Avijit Sengupta, Azeem Siddiqui, Preeti Singh, Meredith Smith, Brett Steel, Rachel Symons, Stuti Tiwari, Ros Walford, Hugo Wilkinson, Tanveer Zaidi.

Special Assistance

Aimee O'Brien at the Greater Boston Convention and Visitors Bureau, who provided invaluable assistance with many Boston sights. Rosemary Barron for acting as food consultant and for food preparation.

Photography Permissions

Dorling Kindersley would like to thank the following for their assistance and kind permission to photograph at their establishments: Courtesy COMMONWEALTH OF MASSACHUSETTS ART: *George Washington* Sir Francis Chantrey, 1827 – 53bl; *Civil War Army Nurses Memorial* Bela Pratt, 1911 – 53ca; *John Hancock Memorial* artist unknown, 1915 – 23cl; *Return of the Colours to the Custody of the Commonwealth*, December 22, 1986, mural by Edward Simmons, 1902 – 53tl; Stained glass window, Main Stair Hall, 1900/details: *Magna Carta seal 43, Seal of the Commonwealth* (pre-1898) 52b.

Museum of Fine Arts, Sackler Museum, Harvard Museum of Natural History, the Fogg Art and Busch-Reisinger Museums, and Franklin Park Zoo.

All other churches, museums, hotels, restaurants, shops, galleries and sights too numerous to thank individually.

Picture Credits

a – above; b – below/bottom; c – centre; f – far; l – left; r – right; t – top.

Works of art have been reproduced with the permission of the following copyright holders: *Here-There Wall* by Kenneth Noland 1985 (c) DACS, London/VAGA, New York 2011 123bc.

The publisher would like to thank the following individuals, companies and picture libraries for permission to reproduce their photographs.

akg-images: Arkivi 24cb. **Alamy Images:** Bill Brooks 59cr; Ian Dagnall 75b; Randy Duchaine 80, 116br; Michael Dwyer 166br; Sarah Hadley 71cr; Andre Jenny 122bl, 141tl; Luscious Frames 85cl; Alan Myers 125br; North Wind Picture Archives 61tr; Old Paper Studios 26cr; William Owens 10cl; Chuck Pefley 11tc; Pictorial Press Ltd 32cl; Prisma Bildagentur AG 29cr; Robert Harding Picture Library Ltd 44bl; Swerve125tl; Jeff Titcomb 123tr; Vespasian 148br; View/Paul Raftery 31cr; Visions of America, LLC 164cr; Jim West 138br. **The Art Archive:** 89bc; **AWL Images:** Alan Copson 68; **Axiom:** 36cl.

Laura Barisonzi Photography/www. photographersdirect.com: 124bl; **Berklee College of Music:** Nick Balkin 99bc; **The Black Rose:** 143tr; **Boston Ballet:** Farnsworth/Blalock Photography 158cr; **Bostonian Society/Old State House:** 55bl, 89cb; *Boston Harbor*, 1853, John White Allen Scott. Purchase 1884 – 8-9.

City Water Taxi: 180bl; **Corbis:** 26tc, Bettmann 27tr, 33tl/br, 74bl, 89cra/bl, 100bc; Edifice, Philippa Lewis 128ca; Kevin Fleming 11cl, 39bl, 158bl, 184tl; Robert Holmes 140cla; Hulton-Deutsch Collection 47tc; Richard T. Nowitz 75c; Photononstop/Calle Montes 56; **Concord Museum www.concord Museum.org:** *A View of Town of Concord April 19, 1775 (1775-1825)* Artist Unknown, oil on canvas, bequest of Mrs. Stedman Buttrick, Sr. 119cr.

David Lyon & Patricia Harris: 30c. **Dreamstime. com:** Americanspirit 90; Jerry Coli 12bl; 28, 166tr, 166cl; Erix2005 102; John Kropewnicki 36br; Thomas Price 13bc; Rcavalleri 40-41; Jorge Salcedo 130-131; Marcio Silva 2-3, 12tr, 75tr, 170b, 172-3; Lee Snider 13tr; Sphraner 42.

L'Espalier Restaurant: 147br.; **The Eliot Hotel and Clio Restaurant:** Eric Roth 135tr. **Fourthree Media:** Justine Flute 178cla.

Getty Images: Boston Globe 145br,146tr; Kim Grant 146bl; Photonica 141c; **Granger**

Collection, New York: 18, 20t/c/bc, 21t/clb/bc, 22tr/clb/bc, 22-23c, 23tl/cra/crb, 24ca, 25tl/crb, 27cla, 32bl, 33c, 67tl, 77br/cr, 85br; **Greater Boston Convention & Visitors Bureau:** US PhotoGroup/Leslie Wood 185cr; **Greyhound Lines Inc.:** 181c; **Grill 23 & Bar:** 138cl.

Harvard University Art Museums: © President and Fellows of Harvard College, courtesy of Fogg Art Museum, Alpheus Hyatt Purchasing and Friends of the Fogg Art Museum Funds *Kneeling Angel* Gian Lorenzo Bernini, c.1674-1675 -115tl; courtesy of the Busch-Reisinger Museum, Gift of Sibyl Moholy-Nagy, *Light-Space Modulator*, Laszlo Moholy-Nagy, 1930 © Hattula Moholy-Nagy/DACS, London 2011 - 114bc; courtesy Fogg Art Museum, Bequest: Collection of Maurice Wertheim *Skating* Edouard Manet, 1877 - 115tr; Peter Vanderwarker 114cla, 115br; **Hulton Getty Collection:** 60cb .

Maggie Janik/www.photographersdirect.com: 124cla.

Lebrecht Collection: The Rodgers & Hammerstein Organization 89br; **James Lemass:** 6cl, 20 tc, 27crb, 37cra/cl/br, 38bl, 39ca, 83tc, 93crb, 120tl, 121br, 165tr, 167tr, 168cla/br.

Massachusetts Bay Transportation Authority: 183b; **Minute Man National Historical Park:** 121cla; **Museum of Fine Arts Boston:** Gift of Egypt Exploration Fund *Egypt, Deir el-Bahri* painted wood 26bl; HU-MFA Expedition *Shawabtis of Taharka* 30br; 106ca, 106cb, Bequest of Mrs. Beatrice Constance (Turner) Maynard in Memory of Winthrop Sargent *Revere Silver Teapot* 106tr; Egypt Exploration Fund *Inner Coffin of Nes-mut-aat-neru* 106clb; Picture Fund *Dance at Bougival* Pierre-Auguste Renoir, 1883 -107bc; Ruth and Carl J. Shapiro Colonnade and Vault *John Singer Sargent Murals* 107cr; Francis Bart-lett Donation of 1900 *Head of Aphrodite*, Greek Late Classical or Early Hellenistic period -107tl; M. and M. Karolik Collection of American Paintings, 1815 – 1865, by exchange, *Boston Harbor* Fitz Hugh Lane 108cla; Bequest of John T. Spaulding *La Berceuse* Vincent van Gogh, 1889 – 108br; Maria Antoinette Evans Fund *Babylonia:Nebuchadnezzar II* 109tl; Gift by Contribution *Horse, early 8th century, China* 109c; Richard Norton Memorial Fund *Fragment of fresco from villa at Contrada Bottaro* 109bc; **Museum of Science:** George Kiley 169tr; Andrew Brilliant 169bc; Kindra Clineff 30tr.

New England Aquarium: 78cl, Bob Kramer 78tr/

bl, 79tc/cra; **No. 9 Park**: Susie Cushner 142bl. **The Oceanaire/Landry's, Inc**: 139tl, 144tr; **Old North Church, Boston**: 73clb; **Omni Parker House**: 58clb; **Used by Permission of Orchard House / The Louisa May Alcott Memorial Association**: 120c; **Paul O'Shaughnessy**: 121ca.

Peabody Museum of Archaeology and Ethnology/Harvard University: © President and Fellows of Harvard College 1976. All Rights Reserved. Photos Hillel Burger 116c; **Courtesy Paul Revere Memorial Association**: 75t.

Puppet Showcase Theatre: Marionettes by Paul Vincent Davis 171tl.

Revere Hotel: 132br, 134bl; **Rialto Restaurant**: 149br; **Robert Harding Picture Library**: Steve Dunwell 40-1.

Sorellina: 148tl; **STA Travel Group**: 175clb.

Taj Boston: 133tl, 136tr; **Topham Picturepoint**: 27bc.

XV Beacon: 137br.

Map front cover: nobleIMAGES.

Front Endpaper: Dreamstime.com: Jorge Salcedo Ltc. **Alamy Images:**. Randy Duchaine Rbl; **AWL Images:** Alan Copson Rtr; **Corbis:** Photononstop/Calle Montes Rbr; **Dreamstime. com:** Americanspirit Lbc.

Jacket
Front and spine top: **Alamy Stock Photo:** nobleIMAGES

All other images ©Dorling Kindersley.
See www.dkimages.com for further information.

Special Editions of DK Travel Guides
DK Travel Guides can be purchased in bulk quantities at discounted prices for use in promotions or as premiums. We are also able to offer special editions and personalized jackets, corporate imprints, and excerpts from all of our books, tailored specifically to meet your own needs.

To find out more, please contact:
in the United States **specialsales@dk.com**
in the UK **travelguides@uk.dk.com**
in Canada DK Special Sales at
specialmarkets@dk.com
in Australia **penguincorporatesales@**
penguinrandomhouse.com.au

Further Reading

Non-Fiction

A Guide to Public Art in Boston: from Newburyport to Plymouth. Carlock, Marty. (Harvard Common Press, 1993.)

AIA Guide to Boston. Southworth, Michael and Susan. (Globe Pequot Press, 1996.)

All about Boston Harbor Islands. Kales, Emily and David. (Hewitts Cove Publishing Co. Inc., 1983.)

Boston Sites and Insights. Wilson, Susan. (Beacon Hill Press, 1994.)

Exploring in and Around Boston on Bike and Foot. Sinai, Lee. (Appalachian Mountain Club Books, 1996.)

Gaining Ground: A History of Landmaking in Boston. Seasholes, Nancy. (Mit Press, 2003.)

Imagining Boston: A Literary Landscape. O'Connell, Shaun. (Beacon Press, 1990.)

Paul Revere's Ride. Fischer, David Hackett. (Oxford University Press, 1994.)

The Fitzgeralds and the Kennedys: an American Saga. Goodwin, Doris Kearns. (Simon and Schuster, 1987.)

26 Miles to Boston: the Boston Marathon Experience from Hopkinton to Copley Square. Connelly, Michael. (Parnassus Imprints, 1998.)

Fiction

The Godwulf Manuscript. Parker, Robert. (Delacorte Press, 1974.)

Make Way for Ducklings. McCloskey, Robert. (Viking Press, 1941.)

Mortal Friends. Carroll, James. (Little Brown & Company, 1978.)

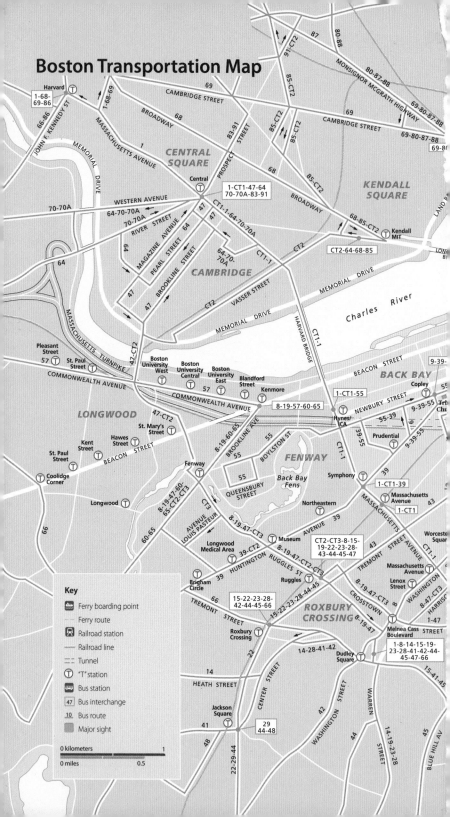